'Laurence Barrett is an entertaining storyteller and has written a sweeping book that includes rich material from his own coaching practice. As a coaching supervisor and an educator, he has a depth and breadth of understanding that is quite unique. He unpacks the symbolic life in a way that I have not encountered so far and the kaleidoscope of ideas he creates is inspiring and extremely valuable. Students, coaches, and analysts from all walks of Jungian psychology would benefit from working with this material.'

Tess Castleman, *Jungian training analyst and former member of the Curatorium of the C. G. Jung Institute of Zurich*

'This book is a profound and original contribution to the coaching field. Laurence brings Jungian psychology to life with clarity, depth, and practical insight, inviting coaches to engage more consciously with symbol, play, and the unconscious. This book doesn't just inform practice; it stretches the coach's capacity for reflection, imagination, and inner growth. A poetically written and a psychologically rigorous work that will leave a lasting impression.'

Verity Hannell, *programme director, professional certificate in executive coaching, Henley Business School*

Coaching the Unconscious

In *Coaching the Unconscious: A Jungian Approach to Working with Symbol*, Laurence Barrett explores how coaches can begin to work with symbol as part of their practice, blending the key principles of Jungian psychology with case studies and practical applications.

The Jungian concept of the symbolic attitude provides a valuable framework for coaches seeking to navigate the complexities of the human mind. It prompts us to notice the rich tapestry of symbols and metaphors arising from the unconscious and reveals what may be happening 'beneath the surface' of the mind. Coaches who have developed a symbolic attitude can better help their clients explore their inner worlds and create a deeper understanding of themselves and their potential. They can support more profound and impactful coaching experiences that go beyond superficial goals to support growth and transformation in more profound ways.

This valuable new resource will be of particular interest for experienced coaches seeking to deepen and extend their practice, as well as coaches who have begun to explore Jungian psychology and are looking for practical ways in which its concepts can be applied. It would also be appropriate for students of coaching and Jungian psychology.

Laurence Barrett has worked internationally in leadership coaching and organisational consulting for over 30 years and has held senior roles in a number of FTSE-30 companies. He holds an MSc in the psychodynamics of human development (Jungian) and trained as a coach and a coach supervisor with the Tavistock Institute.

Coaching the Unconscious

A Jungian Approach to Working with Symbol

Laurence Barrett

Routledge
Taylor & Francis Group

LONDON AND NEW YORK

Designed cover image: Getty Images

First published 2026
by Routledge
4 Park Square, Milton Park, Abingdon, Oxon OX14 4RN

and by Routledge
605 Third Avenue, New York, NY 10158

Routledge is an imprint of the Taylor & Francis Group, an informa business

British Library Cataloguing-in-Publication Data
A catalogue record for this book is available from the British Library

ISBN: 978-1-032-73247-3 (hbk)
ISBN: 978-1-032-73244-2 (pbk)
ISBN: 978-1-003-46326-9 (ebk)

DOI: 10.4324/9781003463269

Typeset in Times New Roman
by SPi Technologies India Pvt Ltd (Straive)

Contents

Acknowledgements

With thanks to

Cornelia Kausch, Anna Reynolds, and Sophia Stewart
For being my manuscript readers

The transcendent 'Bombay' Bob Giles
For being my inspiration

The Unconscious

The familiar ghost that walks with me,
Though I have never yet seen its face,
At times I greet with disgust,
And many other times, I anxiously watch and follow,

It is a silent ghost, austere, and old,
Who doesn't want to converse
…Before that figure, ascetic and composed,
I open my mouth a thousand times… and say nothing.

Only once did I dare to question it:
'Who are you?' (I asked, deeply shaken)
'Ghost whom I both hate and love?'

'Your brothers,' it replied, 'vain humans,
Have called me God for over ten thousand years
…But I myself do not know what I am called…'

Antero de Quental 1886 (trans. Laurence Barrett 2025)

Introducing Symbol

An Introduction to the Importance of Symbol in Human Development

We like to think of ourselves as self-aware, objective, and rational. We believe we are masters of our own destinies as we solve the complex problems of the present and prepare for an even more complex future. We have developed innovative technologies from pottery and the wheel to antibiotics and the internet. We have used these technologies to sustain life in harsh and unforgiving environments, and we have developed complex languages to communicate our increasingly complex ideas. We have created dictionaries, grammar, and syntax to ensure that those communications are as clear and precise as possible. We like to think of ourselves as fully conscious.

Our rational capacity, however, has been accompanied by something far more mysterious that we often find hard to acknowledge, at least in our modern world. Beneath our conscious minds lies the unconscious, a place of intense, confusing, and often quite challenging emotions, coupled with strange associations and intuitive leaps of faith. We write poetry that has no other purpose than to stir the soul. We dance and sing. We believe in gods that we have never seen, and we follow their rules without question. We use our extraordinary technologies to wage wars against people we do not know and who offer no existential threat to us. We use the awesome power of the internet to watch pornography and videos of funny cats.

When we spend time studying ourselves, we discover fairly quickly that most of our thinking happens below the level of awareness and is very different from the linear and logical processes of consciousness. We are forced to acknowledge that we are not primarily rational creatures and instead respond quickly and intuitively to stimuli in ways that we do not think about and, even when we do, do not fully understand.

Shame, Friendship, and the Illusion of Luxury

Research has suggested that people who were asked to think about shameful situations are more likely to see the word fragments 'w_ _s' and 's_ _ p' as 'wash' and 'soap' than as 'wish' and 'soup' and are also more likely to purchase disinfectant than batteries (Kahneman 2011). The relationship between our

DOI: 10.4324/9781003463269-1

emotional state, the symbols we gravitate towards in mind, and the actions we then take is a powerful one. The words 'wash' and 'soap' and the disinfectant have far more than a literal significance when we are feeling shame. These symbols reflect our inner theatre as much as they are conscious and practical artefacts. While we still may need to wash or buy disinfectant, we prioritise it because of a strong but loosely associated emotional state. We recognise Lady Macbeth's compelling need to wash her hands, after she has persuaded her husband to murder the king, because we can all make that same symbolic connection. We know what it is to feel shame, and at some unconscious level, we all hope to wash it away.

> Out, damned spot: out, I say…who would have thought the old man to have had so much blood in him?… What, will these hands ne'er be clean?… Here's the smell of the blood still. All the perfumes of Arabia will not sweeten this little hand.
>
> (*Macbeth*, Act 1, Scene 5)

The increasing use of artificial intelligence (AI) has provided us with a fascinating example of this interplay between the unconscious and the conscious mind. AI is a complex mathematical simulation of human thought, which has the capacity to learn and evolve based on the way it is trained and the outcomes it achieves. It has no sense of consciousness, empathy, or subjective experience, and although it can identify and respond to emotional data, it does so without any felt personal connection. However, when interacting with some forms of AI, we often tend to anthropomorphise it; that is, we imbue the real or imagined behaviour of nonhuman agents with humanlike characteristics, motivations, intentions, or emotions. Human beings have a wonderful capacity for fantasy, and from our first teddy bears, we project human traits onto anything that vaguely reminds us of ourselves. Anthropomorphism is a great defence against an unknown world and the terrors of being helpless and alone. It may help us through dark times by providing suitable objects for projections which remind us that we can survive. These objects may allow us to make sense of the world, develop our feelings of agency, and become more able to find relationships.

There are three primary factors which drive our anthropomorphic fantasies (Epley et al. 2007), the first of which is 'sociality motivation', or our need for relationships and social interactions. Human beings do not like being alone as a general rule, and the lonelier we feel, the more we project human traits onto non-human objects. Our 'imaginary friends' can provide the feeling of safety and connection. We feel our teddy bears love us, and we believe that a collection of algorithms is genuinely interested in us. The second factor is 'effectance motivation', or the desire to influence the object in our interactions with it. If we need the object to respond to us, we are more likely to interact with it as if it were like us. We believe that the more like us it is, the more we can influence it. The more helpless we feel, the more human the object becomes. We cuddle our teddy bears, and we find a conversation with AI to be comforting. The third factor is 'elicited agent knowledge', or how much we know about an object and how easily we can apply that knowledge to make judgements. The less we know about something, the more likely we are to give that thing human traits. We can reduce our unconscious fear of the unknown other by making it more like we are. A teddy bear can become our friend and confident. A collection of algorithms can become a coach or a romantic partner. This final factor is particularly significant, as the less we know about AI, the more likely we are to view it as having almost magical qualities (Tully et al. 2025). This tendency appears to be systemic and consistent across groups, and people in professions or societies with lower average AI literacy seem to be more likely to be receptive towards uncritical AI adoption than those in groups with higher AI literacy. When the conscious mind is in a weaker position (supported by less data and without any rational foundations), the more likely we are to be influenced by the unconscious.

The importance of the unconscious has been leveraged particularly well in brand marketing, where the emotional, symbolic value of the product is often recognised as being worth far more than its practical value alone. We know that colours and smells significantly influence our choices. The colour red, for example, appears to suggest power, confidence, and sexuality. It can lead men to view women as more attractive (Elliot and Niesta 2008) and can make us all hungrier (Berman 2007). Blue seems to be calming and reassuring (Conway et al. 2010) and may even lead to associations with wealth and security (Lichtlé 2007). Casinos meanwhile use scents to encourage us to relax or to gamble, depending on whether we are buying food or sitting at the tables (Hirsch 1995). Research has even suggested that the way that the phonetic structure of the name of a product or brand, the way we experience it rhythmically, is significant. An emphasis on the front vowels of a name tends to elicit positive associations, such as beauty or tenderness, while the back vowels lead us towards negative associations, such as ugliness or bluntness (Duduciuc 2015).

We don't then buy a Burberry trench coat simply because we want to keep the rain off. While it may be partly true from a conscious perspective, other factors encourage us to make this rather expensive decision. We may be interested in the glamorous heritage or the excellent craftsmanship or perhaps in the models in the advertising who are (as a rule) both younger and more attractive than we are. The high price itself may also be a factor, reminding us of the value of money as an object of status and suggesting that we matter simply because we can afford it. This appeal is to our deepest sense of identity and reminds us not simply of the need to protect ourselves from the weather but of who we are or who we aspire to be (Elliot and Wattanasuwan 2015). It would appear that the gap between the utility value of the coat and the price we are prepared to pay for it is filled with the unconscious. As Luciana

Penteliuc-Cotoşman has suggested in her exploration of the use of symbolic imagery in luxury brands:

> Luxury…answers to the existential anxiety about time and death, trying to overcome it and to improve the situation of man in the world…The luxury brand has a mythical dimension and the luxury product, endowed with this singular glow specific to magic objects, has a very strong symbolic value.
>
> (Penteliuc-Cotoşman 2018, p. 128)

Introducing Symbol

In the gap between the wild impulses of the unconscious and the considered thoughts of the conscious mind, we find symbol, forming the bridge that connects the real and the felt. Through symbol, complex emotions can be associated with more tangible ideas and given form and life, and stimuli from the outer world can shape our inner world. More than any other quality, our capacity to create, interpret, and live within symbols defines us as human. We are symbol-bearing creatures, and our symbols are not just decoration for the psyche; they are its deepest language. To be human is to live in a continuous symbolic dialogue. Every encounter, every experience, every object can carry meaning beyond itself in symbolic form. Through symbols, we find expression, not in rational terms but in the language of the soul.

> Symbols are the essential message carriages from the instinctive to the rational parts of the human mind, and their interpretation enriches the poverty of consciousness so that it learns to understand again the forgotten language of the instincts.
>
> (Jung 1964, p. 52)

Symbols take many forms and carry many different ideas. They often appear in clusters and in unpredictable, obscure, and highly subjective ways. Symbols that move some of us can be safely ignored by others. They are found in the words we use and the products we buy. They appear in our myths, our poetry, our art, and our religions. We have gone to war for them and dedicated our lives to them. From the earliest religious icons to the quiet habitual rituals we perform every morning, we navigate our reality through symbols, as a combination of both the unconscious and the conscious mind, of our feelings and our thoughts. A wedding ring is not then just a loop of metal. A national flag is not just a piece of dyed cloth. Disinfectant does not just clean our floors, an AI chatbot is not simply a piece of mathematics, and a coat is not just to keep the rain off. Whatever form symbols take, they speak to us and for us. Symbols provide the impetus and emotional energy to inspire and provoke, moving us to action and revealing our underlying motivations.

This symbolic layer of life is not always easy to notice in the chaos of a modern world. We are surrounded by noise, and when we do notice symbols, we have learned not to take them seriously. Our addiction to literal interpretation and absolute answers has confined the symbol for the most part to dreams and leisure activities. However, we are still restless, scrolling endlessly, not for information but for something that feels resonant: an image, a quote, a story that stirs something vital and significant. This is the voice of the unconscious trying to be heard.

> It is only possible to live the fullest life when we are in harmony with these symbols; wisdom is a return to them.
>
> (Jung, 1960, CW8, para. 794)

Symbol and Coaching

The ability to work with symbol is then an essential part of any coaches toolkit. While we may deny the unconscious (perhaps overcome by our own 'fear of the dark'), it will be a continual presence for both coach and client. It will shape our work whether we like it or not. As the psychoanalyst W. Gordon Lawrence has suggested:

> Lurking in every executive coaching session, every role consultation, and, indeed, every social relation, is the presence of unconscious thinking. That presence can be like an unattended absence, but it is always there, for it cannot be wished away.
>
> (2006, p. 104)

When we are working with any form of personal change, we are working with the feelings and associations of the unconscious. If we are unable or unwilling to acknowledge them, they will have their effect anyway, and at some point or other, we will need to face them. The unconscious is alive in every coaching session, no matter how superficial and prosaic the conversation.

Coaching has often placed its emphasis on the development of those superficial behaviours and habits which may be easily observed and which may be easily linked to the delivery of clear and defined goals. As a result, many coaches do not pause to wonder why their clients behave like they do and what unconscious factors may be shaping them. We often assume that 'coaching focuses on what clients want' (Whitworth et al. 1998), without acknowledging that clients may not always be consciously aware of what they want and perhaps at an unconscious level may in fact want something very different from those things they are able to voice (Kegan and Lahey 2009).

However, a great deal of our work as coaches may instead focus on much more complexed and nuanced issues, particularly when those issues threaten our established personal or professional identity (Ibarra et al. 2005). Here the emotions that lie beneath the surface may be very powerful indeed, and our awareness of them may be very limited. When we move from being a functional specialist to a departmental manager, become a parent, or perhaps leave corporate life to take another course, we are challenging our identities and our very sense of self. We may be questioning beliefs that we have long held close, perhaps since childhood, or simply be facing the overwhelming fear of an unknown future. We may be asked to consider perspectives that we may not realise exist or do not yet fully understand (Charan et al. 2005). We may experience a difficult period of identity loss and an 'unlearning' of the behaviours and habits that have served us well in the past. As we enter a new world, we may then find ourselves unequipped to deal with its new challenges and may begin to wonder, what if we are not good enough? What if we don't 'fit in' to the new community that comes with the new identity? What if that new community realises that we are afraid and incompetent and then rejects us? These underlying fears may not be rational and may not even be conscious, but they will shape how we behave. As Jung suggested:

> The secret participation of the unconscious is everywhere present without our having to search for it, but as it remains unconscious we never really know what is going on or what to expect. What we are searching for is a way to make conscious those contents which are about to influence our actions, so that the secret interference of the unconscious and its unpleasant consequences can be avoided.
>
> (1960, CW8, para. 158)

In these moments, a sensitivity to symbol may be essential if we want to make sense of what is happening below the surface for our clients and ourselves. By being aware of the possible symbolic value of the things they do and say, the things they wear, and the associations that come to mind, we can start to notice and wonder why and may even be able to work more intentionally with the unconscious. While symbols may still raise as many questions as they provide answers, through their guidance we can at least find ourselves looking in the right direction.

References

Berman M 2007, *Street smart advertising: How to win the battle of the buzz.* Lanham, MD: Rowman & Littlefield.

Charan R, Drotter S and Noel J 2005, *The leadership pipeline: How to build the leadership powered company.* San Francisco, CA: Jossey-Bass.

Conway CM, Pelet J-E, Papadopulou P and Limayem M 2010, Coloring in the lines: using color to change the perceptions of quality in e-commerce sites. *ICIS 2010 Proceedings, Paper 224.*

Duduciuc A 2015, Social psychology applied to advertising: The effect of sound symbolism on perceived characteristics of brands. *Psihologia socială* 35: 53–61.

Elliot AJ and Niesta D 2008, Romantic red: Red enhances men's attraction to women. *Journal of Personality and Social Psychology* 95(5): 1150–1164.

Elliot R and Wattanasuwan K 2015, Brands as symbolic resources for the construction of identity. *International Journal of Advertising* 17(2): 131–144.

Epley N, Waytz A and Cacioppo JT 2007, On seeing human: A three-factor theory of anthropomorphism. *Psychological Review* 114(4): 864–886.

Hirsch AR 1995, Effects of ambient odors on slot-machine usage in a Las Vegas casino. *Psychology & Marketing* 12(7): 585–594.

Ibarra H, Snook S and Guillen Ramo L 2005, Identity based leader development. In N Nohria and R Khurana (eds.) *Handbook of leadership theory and practice: A Harvard Business School Centennial Colloquium*. Boston, MA: Harvard Business Press.

Jung CG 1960, *The structure and dynamics of the psyche*. CW8.

Jung CG 1964, *Man and his symbols*. Garden City, NY: Doubleday & Company.

Kahneman D 2011, *Thinking fast and slow*. London: Penguin.

Kegan R and Lahey LL 2009, *Immunity to change: How to overcome it and unlock the potential in yourself and your organisation*. Boston, MA: Harvard Business Press.

Lawrence GW 2006, Executive coaching, unconscious thinking and infinity. In H Brunning (ed.) *Executive coaching: A systems-psychodynamic perspective*. London: Karnac.

Lichtlé M 2007, The effect of an advertisement's colour on emotions evoked by an ad and attitude towards the ad. *International Journal of Advertising* 26(1): 37–62.

Penteliuc-Cotoşman L 2018, Symbolic image and social imaginary in the luxury brands communication and marketing. *Anale. Seria Ştiinţe Economice. Timişoara* 23: 128–137.

Tully SM, Longoni C and Appel G 2025, Lower artificial intelligence literacy predicts greater AI receptivity. *Journal of Marketing*.

Whitworth L, Kimsey-House K and Sandahl P 1998, *Co-active coaching: New skills of coaching people toward success in work and life*. Mountain View, CA: Davies-Black Publishing.

Chapter 1

The Location of Symbol
Introducing a Jungian Model of the Psyche

Our knowledge of the world is dependent upon our lived experience in the world. While we may have an informed understanding of anatomy and genetics, psychology, or social systems, we do not know ourselves in the same way that a doctor or a psychologist or a social scientist may know us. We know ourselves from within and this knowledge is often intuitive, unformed, and emotionally charged. We may have no words for it, only associations or feelings which we can never completely define or describe. Any sense of reflective distance and rational objectivity that we can create rests upon this subjective 'felt' experience.

Our knowledge is also inextricably bound up with the world around us. The world is dynamic and often unpredictable, and our lives may depend on our adaption to it. We take in a complex and often overwhelming array of images and sensations, which in turn provoke responses within us which we may not always be able to acknowledge or understand. We exist not as a predictable landscape of defined psychological structures and traits but as a turbulent and evolving seascape of changing perceptions and influences, with often mysterious and terrifying depths. Even when we find a moment of stability, the next storm threatens to disturb our fragile and precarious peace and perhaps even destroy us. Jung brings this confusion to life:

> It is my mind, with its store of images, that gives the world colour and sound; and that supremely real and rational certainty which I call "experience" is, in its most simple form, an exceedingly complicated structure of mental images. Thus there is, in a certain sense, nothing that is directly experienced except the mind itself. Everything is mediated through the mind, translated, filtered, allegorized, twisted, even falsified by it. We are so enveloped in a cloud of changing and endlessly shifting images that we might well exclaim with a well-known sceptic: "Nothing is absolutely true— and even that is not quite true."
>
> (Jung 1960, CW8, p. 623)

DOI: 10.4324/9781003463269-2

Any conscious assessment of our lived experience can then only ever be provisional and emergent. We cannot isolate ourselves from the world, and as the world around us changes, so do we. Using the only instrument available to us, our conscious mind, we develop and adopt hypotheses and frameworks that seem meaningful and crucially provide us with the mental models we need to survive. However, as we attempt to make these models more concrete and tangible, it becomes obvious that they can never truly represent the richness and vitality of our lived experience. We can explain the abstract structures and processes which allow us to make conscious sense of a piece of music, but we cannot fully articulate how and why that piece fills us with joy or reduces us to tears.

Jungian psychology would suggest that, with this chaotic, complex, and perhaps rather inconvenient backdrop, the best route to understanding ourselves begins with understanding symbol. The images and associations that arise within us, and that we notice in the world around us, can provide a bridge between the unformed impulses and intuition of the unconscious and the rational order of the conscious mind. If we pay attention to symbol, we have a compass to help us explore our lived experience and to make meaning in the world.

To understand why Jungian psychology values symbol so highly, we must begin by locating it within Jungian model of the psyche, a term used to describe our whole psychology, extending beyond the conscious mind to include the depths of the unconscious.

Space and Time

We find the origins of psyche in what Jung termed the psychoid unconscious (Jung 1960, CW8, para. 417–418), a permeable border zone which both separates us from and connects us to the world. Through the psychoid we have a 'felt experience' of existence where body and psyche are entwined, continuously influencing each other in a way that we could describe as simultaneously psychosomatic and somatapsychic (Carvalho 2020). The psychoid is a bridge between the psyche and the world beyond, which mediates and influences the way in which we experience ourselves in the world and the world in us. It can never be made fully conscious and instead is something we 'know' but cannot adequately describe. It reminds us, at a profoundly visceral level, that we are alive and part of a living world. Overturning Descartes famous aphorism (2005), the psychoid suggests 'I am, therefore I think'.

We may imagine the experience of the womb and the effect this has upon the psychology of both mother and infant. In the womb, we are simultaneously separate and whole, a shared physical experience which creates a profound sense of intimacy and connection. The mother becomes a nurturing container (Neumann 1963, pp. 44–45) providing the conditions for life, while the infant is unconditionally contained as psyche begins to develop. The rhythmic sounds of the mother's heartbeat, the gentle swaying of her movements, and shared biochemical signals then create a foundation for a post-natal bond and for the longer-term psychological development of both. Through the physical experience of the womb, we lay the foundations for our lives beyond the womb (Piontelli 1992).

> Developmental potential is bound up in these earliest interweaving skeins of physical and psychic life, in the connections and disconnections between mother and baby, already so deep and so subtle.
>
> (Waddell 1998, p. 21)

Although we may think of the psychoid as being 'deep' within the unconscious, its depth is not then distant and lifeless but is filled with a pervasive and vital energy. This energy, which Jung termed 'libido', is the dynamic energy of life itself. It fuels our primal instincts and raw emotions and ultimately assembles the complex web of drives and behaviours that we can call personality. At the level of the psychoid, the intensity of this energy is often experienced as 'numinous', a term first used by the theologian Rudolf Otto (1923) to describe the presence of the divine. Numinous experiences carry a profound sense of awe and a compelling suggestion of meaning, meaning which cannot yet be given a clear and recognisable form but which nonetheless demands our attention. They have the power to inspire profound psychological and spiritual change and transformation. They suggest a sense of connection to something much greater than us and through the intensity of this connection they possess a timeless quality.

Like Freud (1900), Jung proposed that the unconscious exists beyond time and that, in the unconscious, the events of the past are re-experienced emotionally in the context of the present. The felt experience of the unconscious is always now. Through the psychoid, psyche reaches back beyond our own lives, or even the lives of our ancestors, to our evolutionary heritage (Brooke 2015). We share the experience of being human with all the other humans who are living and have lived and, perhaps to some degree, the experience of being alive with all other living beings (Jung 1960, CW8, para. 321). We cannot easily describe the psychoid, but through it, we know with certainty that we are part of something much larger and more significant than ourselves. Jung challenges us to look further and ask:

> The question is, in short: shouldn't we give up on space-time categories altogether when we are dealing with psychic existence? It might be that psyche should be understood as unextended intensity, not as a body moving in time.
>
> (Jung 1975, p. 45)

Through a Jungian lens, we can then view time in the psyche as being governed simultaneously by two dimensions. Chronos represents linear time, as experienced by rational consciousness, where our movement through time and space is exact and quantifiable. It is the time through which we measure our days and mark the mortal limits of our lives. Chronos reminds us that the clock is ticking and that progress demands action. Kairos by way of contrast represents the amorphous, spiral time of the unconscious. It evokes moments of meaning and possibility that connect us with the broad and timeless patterns of life. In Kairos, linear time stands still, and we stand still with it. It is a numinous moment of prayer, of awe, of terror that suggests that something significant is about to happen. In Kairos, we are connected to the whole, as the feelings of the past are re-experienced in the present as a suggestion of future possibility. As the novelist William Faulkner observed, 'the past is never really dead. It's not even past' (1951, p. 73), and in the kairotic nature of the unconscious it is lived again as now. This contrast is a fundamental challenge for mind and goes to the heart of Jungian psychology. In our connection with both Chronos and Kairos, we must navigate the tension between the limited and definable reality of consciousness and the vast but mysterious experiences of the unconscious: 'between a knowing unknowing and an unknowing knowing' (Zabriskie 2004, p. 271). The paradox of mind is that we can only begin to make conscious meaning from the experience of the unconscious by allowing ourselves to acknowledge its timeless intensity and to be open to its potential.

Symmetries and Schemas

This potential begins to form around the psychogenetic structures that Jung termed archetypes: 'an inherited organisation of psychic energy...which not only gives expression to the energetic process but facilitates its operation' (Jung 1971, CW6, p. 754). The archetypes form a potentially infinite and overlapping array of instinctual and overlapping basic schemas, which shape how we perceive and relate to the world (Hillman 1975). These schemas are not simply a reaching back to the past but a meaningful suggestion of the future. When experienced in the present, the archetypes provide the provocation and energy that propel us forwards. They are responsible for what Jung termed the 'teleological' or purposive nature of the psyche (Papadopoulos 2006).

Archetypes arise in the psychoid as a timeless accumulation of our evolutionary experiences and contain both the physiological reality of those experiences and our psychological responses to them. Jung drew an analogy with the electromagnetic spectrum, suggesting that the archetype had two opposing poles which we experience in different ways: an invisible 'infra-red' end that represents the physical aspect and a visible 'ultra-violet' end that represents the psychological aspect (Jung 1960, CW8, para. 420). This connectedness between the physical world and the psyche has suggested parallels with the 'symmetries' of physics where the behaviour of the physical world is understood not in its separate parts but in its underlying patterns (Peat 1991, Stevens 2004). The physicist David Peat has proposed that

Just as the elementary particles are maintained by a dance that transcends the world of matter, so too, is mind sustained by dynamics that lie beyond mind and matter. Beyond mind and matter are therefore symmetries that that have a generating and animating effect.

(Peat 1987, pp. 111–112)

If we then return to the very human experience of mothering, we know we are helpless at birth. We cannot feed and protect ourselves. We cannot stand or crawl or run. For a human being to live more than a few days, we need care and support. In our early years, we are wholly reliant on another, and if we are able to read this chapter, we have experienced care in some form. We have an innate need to give and receive care, and without this need we would not exist as a species. We have developed instinctive responses to ensure that this need is met, from the crying that alerts our parents to our distress, to the reflexive smiles that support the bond between infant and caregiver (Stevens 1982). We may think of this need as archetypal, with roots that reach down through the psychoid to our genetic inheritance and with implications that reach up to the complex social structures of the modern world. It is an archetype that compels us to provide and receive support, from the basic reality of parenting through to complex social health provision. Its numinous energy reminds us that it is of fundamental importance to our survival. We can refer to this archetype as the 'Great Mother', but there are many other names that would also apply, none of which would be able to fully capture its potential breadth. Similarly, there may be archetypes that represent the experiences of relationship, sex, hierarchy, achievement, transformation, violence, or death, all of which have profoundly shaped our evolution and history and which seem to define humanity. The archetypes arise both from experiences of trauma and from ordinary everyday events: the 'immediate realities like husband, wife, father, mother, child…which are eternally repeated, [and] create the mightiest archetypes of all, whose ceaseless activity is everywhere apparent even in a rationalistic age like ours' (Jung 1960, CW8, para. 336). Through the stable and enduring templates of the archetypes, we instinctively know what it is to be human.

All these possible archetypes cannot, however, be easily defined. They are ambiguous, 'felt' experiences, and they will assume different forms depending on the context in which they appear. They may change and adapt over time while retaining their essence.

No archetype can be reduced to a single formula. It is a vessel which we can never empty, and never fill. It has a potential existence only, and when it takes shape in matter it is no longer what it was. It persists through the ages and requires interpreting ever anew. The archetypes are imperishable elements of the unconscious, but they change their shape continually.

(Jung 1959, CW9i, para. 301)

Although they are not themselves symbols, it is through the archetypes that symbols begin to appear in the psyche. Like the psychoid from which they arise, the 'the real nature of the archetype is not capable of being made conscious' (Jung 1960, CW8, para. 417). We know them, but we cannot easily explain our knowing. For this reason, Jungian psychology makes a distinction between the 'archetype-as-such' and the archetypal symbols through which the archetype is understood in a particular context (Stevens 1982, Knox 2003, Hogenson 2004). The 'archetype-as-such' is simply an energetic organising principle and a nucleus around which symbols begin to accumulate as the archetype establishes itself in the psyche. The symbol gives the archetype a more concrete form and a more discernible voice. A symbol may appear in many different forms, perhaps as a visual image or a sound or a movement of the body or perhaps as something half formed and elusive. They may exist in overlapping clusters, which reveal the archetype through their overall pattern rather than the individual images themselves. Symbols do not simply represent ideas in the inner or outer world; they also represent each other and need to be considered in context. However they appear, they will always carry a level of energy that draws our attention to them, and the closer they are to the archetype, the more numinous and overwhelming this energy will be. It is through this accumulation of symbol and energy that we begin to create complexes, the basic building blocks of the psyche.

The Feeling Toned Complexes

A complex is a loose arrangement of implicit memories, emotional responses, and associated symbols drawn together through lived experiences and clustered around an archetypal core (Knox 2004). This core provides a sense of coherence and order, to create a generalised 'mental map' which in turn helps navigate the challenges of an often-hostile world. These maps are not fixed and conscious but dynamic and unconscious, and they allow us to respond quickly and intuitively to changes in our environment. They provide the generalised schemas upon which we build our personalities and our relationships. The symbols that provide their waypoints have both a concrete origin, derived from the real experiences of the outer world, and an associated emotional energy, derived from felt experiences of the inner world. A complex may have both positive and negative emotional associations and may change over time, as the experiences of our lives change or reinforce those associations. They are importantly not unusual or even necessarily problematic and instead may be considered to be

> focal or nodal points of psychic life which we would not wish to do without; indeed, they should not be missing, for otherwise psychic activity would come to a fatal standstill.
>
> (Jung 1971, CW6, para. 925)

Each complex is an autonomous structure, with its own origins, energy, and intent, and each will function as 'a small secondary mind' (Jung 1992a, CW2, para. 1352). They behave like 'independent beings' (Jung 1960, CW8, para. 253), and whether we are aware of them or not, they shape our behaviour and may even influence our physical state:

> A complex with its given tension or energy has the tendency to form a little personality of itself. It has a sort of body, a certain amount of its own physiology. It can upset the stomach. It upsets the breathing, it disturbs the heart—in short, it behaves like a partial personality. For instance, when you want to say or do something and unfortunately a complex interferes with this intention, then you say or do something different from what you intended. You are simply interrupted, and your best intention gets upset by the complex, exactly as if you had been interfered with by a human being or by circumstances from outside.
>
> (Jung 1977, CW18, para. 149)

Each complex will function in its own way, according to its own energy and symbolic associations which provoke intuitive and often rapid responses. We have many possible complexes, potentially as many as there are archetypes, and each brings a distinct dimension to our personalities. Complexes may appear in clusters with shared symbols, often with many different associations which may even create feelings of inner conflict and turmoil. The symbols attached to each complex serve to shape and direct its emotional energy in a process Jung described as the 'canalisation of libido' (Jung 1960, CW8). We may imagine a complex as a psychological river, where the archetype forms the bed and the banks made up by symbols, which then guide a dynamic flow of energy and affect. It is through the canalisation of libido that we form the habits and patterns that define personality and behaviour. The more the river of the mind flows along a particular path, the more entrenched these habits and patterns become. Some complexes lurk quietly in the corners of the mind, while others lie close to the surface as 'habitual' or 'staple' complexes (Jung 1964, pp. 28–29) and react quickly and frequently to the everyday events of our lives. The everyday flow of the complex may be subtle or powerful, but given the right stimuli it will overwhelm the rational mind. The complex will intensify or 'constellate', and we will 'act it out', driven by its emotional energy to behave in often surprising and extreme ways. Their potential power over us was emphasised by Jung:

> Everyone knows nowadays that people "have complexes". What is not so well known, though far more important theoretically, is that complexes can have us...Every constellation of a complex postulates a disturbed state of consciousness. The unity of consciousness is disrupted, and the intentions of the will are impeded or made impossible. Even memory is often noticeably affected, as we have seen.
>
> (Jung 1960, CW8, para. 200)

As the complex constellates, its symbols are released in more tangible forms, and if we pay attention to them, we can hear the voice of the unconscious. We can begin to understand the feelings aroused by the past events from which the complex was born, the influence they then have on our present behaviour, and the possible futures that they point towards.

The Collective Mind

Our complexes begin not with our personal experiences of the world but in the shared experiences of humanity that Jung termed the collective unconscious: 'a record in, and of, the psyche of humankind going back to its remotest beginnings' (Jung 1959, CW9i, para. 90). These experiences inform and are informed by the archetypes and by the symbolic associations that that have gathered around them during the lives of our ancestors. We can imagine the first symbols as a primitive expression of our early consciousness, bridging the gap between the intangible and the tangible, in an attempt to grasp the essence of human experience. These symbols link us to a common instinctual and psychological heritage and provide a timeless wellspring for the iconography and myths which form the foundations of human history and culture. The collective unconscious is part of us, informing the processes of our own minds, and yet does not belong to us as individuals. It carries feelings and associations that profoundly resonate with us but do not have their origins in our own experiences. The intensity of these feelings and associations ensures that the collective unconscious is not 'a dead deposit, a sort of abandoned rubbish heap, but a living system of reactions and aptitudes that determine the individual's life in invisible ways' (Jung 1960, CW8, para. 339). Within the collective unconscious, we can begin to see the earliest formations of symbol and the nascent complexes of humanity. The symbols of our distant ancestors, painted on the walls of caves or carved from bone and ivory, evoke feelings within us that may be unique to us but are also shared with them.

The Willendorf Venus may be one such symbol. Carved from limestone and tinted with red ochre, it is a small sculpture around 11 cm in height that was made between 25,000 and 30,000 years ago. It depicts a woman with large pendulous breasts and pronounced genitalia who seems to be 'weighed down with fertility, so rooted in the earth that she seems to be part of it' (Baring and Cashford 1991, p. 10). We can never know why she was made or what purpose she served. Perhaps she was a symbol of the act of creation and birth or of the milk that sustains life. Perhaps she was a symbol of the womb, as a container and the mysterious source of life itself. Perhaps she had a name, as an ancestor or a goddess who somehow embodied some of those attributes, or perhaps she was an image of all women. Whatever the case, her enduring power was enough to have encouraged one of my clients to hold a replica of her image during the birth of her first child, inspired and comforted by the idea of eternal womanhood. While the exact meaning of the Willendorf Venus and of similar 'mother goddess' symbols may elude us, they evidently still provoke something within us which connects a profound archetypal abstraction to a present felt reality.

These primal collective complexes then inform the development of communities, whose lived experiences in turn add new images and associations to their shared unconscious. The 'group' (Von Franz 1985), 'tribal' (Castleman 2004), or 'cultural unconscious' (Henderson 1990) begins to emerge as a storehouse of images and associations specific to a particular community. With each generation, the symbols of the collective are refreshed, and new symbols are added to provide new nuances of meaning. Although the archetypal core of a complex may remain essentially the same, the symbolic meaning that surrounds it becomes more localised and we may experience the archetype in new ways. The collective complex may then become a cultural complex (Singer and Kimbles 2004) which defines our shared identity, reminding us through the symbols and myths of who we are as a society and of how we should behave. The cultural complex provides us with a shared symbolic language that holds a group together as a group. If the history of a society has involved a particular experience of the archetypal mother, then the representations of that archetype may take on new symbols with meaning that is specific to that society. If the experience was negative, for example, the maternal archetype may feel dark and devouring (Neumann 1963, Stevens 1982). We may embrace this new feeling in new symbols and esoteric cults, where we worship the cycle of life and death in female form, or we may reject it, persecuting midwives and healers (themselves symbols of the mother) as dangerous witches. With each choice we make, the archetype is re-energised and continues to evolve, shaping history and being shaped by it. The cultural unconscious in turn provides a source of symbolic meaning around which we can begin to locate and inform the events of our own lives, and our personal unconscious begins to emerge. Jung suggests that

> The personal unconscious consists firstly of all those contents that became unconscious either because they lost their intensity and were forgotten or because consciousness was withdrawn from them (repression), and secondly of contents, some of them sense-impressions, which had never sufficient intensity to reach consciousness but have somehow entered the psyche.
>
> (Jung 1960, CW8, para. 321)

Here we collect more symbols or give an enriched personal meaning to the symbols already present in the cultural or collective unconscious, and these are bound up with the emotional energy associated with our own life events. They combine or recombine with existing complexes or perhaps form new ones. To the collective complex of the eternal mother and the cultural complexes of our community, we may now add our own symbolic associations for the experience of care, which will in turn shape our own behaviours as caregivers, adding our part to the development of the complexes of future generations.

The Emergence of Consciousness

Within this vast and dynamic space, the ego begins to form as the foundation of the conscious mind. Faced with the limitations of our bodies and the realities of our environment, we become increasingly conscious of our own existence. As we separate from the primal connection with our mothers, we develop a sense of 'I' as a bounded entity that exists in time and space and which is different in kind from the 'other' that surrounds it. In the unconscious mind, we are part of a 'participation mystique' (Jung 1971, CW6, para. 781) where we are fully immersed in a fluid and unbounded world. In the conscious mind, the ego places itself at the centre of its own universe and we become the distinct subject to which all other objects are related.

The development of the conscious mind may feel to us like the taming of fire may have felt to our ancestors. Before they learned to make fire, their nights were spent in the world as part of its darkness. With fire, they became separate, living in their own circle of light. With fire, the darkness beyond was intensified and became a place of the 'other', to be feared and rejected. While they stayed near their fire and remained vigilant, they were safe from the dangers that they now imagined lurking beyond. But no matter how hard they stared into the flames, the creatures in the darkness remained, and the fire could still go out. The fire became an essential symbol for the comfort of the known, and the darkness beyond a symbol for the terror of the unknown, of death itself. Here time as Chronos begins, in the wait for the certainty of daylight to return and in the fear of the next setting sun. Here we began to perform rituals and invent gods to keep us close to the light.

In this way, the ego presents us with the essential paradox of human psychological life. Through the consciousness of the ego, we are able to reflect rationally on our inner world, but the ego still prefers to deny the unconscious and to reject those things that are incompatible with its illusion of omnipotence. Mind is afraid of its own potential depths. It believes itself to be a decision maker, while research consistently suggests otherwise (Norretranders 1998, Wegner 2002, Wilson 2002). We know empirically that we know that consciousness does not make decisions but instead deploys post rationalisations for decisions that have already been made by the unconscious (Libet 2004), and the ego works hard to resist this existential threat. As Jung suggests:

> Anything unexpected that approaches us from that dark realm [the unconscious] is regarded either as coming from outside and therefore as real, or else as an hallucination and therefore not true. The idea that anything could be real or true which does not come from outside has hardly begun to dawn on contemporary man.
>
> (Jung 1992b, CW10, para. 387)

However, despite its capacity for rational reflection and self-awareness, the ego is still a complex and like all complexes, it maintains its continuity through the feeling-toned symbols of the unconscious. These symbols that define the ego may represent core aspects of our personal identity, such as gender or race, or they may be images of social or professional roles. They may be shared with other complexes and be bound up with the complexes that may define our cultures and our institutions. Whatever form they take, they will mark the ego's boundaries and direct the flow of its energy, reminding us of who we *feel* we are and who we *feel* we are not. Although the ego imagines itself to be rational and in control, it is in reality 'pushed around like a figure on a chessboard by an invisible player' (Jung 1928 CW7, para. 251). Any challenge to the continuity of the ego will therefore be met with an emotional resistance, and when the associated symbols are archetypal or related to more collective cultural or group complexes, the reaction may particularly intense.

During a group supervision session, it had been suggested to a participant that her behaviour in the group was shaped by her national culture. Her immediate response was explosive and charged with a level of intense anger that was striking, given that the suggestion had seemed well intended and balanced. As the group explored what had happened, she revealed that she was part of a religious minority that had historically been subjected to oppression within her country. She described how her grandparents had been forced to flee from their homes during a particularly brutal period of persecution. Although her own life had been comfortable, the trauma of her ancestors was experienced as personal and in the present. Her remembered past also came with strong matrilineal associations, as the stories told to her by her mother and grandmother had emphasised that it was only through the strength and endurance of women that her family had survived. While she understood rationally that she held her nations passport, she rejected the idea that she was part of its culture. Any association with her country as a symbol of identity was received as an attack not simply on herself but on her community and perhaps even on the maternal archetype itself. It caused a complex to constellate that was personal, cultural, and collective and carried all the numinous energy that implies.

As we develop, the ego faces a threat not only from the turbulence of the psyche within us but from the reality of the world beyond us, and it takes further steps to protect itself. The complex of the persona begins to form as a functional adaption to a social world. It protects the ego from the rough and tumble of external relationships and acts as an additional layer of insulation from the unconscious. It provides an idealised mask, rich with its own symbols, that mediates our relationships and reminds both ourselves and others of how we want to be seen. Those parts of us that are incompatible with our rational and social existence are then returned to the personal unconscious where they find a home in the developing shadow complex, an accumulation of those symbols that represent 'the dark, unlived and repressed side of the ego' (Von Franz 1995, p. 3). In the shadow lurk those ideas that we cannot allow ourselves to face in ourselves, and their symbols embody the 'other'. These ideas are not simply repressed aspects of the conscious mind but things we fear and despise as a direct threat to our sense of self. The shadow complex also has an arche-typal core, that of absolute evil, which is ready to provide its numinous energy to otherwise everyday associations.

Lying at the core of the ego complex but also encompassing the whole psy-che is the archetype of the Self. This is the embodiment of the sense of possi-bility and wholeness that stimulates our search for meaning in a fragmented and potentially meaningless world. It is through the numinous energy of the Self that the ego finds the impetus to transcend its own limitations and to face the paradoxical mystery of the unconscious. The Self gives us purpose by reminding us of the possibility of an integrated psyche which contains all that we have been, are now, and could perhaps become.

> The self is not only the centre, but also the whole circumference which embraces both conscious and unconscious; it is the centre of this totality, just as the ego is the centre of consciousness.
>
> (Jung 1968, CW12, para. 444)

For this reason, Jung referred to the Self as the 'god image' (1928, CW7, para. 248), and its often-circular symbols can be found in many of the spiritual and religious traditions of the world. In Hinduism and Buddhism, mandalas are intricate geometric designs often used in meditation to symbolize the divine wholeness of the cosmos. In Islam and Orthodox Christianity, the great domes of mosques and churches remind us of the celestial heavens and the presence of the divine. Native American cultures, such as the Navajo, incorporate circu-lar sand paintings in ceremonies, reflecting the sacred interconnectedness of all living things. Many traditions across the world, from ancient Egypt to the Norse myths of the Viking age to the Gnostics of the Middle Ages, have also made use of circular images of the uroboros (Neumann 1954), a snake eating its own tail as a reminder of the eternal cycle of life and death. Even the spiral carvings and stone circles of palaeolithic and neolithic sites (Lewis-Williams and Pearce 2005) point towards a universal symbol of something beyond us, something which transcends cultural boundaries and which seems to demand transformation.

The archetypal and collective nature of these symbols was emphasised by the child psychiatrist and Jungian analyst Michael Fordham (Astor 1995), who observed that young children often spontaneously drew circles as an apparent aid to give form to and then integrate their emerging sense of self. In one case, he described a two-year-old girl who clung to her mother and found the possi-bility of separation to be almost unbearable. One day she drew a circle and said, 'me', and 'almost at once her whole manner changed and she got down off her chair and played with some toys for several minutes' (Fordham 1957, p. 149). Fordham likened the mandala to the breast and suggested that the child's ability to create this symbol for themselves allowed them to replicate the feeling of wholeness in the relationship with the mother (Astor 1995). In creating circles, we are apparently able to (at least temporarily) resolve the paradox of the separate reality of the conscious mind and the collective depths of the unconscious.

Reflections and Implications

The psyche, then, can be seen as a dynamic and energetic system that extends far beyond the limitations of the conscious mind. Despite the best efforts of the ego to convince us otherwise, mind is located not beyond our physical and social systems but within them. We are continually influenced by them, and this influence may be based upon experiences that may not always be our own. The psyche gathers up the collected experiences of the past in 'feeling toned complexes' of symbolic associations, which then reach through time and space to shape our personality and behaviour, as individuals, groups, and societies. This past is not limited to our own experiences but may extend to include the experiences of those around us, to our societies, and perhaps even to other living beings. For this reason, Jung has depicted mind as a series of islands (Figure 1.1, McGuire 1989, p. 154), emerging from a foundation of collective experiences, which includes our 'animal ancestors'.

For coaches working within the Jungian tradition, the primary focus is on making sense of what is happening 'below the surface' of the conscious mind. We must help our clients locate themselves in the vast collective system that surrounds them and understand the timeless forces that shape them. With a more nuanced appreciation of the voice of the unconscious, they can begin to understand why they behave as they do and examine their relationships, to themselves, to their families, organisations, or cultures, or simply to

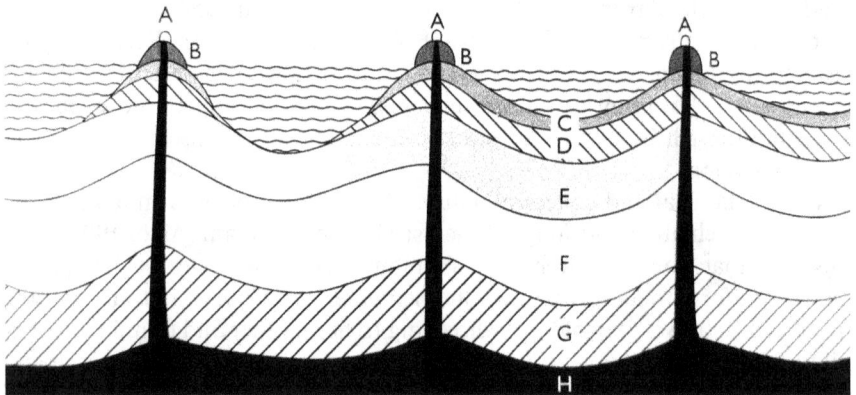

Figure 1.1 Diagram of the psyche, used with permission from Princeton University Press.

A = Individuals, B = Families, C = Clans, D = Nations, E = Large Group (European man for instance), F = Primate ancestors, G = Animal ancestors in general, H = "Central fire."

the complex reality of being human. They can begin to make more conscious choices about who they want to be and how they live their lives. With a greater awareness of the whole psyche, they can draw upon the intuition, inspiration, and energy of the unconscious without being swept along by it. They may still act out their complexes as a reflex, but they will return to conscious awareness more quickly and regulate their responses more easily (Knox 2004).

In Jungian psychology, this process is termed 'individuation', a lifelong journey of development through which we begin to realise our potential and make more conscious choices about our lives. It is a process through which we may better understand and mitigate the unexamined effects of the unconscious while listening to its voice and drawing inspiration from it. Individuation is a movement towards the archetypal image of the Self, not simply as the centre of the ego but as the circumference of whole psyche. While we can never attain the full potential of the Self, it provides an imagined goal to which we are continually drawn, through an increasing understanding of who we are and of who we may become. Individuation is a natural process, and over the course of our lives, many of us will be drawn to wonder about ourselves and our place in the world. It may also be a confronting and demanding process, as we are forced to question deeply held beliefs and assumptions and perhaps face aspects of ourselves that we have denied or never even considered. As Jolande Jacobi has suggested, we know that 'no saint is spared wrestling with his inner demons, and that no great artist ever accomplished his work without toil and sweat' (1967, p. 17). It may, however, be a little less lonely with a psychotherapist, a coach, or just a good and insightful friend alongside us.

The key to individuation is an awareness and an appreciation of symbols as the voice of the unconscious. Through what is termed a 'symbolic attitude' (Jung 1971, CW6, Hubback 1969), we can pay more attention to the symbols of the unconscious and develop an appreciation for their possible origins and for the energy they carry. Symbols provide a focal point for the conscious mind to begin to make sense of what otherwise would simply be an inexplicable feeling or an impulse to act. Through symbols, we can reflect on what belongs to us, on what belongs to our culture, and on what may even be simply part of being human. We can begin to imagine what the unconscious is trying to do and why, as it re-enacts its timeless, often archetypal strategies. We can start to appreciate the importance of our bodies and of our connection with the physical world. In noticing these symbols, we can perhaps be less overwhelmed by the energy and associations they often carry with them. We may become less fearful, less angry, or less ashamed and can work constructively with the energy of their associated complexes rather than simply being taken by them. Symbols allow the intangible to be given form and so allow us to make more conscious choices. If we want to move closer to our potential, it is symbol that will show us the way.

As you read this chapter:

* What images or associations come to mind?
* What feelings are evoked in you by these images? How intensely do you feel them?

References

Astor J 1995, *Michael Fordham: Innovations in analytical psychology*. London: Routledge.

Baring A and Cashford J 1991, *The myth of the goddess: evolution of an image*. London: Viking.

Brooke R 2015, *Jung and phenomenology*. New York: Routledge.

Carvalho R 2020, Somapsyche. *British Journal of Psychotherapy* 36: 586–596.

Castleman T 2004, Threads, knots, tapestries: How a tribal connection is revealed through dreams and synchronicities. Einsiedeln, Switzerland: Daimon Verlag.

Descartes R 2005, *Discourse on method and the meditations*. London: Penguin Classics.

Faulkner W 1951, *Requiem for a nun*. New York: Random House.

Fordham M 1957, *New developments in analytical psychology*. London: Routledge and Kegan Paul.

Freud S 1900, *The interpretation of dreams*. SE4.

Henderson J 1990, *The cultural unconscious, shadow and self*. Wilmette, IL: Chiron Publications.

Hillman J 1975, Revisioning psychology. New York: Harper & Row.

Hogenson GB 2004, Archetypes: Emergence and the psyche's deep structure. In J Cambray and L Carter (eds.) *Analytical psychology: Contemporary perspectives in Jungian analysis*. Hove: Routledge.

Hubback J 1969, The symbolic attitude in psychotherapy. *Journal and Analytical Psychology* 14(1): 36–47.

Jacobi J 1967, *The way of individuation*. New York: Harcourt Brace Jovanovich.

Jung CG 1928, *Two essays on analytical psychology*. CW7.

Jung CG 1959, *The archetypes and the collective unconscious*. CW9i.

Jung CG 1960, *The structure and dynamics of the psyche*. CW8.

Jung CG 1964, *Man and his symbols*. Garden City, NY: Doubleday & Co.

Jung CG 1968, *Psychology and alchemy*. CW12.

Jung CG 1971, *Psychological types*. CW6.

Jung CG 1975, *Letters, vol. 2: 1951-1961* (eds. G Adler and A Jaffe). London: Routledge & Kegan Paul.

Jung CG 1977, *The symbolic life*. CW18.

Jung CG 1992a, *Experimental researches*. CW2.

Jung CG 1992b, *Civilisation in transition*. CW10.

Knox J 2003, *Archetype, attachment, analysis: Jungian psychology and the emergent mind*. Hove, East Sussex: Brunner-Routledge.

Knox J 2004, Developmental aspects of analytical psychology: New perspectives from cognitive neuroscience and attachment theory. In J Cambray and L Carter (eds.) *Analytical psychology: Contemporary perspectives in Jungian analysis*. Hove, Easy Sussex: Routledge.

Lewis-Williams D and Pearce D 2005, *Inside the neolithic mind*. London: Thames & Hudson.

Libet B 2004, *Mind time: The temporal factor in unconsciousness*. Cambridge, MA: Harvard University Press.

McGuire, W 1989, *Bollingen: An adventure in collecting the past*. Princeton, NJ: Princeton University Press.

Neumann E 1954, *The origins and history of consciousness*. London: Routledge and Kegan Paul.

Neumann E 1963, *The great mother: An analysis of the archetype*. Princeton, NJ: Princeton University Press.

Norretranders T 1998, *The user illusion: Cutting consciousness down to size*. New York: Viking.

Otto R 1923, *The idea of the holy*. London: Oxford University Press.

Peat FD 1987, *Synchronicity: The bridge between matter and mind*. New York: Bantam.

Peat FD 1991, Introduction to Pauli, physics, and psychology. *Psychological Perspectives* 24: 17–18.

Papadopoulos RK 2006, Jung's epistemology and methodology. In RK Papadopoulos (ed.) *The handbook of Jungian psychology: Theory, practice and applications*. Hove, East Sussex: Routledge.

Piontelli A 1992, *From foetus to child: An observational and psychoanalytic study*. London: Routledge.

Singer T and Kimbles S 2004, *The cultural complex: Contemporary Jungian perspectives on psyche and society*. Hove, East Sussex: Routledge.

Stevens A 1982, *Archetypes: A natural history of the self*. London: Routledge.

Stevens A 2004, The archetypes. In RK Papadopoulos (ed.) The handbook of Jungian psychology: Theory, practice and applications. Hove, East Sussex: Routledge.

von Franz M-L 1985, The transformed berserk: Unification of psychic opposites. *ReVISION* 8(1): 17–26.

von Franz M-L 1995, *Shadow and evil in fairy tales*. Boston, MA: Shambhala Publications.

Waddell M 1998, *Inside lives: Psychoanalysis and the growth of the personality*. London: Karnac.

Wegner D 2002, *The illusion of conscious will*. Cambridge, MA: MIT press.

Wilson T 2002, Strangers to ourselves: Discovering the adaptive unconscious. Cambridge, MA: Harvard University Press.

Zabriskie, B 2004, Endnotes: Whence and whither. In J Cambray and L Carter (eds.) *Analytical psychology: Contemporary perspectives in Jungian analysis*. Hove, Easy Sussex: Routledge.

Chapter 2

Form and Function

The Many Faces of Symbol and Its Significance for Our Development

A symbol begins as an association, a bridge between an inner 'felt experience' and an image (or collection of images) from the outer world. It is a psychological echo of real events, which allows the learning from the past to be easily stored and accessed to support our lives in the present. The symbol represents not literally its concrete and real-world inspiration but its emotional significance to us. We feel something and associate it with an image in mind that is then able to evoke the past in the present. We are quickly reminded by the symbol of how we should feel and react in response to a particular stimulus. Because the symbol begins in the emotionally charged depths of the unconscious, it cannot easily be defined and can never be more than a partial representation of its possible associations. It is an elusive and intangible artefact which may contain many different and often conflicting faces. Jung suggested that a symbol was simply 'the best possible explanation for a complex fact not yet clearly apprehended by consciousness' (1927, CW8, para. 69) and 'an intuitive idea that cannot yet be formulated in any other way' (1956, CW5, para. 77).

The mysterious nature of a symbol is then compounded as its origins may lie not always in our personal experience but in the shared experiences of our communities and our cultures and perhaps even of humanity itself. They may represent not only those things that have happened to us but the things that have happened to those around us and to those that have gone before us. The symbol may have begun its journey in the impersonal psychological storehouse of the 'collective unconscious', as a record of typically human experiences and associations. Here we may encounter 'symbols which are older than the historical man, which are inborn in him from the earliest times, and, eternally living, outlasting all generations, still making up the groundwork of the human psyche' (Jung 1927, CW8, para. 794). These symbols may be 'archetypal', as representations of the basic themes that define what it is to be human and which provide a 'stock of inherited possibilities of representation that are born anew in every individual' (Jung 1956, CW5, para. 264). However, symbols are not archetypes, which 'manifest themselves only through their ability to organise images and ideas' (Jung 1927, CW8, para. 440). They are only partial

DOI: 10.4324/9781003463269-3

images of an archetypal idea which simply provides an inherited general core, partly physiological and partly psychological, around which associated symbols begin to cluster and organise themselves. Symbols help channel the energy of an archetype but are not a complete representation of them.

> The symbols [the psyche] creates are always grounded in the unconscious archetype, but their manifest forms are moulded by the ideas acquired by the conscious mind. The archetypes are the numinous, structural elements of the psyche and possess a certain autonomy and specific energy which enables them to attract, out of the conscious mind, those contents which are best suited to themselves. The symbols act as transformers, their function being to convert libido from a 'lower' into a 'higher' form.
>
> (Jung 1956, CW5, para. 344)

The symbols of popular psychology, like the Heroic Warrior or the Great Mother, are inspirational and draw on archetypal energies, but they have many forms and always exist in the context of the cultures and personal lives of those they touch. They are intertwined with the history and social structures of our communities to form the 'cultural unconscious' (Henderson 1990) as symbols that represent the ideas and beliefs of a particular group of people. It is to this accumulation that we then add our own associations, with our own particular nuances and meanings.

When a symbol has a close connection to the collective and cultural unconscious, its energy may feel particularly intense or 'numinous', prompting an emotional response that may appear disproportionate to the symbol itself. We may find ourselves drawn to a mythological motif or a religious icon with a fascination that extends far beyond the superficial image. In describing the impact of symbol upon us, Jung writes:

> Their pregnant language cries out to us but they mean more than they say. We can put our finger on the symbol at once even though we may not be able to unriddle its meaning to our entire satisfaction. A symbol remains a perpetual challenge to our thoughts and feelings.
>
> (Jung 1971b, CW15, para. 119)

It was this fascination that first led me to Jungian psychology. At the age of 21, I was studying palaeolithic cave art in France, with a particular focus on hand stencils. These images cover the walls of caves and were made around 14,000 years ago by blowing pigment over the hand while it was placed on the rock. Although I had no real idea why they had been made (perhaps as a signature or part of a ritual), I found I was touched by an increasing sense of connection and wonder. There was something primal and archetypal about the images. They felt like a statement of presence, agency, and identity and made me want to place my own hand over them and touch the same rock that the maker had touched. The images felt charged with an intent that drew me in, but their meaning seemed just out of sight. I was captivated by them because they raised so many questions but gave me no answers. It does not seem to matter whether the handprints were eternally collective symbols, existing beyond time and space, or whether they were just personal symbols arising from my own experiences and challenges. Did they draw me into a human experience, or did I project my own fantasies into them? What does matter is that they moved me.

We can then best know a symbol by the emotional intensity it seems to evoke with us. In a process that Jung called 'canalisation' (1927, CW8, para. 79), symbols form the 'banks' through which the energy of life flows and the underlying psychological structures of complexes are organised and directed. In this way, symbols are an intrinsic part of the basic building blocks of our personality and behaviour. They shape and define how we organise our understanding of the world and how we respond to it. As the energy bound up with the symbol is activated by an association to changes in our inner or outer worlds, the symbol begins to 'constellate' or return to conscious form, perhaps with subtle changes to its structure or associations. Here it demands our attention and provides a locus for our reactions, channelling energy into our responses. It is not until we have spent time with it that its power seems to dissipate, and even then, it may continue to remind us of something we have not quite grasped. Symbols seem to arouse and compel us to action. They are a carrier of subjective meaning, and if we reflect on the symbols and the way they shape our behaviour, we may begin to better understand the hidden depths of the unconscious. Through symbols, we can become aware of our unexamined and yet defining emotions and motivations.

The energetic and elusive quality of symbols suggested by Jungian psychology contrasts with a traditional psychoanalytic perspective and the simplistic interpretations of popular psychology. Freud imagined the unconscious as a storehouse of coded images, which could be reduced through interpretation to a clear and unambiguous set of meanings. In contrast, Jung saw it as a dynamic and living system, reaching from an unknowable past through an experienced present to an emerging future. In this context, he took care to distinguish symbols from signs: the former play an active and emotionally resonant role in shaping our lives, and the latter simply denote the objects they represent, like an arrow on a map indicating 'you are here'. As Jung suggests:

> A sign is always less than the thing it points to, and the symbol is always more than we can understand at first sight. Therefore, we never stop at the sign but go on to the goal it indicates; But we remain with the symbol because it promises more than it reveals.
>
> (Jung 1977, CW18, para. 482)

The energetic quality of symbol is highly subjective, as it is driven by our early associations with the symbol in mind. Whether their origins lie in collective or purely personal experiences, symbols may have a very different resonance, association, and meaning for each person who encounters them. Although they may point to similar and often archetypal associations, the particular meanings they evoke can really be considered only in a particular context. Though writing about dreams, Jung could have been writing about any manifestation of symbol when he suggested that 'no dream symbol can be separated from the individual who dreams it, and there is no definite or straightforward interpretation of any dream' (1964, p. 53). Although the symbol of a hand may have collective associations, I encountered the symbol at a time when I was wondering about my own place in the world. As I prepared to leave university, I was faced with the questions of what I would do with my life and who I would become. What would my handprint be? The more I observed and studied these images, the more this question seemed to haunt me, although I was consciously aware of their symbolic impact only in retrospect. At the time, I felt their presence and was moved by it but did not deliberately reflect on it. The meaning of the handprints and the unconscious effect it had on me at the time became clear only as I reflected on those symbols in the years that followed. While it feels likely that at least some part of that meaning, as archetypal images of self and agency, may have been shared with their creators, all I can describe with any certainly is their effect upon me.

Forms and Faces

When we imagine a symbol, we often imagine a single visual image, such as a mandala or a religious icon or the images of art or film, but a symbol may take many forms, including 'symbolic thoughts and feelings, symbolic act and situations' (Jung 1964, p. 55). They may appear in clusters or build progressively on each other to provide a kaleidoscope of ideas and associations that somehow combine and align in meaningful ways. We may discover them in 'the hand that guides the crayon or the brush, the foot that executes the dance-step, with the eye and the ear, with the word' (Jung 1927, CW8, p. 343). Their defining quality as symbols is always found in the energy and associations bound up with them. Symbols are experienced in their effect and the attention and reaction they demand from us. Anything then may be a symbol provided it has the potential to carry more meaning than its literal form suggests: to state or signify 'something more and other than itself' (Jung 1971a, CW6, para. 817). The sounds of seagulls evoke the memories of childhood holidays with my grandparents, and I am reminded of happy times of ice creams and long walks on sandy beaches with a plastic bucket and spade. The smells of wet dog resurrect much-loved family pets, long muddy walks in the woods, and log fires. Through symbol in all its many forms, the associations of the past come flooding back, to be lived again in the present.

Symbol may also be physical in nature, perhaps appearing as an intentional act like a handshake or a hand-on-heart greeting. These may, of course, appear as reflexive social norms but may still also carry a deeply symbolic personal or cultural meaning and perhaps also a collective need. Following the COVID pandemic, where touch had been socially and sometimes legally proscribed, many people seemed to find found the experience of a handshake or a hug to be a particularly cathartic one. After months of social distancing, physical contact became a sometimes awkward, sometimes fearful and often deeply satisfying reestablishment of relationship through a symbolic act.

A physical symbol may also appear unintentionally as a parapraxis (Laplanche and Pontalis 1988), an unwitting 'slip' which reveals an underlying unconscious complex or state without a conscious awareness of the act itself. The Jungian analyst Arnold Mindell has proposed the existence of a 'dreambody', or a manifestation of the psychological in the physical. Mindell suggests that just as the dream expresses the unconscious with symbols in the mind, the 'dreambody' expresses the unconscious with symbols in the body, through movements, sensations and symptoms. To work with these symbols, Mindell developed an approach, termed 'process work' (1988) where physical impulses were encouraged and amplified, making them easier to explore. If a leg needed to kick, the client was encouraged to kick harder and if a finger needed to scratch, the client was encouraged to scratch more:

> While I was talking with the patient, his right-hand index finger continuously went to his head and scratched his scalp. Instead of asking him what he was doing, I told him to let his hand continue what it was doing and to let his finger speak. To make the story short, the finger said it was not really scratching the scalp but trying to massage it, because it was tense. It did not let the blood run through up into the hairs and would not let thoughts through. In other words, this person was 'narrow' minded in the sense that he did not let his thoughts flow.
>
> (Mindell 1984, pp. 98–99)

Symbols may be musical, evoking associations and emotions through different keys, rhythms, and melodies. Auschwitz, like many concentration camps in the 1940s, had an active camp orchestra which played as prisoners left the camp to work and then returned at the end of the day, often carrying the bodies of their comrades who had died during the shift. A number of pieces of music were composed and played by this orchestra, and notable among these was the tango entitled 'Dream of Haiti'. The tango was a popular dance hall tune in the 1930s and 1940s across Europe but seemed to have a particular symbolism for both prisoners and guards. It originated in the slums of Buenos Aires and drew from a colourful cultural palette of Italian, Spanish, Polish and Jewish immigrants. During the 19th century, Argentina saw massive waves of the poor and the dispossessed and became a melting pot of marginalised people, all desperate to change their lives. The tango reminded these people of their alienation from their roots, and their hopes for a better future. It was a dance of companionship and frustrated love, that also spoke 'of fatality, of painful des-tinies; of an unlikely ideal world' (Czackis 2003, p. 45). The tango was permit-ted by the camp guards who saw it as being less rebellious than jazz and as providing inmates with a 'willing preoccupation with the dance as an oblivion of the self rather than as an incentive to disobedience' (Czackis 2003, p. 51). Because of its prominence in the camps, particularly as an accompaniment to formal executions, any music played by the camp orchestra ultimately became known as a 'death tango'. This symbolism then takes on even greater depth and resonance when the title of this particular piece is considered. Haiti is the only nation in history that was founded, following a successful revolution, by its slaves, and it is easy to imagine the prisoners in Auschwitz having a similar dream. We can only wonder whether the title of the piece was discussed secretly in the camp, accumulating new ideas and associations, or whether it remained in the collective unconscious as an unacknowledged symbol of hope in enslavement.

Language may also provide a source of powerful symbols, allowing often abstract ideas to be layered with complex meaning and associations. Words may also be clustered together to form metaphors, but even simple words that are superficially clear and defined may be symbolic for a particular individual or group in the right context. Some words may also have a close archetypal association, conjuring a profound and often psychoidal experience, that speaks to both the physiological and psychological inheritance of being human. It is on this foundation that literature and poetry is built, separating these combina-tions of words from those of instruction manuals and legal documents. When T.S Eliot writes 'this broken jaw of our lost kingdoms' (Eliot 1977, p. 84) he is not describing a simple and literal injury, but the physical and psychological desolation in Europe that followed the First World War. Even for generations too young to have experienced the devastation of this period, the line evokes a sense of visceral pain and a nostalgic loss that still moves us.

> The eyes are not here
> There are no eyes here
> in this valley of dying stars
> in this hollow valley
> this broken jaw of our lost kingdoms
> in this last of meeting places
> we grope together
> and avoid speech
> gathered on this beach of the tumid river'
> TS Eliot (1977, p. 84 from The Hollow Men)

The Word Association Test (WAT) is a technique developed by Jung early in his career to explore language as a symbolic route to understanding the unconscious. It involves presenting a series of words to participants, who then respond with the first word that comes to mind, while the person carrying out the test observes both the words used, and the underlying energy or physical 'tics' that colour the response. Jung believed that analysing a person's responses could uncover hidden conflicts, complexes, or aspects of the psyche not readily accessible to conscious awareness. I was working with this test with a coach, who had come to me for supervision. I had mentioned the WAT in an earlier conversation, and he was intrigued, and had asked to experience it. As we began the test, he appeared confident, articulate, and relaxed, but he noticeably stumbled when I mentioned the word 'magic'. He coughed and spluttered before suggesting (with some irritation) that it was a 'stupid word in include' in a supervision conversation. We discussed why this word had created such a strong response and he told me that he did not think 'magic' had anything to do with coaching or coaching psychology. The very idea of the word seemed to annoy him, and he was keen to dismiss it along with the WAT itself. As we explored the meaning of the word however, he revealed that, although he loved coaching when he had started out, he had come to find it dull and uninspiring. He had lost any emotional connection with his work and his clients, and as he began to approach the last decade before retirement, he felt he was just 'going through the motions'. The word 'magic' felt like a symbolic reminder of what he had lost, and the WAT had revealed an inner conflict that was being played out in my client's professional life. On the one hand was the idea of work and responsibility, perhaps gathering around a patriarchal archetype, where the image of a stern father demanded a rational 'seriousness'. Here the rigid dogma of psychology as science, excluded any possibility of 'magic' in my client's working life. On the other hand, was the mystery of relationship and the human mind, that had drawn him to coaching in the first place, as part of his own development journey. Our subsequent conversations then focused on how these two ideas could be brought together, and how he could rediscover a little 'magic' to inspire him again. In our day-to-day lives and work, we may not use a formal process like the WAT but if we pay attention, we may still discover the symbolic significance of language. In our conversations we may notice that we use particular words frequently or in unusual ways or have strong emotional reactions to words or phrases which seem misaligned with the superficial meaning of the words themselves. In Jungian psychology:

> The symbol is the word that goes out of the mouth, that one that does not simply speak, but that rises out of the depths of the self as a word of power and great need and places itself unexpectedly on the tongue. It is an astonishing and perhaps seemingly irrational word, but one recognises it as a symbol since it is alien to the conscious mind. If one accepts the symbol, it is as if a door opens leading into a new room whose existence one did previously not know.

(Jung 2009, p. 311)

The Stories We Tell

Once we acknowledge the symbolic significance of our words, we can become more sensitive to the way in which we use them in the stories we tell ourselves and others. Human beings have after all told stories for as long as we have had the language to do so. Our stories are filled with creation myths of gods, the battles of heroes, and the daily struggles of ordinary people. Sometimes magical and sometimes prosaic, they help us to orient ourselves and find our place in an often turbulent and confusing world. They remind us of where we have come from, of who we are and of what we may become. They are not simply descriptions of half-remembered events but are a medium through which we create and recreate our sense of self. Their power is derived from the symbols they contain (Covington 1995), which allow us to express feelings and intuitions that cannot be adequately expressed in any other way.

In his seminal study of the stories told by people facing serious illness, the sociologist Arthur W Frank (1995) describes how stories can be used to find a way through the 'narrative wreckage' of cancer, by restoring some sense of continuity and meaning. When 'the present is not what the past was supposed to lead up to, and the future is scarcely thinkable' (Frank 1995, p. 55), stories and their symbols can help us to ground and then reimagine ourselves. Frank describes symbols of denial, where the emphasis is placed on the promise of a cure and the body is described as something separate and distinct from the individual. Here, any real subjective experience of the present is simply ignored; 'I am fine but my body is sick and it will be fixed soon' (Frank 1995, p. 86). He describes symbols of chaos, where the narrative is disjointed and the symbols feel disordered, as a reflection of an unresolved inner turmoil. One woman with a chronic illness seems to use the frustrations of living with her mother as a symbol of the psychical way in which her own body gets in the way of her life: 'And if I'm trying to get dinner ready and I'm already feeling bad, she's in front of the refrigerator…and then she's in front of the microwave and then she's in front of the silverware drawer' (Frank 1995, p. 99). Finally, he describes symbols of hope, where the illness may be seen as somehow redemptive, offering new meaning for life. Here a woman sees herself, following a mastectomy, as an 'Amazon of Dahomey' whose initiation involved having one breast removed, to better shoot a bow. The mastectomy represented for her a rebirth as a warrior who needed to lose something of herself to become more fully herself.

Listening to stories is particularly important in coaching work, as they provide a window into the inner theatre of our clients and the narratives that define and shape their sense of self. I often begin a coaching relationship by asking my clients to tell me their stories and where they begin is usually in itself highly symbolic. Some stories begin with an ancestral journey, and the leaving of a homeland through war or famine, or just in search of a better life. They acknowledge a wound or a redemption, or perhaps the experience of being an outsider and the strength of character needed to survive. Some tell stories about the lessons learned from their parents or their childhood dreams, perhaps with a nostalgia for what might have been or a hope for what may still be possible in some form. For some the real stories begin in early adulthood with the challenges of leaving home and finding work and for others there are a series of impactful events through which they have emerged. The stories may focus on particular hobbies or achievements. These stories may have been consistent throughout their lives, providing reliable templates to remind them of who they are or they may be remembered in new ways, with new imagery to reflect changes in circumstances and inner theatre. The stories both contain symbols and are symbols themselves, held together by a single, archetypal theme.

A good friend and colleague was brought up in a hotel that had been in her family for generations. Some of her earliest memories are of helping her parents tend to their guests, and she has also worked most of her adult life in the hotel industry. To listen to her life story is to experience a vocation that goes far beyond a simple commercial exchange of a bed for money and is instead steeped in a pervasive image of a welcoming maternal warmth. The 'Great Mother' archetype has provided her with the foundations of a highly successful career. Hotels have not simply been her places of work, but the places of her identity.

> Once upon a time, I discovered I had a natural instinct for leadership. Not because of a title or training, but because people chose to follow me. Much of that came from mirroring my mother who was a strong woman with a clear vision, and the warmth I felt when I was liked, when I stood for something. Courage came naturally. I stood up for what I believed in. In school, I was the centre of energy, not because I demanded it, but because I created space for others to feel seen. That role, of being present, visible, leading from the front, became my anchor, especially when life at home revolved around the demands of our family business. In hospitality, you meet people from every walk of life. That multicultural, ever-changing environment became my safe space. A space where I didn't just lead a hotel: I created a home, for my guests, my teams, my partners.

A Psychic Prison

Whatever form they take, symbols allow a rapid and reflexive response to our environment. Through symbols we can quickly interpret what is happening to us, and have our choices made for us by the unconscious without any need for conscious intervention. They hold our complexes together and direct their flow, ensuring a degree of continuity between the past, present and future. Symbols help defend us from the threats from the past, and direct us to action, often without a conscious acknowledgement of their presence. They guide predictable shortcuts which allow us to respond without needing to consider all the possible choices we could make. They keep us safe, but we may also become trapped. We may be defined by the energy and associations bound up with them, and we may never stop to wonder why we have taken a particular path. Through symbols we once again live out the experience of the past in the present, as an unconscious reflex.

During a supervision conversation, a coach described a piece of consultancy work where she had been asked to observe an executive team, led by a powerful and charismatic CEO. As she had entered her clients' offices she had felt as though she was being watched, and this feeling intensified as the first meeting began. She felt unusually uncomfortable upon entering the room and mentioned that 'all eyes were on her'. She found herself avoiding eye contact, and wondering if she was being judged by participants, and by the CEO in particular. The more she became aware of the eyes of the others, the more withdrawn she became. She began to doubt her ability to work with the group and when she debriefed with the CEO felt clumsy and inarticulate. Again, she was aware of his eyes observing her. When we discussed the symbol of the eyes, she remembered her own father's eyes when he scolded her for not being good enough. As a child recognition was 'given through achievement, when there was no achievement, there was no love'. She had come to associate being noticed with a feeling of inadequacy, and the eyes of others became a power symbol that drove her back into her herself. The act of observing a patriarchal authority figure had surfaced the feelings of the past and the symbol of the eyes which evoked a sense of inadequacy, urging her to hide. The symbol was, of course, personal but may also have carried a numinous energy. In myths and folk tales, the eye may have many often-conflicting associations, including wisdom, power, and the threat of evil, all of which seem to focus on the archetypal experience of seeing and being seen, perhaps by another human and perhaps by a predator. For my client, this primal image had become associated as a complex with the judgemental eyes of her father and then with authority figures in general.

Symbols may also help lock us into the belief systems that shape our identities, reminding us of who we are (and who we are not) as individuals, groups, or cultures. Symbols may be found in the way we dress, our possessions, and our particular mannerisms. We apply labels to ourselves that have an emotional resonance extending far beyond the literal fact. These labels may have both personal and collective origins and may be charged with archetypal, numinous energy. The symbolism of being a 'mother' or a 'teacher' is likely to evoke more associations than the simple reality of having produced children or being responsible for the transfer of knowledge. Our race or nationality may evoke feelings of belonging that transcend the simple accidents of birth and connect us with a timeless community whose norms and assumptions then define us. The events that shaped our ancestors, families, and colleagues will live on in symbolic form to shape us in turn. It is through symbols that our identity then becomes an 'unconscious conformity' (Jung 1971a, CW6, para. 742) where we subscribe unquestioningly to a particular way of being. We are defined by the symbols that surround us, but we rarely wonder about what they really mean. They direct our libido, the energy that shapes our behaviour, but we rarely allow ourselves to wonder if we have different choices. The unconscious past becomes our destiny.

A Catalyst for Transformation

However, as the symbol becomes conscious and begins to constellate, it gradually loses its hold over us. Its energy dissipates, and as we start to understand what is happening in the unconscious, we can begin to make different choices. We may begin to see the symbol differently and make new associations which take us down slightly different paths. We may also notice new symbols which make us stop and wonder, as they first appear to be quite at odds with the familiar patterns and habits that have shaped our life's journey so far. These symbols may provoke new thinking and energy that provide a bridge between old habits and new possibilities, not as a compromise but as a 'third living thing…a living birth that leads to a new level of being, a new situation' (Jung 1927, CW8, para. 189). In Jungian psychology, this is referred to as the 'transcendent function', a confrontation of opposing ideas, from which emerge a new position or perspective and 'a progressive development towards a new attitude' (Jung 1966, CW7, para. 159).

This confrontation is not a peaceful one and usually creates a tension and inner conflict which goes to the very heart of development work. It reflects the need of the conscious mind, the ego complex, to defend itself and to maintain the illusion of order and control. The ego prefers the status quo and the familiar paths of our established complexes, held in place by their symbols and associations. However, when faced with changes in our environment or perhaps simply the suffocating inflexibility of the conscious mind, the psyche may offer up a symbol as an intuitive demand. This symbol may capture our attention for a moment and interrupt the natural course of events with an idea that carries new meaning and new possibility. It may be charged with the numinous, archetypal energy of the collective unconscious. We can describe this as a moment of kairos, a meaningful moment that transcends linear time and space and reminds us that we are connected to something larger than ourselves. Here the symbol offers access to the collective themes and wisdom of humanity. We are faced with the challenge and possibility that others have faced before. The symbols that activate the transcendent function usually appear in the moment that we need them to. We will resist them, as a reaction to their potential for disruption and the risk of the unknown, but if we are able to overcome our anxiety and stay with the image, it will help us move to a new and previously unimaginable way of being. Symbol allows us to confront and then develop those ideas that we would otherwise avoid. It helps us live a more whole and more integrated life and provides a provocation (through the transcendent function) which may reveal new possibilities and unimagined potential.

> Say you have been very one-sided and lived in a two-dimensional world only, behind walls, thinking that you were perfectly safe; Then suddenly the sea breaks in: you are inundated by an archetypal world and you are in complete confusion. Then out of that confusion suddenly arises a reconciling symbol... Which unites the vital need of man with the archetypal conditions. So you have made a step forward in consciousness, have reached a higher level; therefore it is of course a transcendent function because you transcended from one level to another. It is as if you had crossed the great flood... or the great river, and arrived on the other bank, and so you have transcended the obstacle.
>
> (Jung 1988, p. 975)

The transcendent function of symbol is founded on an important aspect of the unconscious which is distinctive to Jungian psychology. For Jung, the unconscious was not simply repository of the half-remembered events of the past but a dynamic system in its own right, which supports adaption and growth. A traditionally psychoanalytic approach to the unconscious would look to the origins of symbol as condensed representatives of the events of the past, a perspective Jung described as 'reductive' (CW, para. 788). In contrast, Jung emphasised what he termed a 'constructive method' where symbols could also bring an intuitive meaning that relates to our 'future attitude' (1971a, CW6, para. 701) and allows us to 'act in harmony with the unconscious' (1971a, CW6, para. 702). Through the lens of Jungian psychology, the events of the past, whether personal or collective, can be continually remembered in new ways and combined with new ideas to offer new possibilities. These possibilities can be carried in symbols. It is through symbols that the unconscious intuitively takes in new information from our context and suggests new ways in which we may adapt and grow. Jung suggests that symbols provide a catalyst for development if we are only able to notice and work with them:

> Consciousness is continually widened through the confrontation with previously unconscious contents, or - to be more accurate - could be widened if it took the trouble to integrate them.
>
> (Jung 1927, CW8, para. 193)

A supervision client was a former military officer from a conservative family background who now worked in a very structured and hierarchical commercial organisation. Over a few years, he had begun to explore other ways of working and became drawn to coaching. He raised with me the subject of a woman he had met on a programme. He described how he had been fascinated by the combination of her playful, flirtatious 'trickster' energy and the self-confidence with which she maintained her boundaries. We discussed the interesting contrast she offered as a symbol, combining a grounded maturity with an almost mystical promise of intimacy and transformation. I was reminded of the goddess Athena, from classical Greek myth, who was a similarly paradoxical figure as a goddess of both war and wisdom and who carried an archetypal 'trickster' energy. It was the cunning interventions of Athena, often in disguise, that allowed Odysseus to return home from the Trojan War and reunite with his young son, Telemachus. Through these interventions and the encouragement of the goddess, Telemachus was also able to achieve his own great deeds (aresteia) and become a man. Unlike other Homeric heroes, who achieve their aresteia through courage and bravery, Odysseus and his son, inspired by Athena, achieve theirs through their resourceful imaginations and their loyalty to her and to each other. As I mentioned my association, my client laughed and showed me an owl, a symbol of Athena, that he had tattooed on his arm a few years previously. We then discussed his intuition to integrate a more relational, playful, and possibly 'feminine' energy into his work, in contrast to the more structured, directive, and 'masculine' approach demanded by his upbringing and career.

A couple of hours after our meeting, I received a message from him. He had been speaking to a potential client who had mentioned during their initial conversation that her team called themselves 'Team Athena' and each member had an owl pendant key ring. It felt as though my client was being reminded of the need to change through what is termed a 'synchronicity' or 'meaningful coincidence' (Jung 1927, CW8, para. 827). Here archetypal, collective symbols often appear in uncanny and apparently unrelated ways to suggest some powerful purpose to which we feel inexplicably drawn. A synchronicity is an unexpected collision with the collective unconscious as a whole system, independent of space and time, during which we are reminded that we are simply a small part of that system. The meaning we seek and sometimes find in our own lives is something that has been lived before by others, and we may learn from their experiences. For my client, we may imagine that the move towards a more 'Athena' consciousness was not simply a personal impulse but something shared with others who have faced or are facing similar archetypal challenges, in this case an integration of both 'masculine' and 'feminine' aspects of the psyche as a movement towards our potential. In Jungian psychology, this integration may be seen as a symbol of the Self as an experience of wholeness, through the merging of the known 'reality' of the conscious mind and the mysterious 'other' of the unconscious (Barrett 2023, pp. 71–85). It is these archetypal experiences, arising from the collective unconscious, that provide the most intense and catalytic symbols for personal development. They supply the energy to move us away from our established patterns into a new way of being. In a structured 'patriarchal' world, there may be a collective need to integrate a more relational 'matriarchal' energy. My client was simply open to that possibility.

Reflections and Implications

Symbols then offer not only a route to understanding the mind but the key to our development. A symbol or cluster of symbols may bring the energy needed to begin the movement of the transcendent function, sparking new creative energies and offering new possibilities. They may appear in dreams, in particular events or synchronicities, or simply in the day to day and carry the potential for continual learning 'in every situation, person, relationship, challenge, thought, and event we face each moment of each day' (Miller 2004, p. 141). However, symbols alone will offer no easy solutions. The emergence of a symbol from the unconscious creates the possibility, but not the certainty, of change, and it is perhaps more likely that we will remain unaware of its significance. The symbols that define us will continue to shape our behaviour without any qualification or consideration, and the symbols that could unlock new possibilities are quickly repressed and returned to the unconscious. For sustainable development to happen, the conscious mind must become engaged. We must become consciously involved with the process of meaning-making and acknowledge that this may not be an easy task or a comfortable experience.

Our initial challenge is the complexity of symbol, in both its dynamic energy and its ambiguity. As the symbol constellates and we become consciously aware of it, it may take many different forms, evolve, or combine with other symbols. These may then draw upon each other for inspiration and appeal to different senses, offering more nuance and new associations. They may compete uncomfortably for space, representing an inner conflict that cannot be expressed in any other way. Some images may appear to be distinct and unique like small icons or single notes, and others as great blurred landscapes or complex musical scores. As Jung has suggested, 'the essence of the symbol consists in the fact that it represents in itself something that is not wholly understandable, and that it hints only intuitively at its possible meaning' (1971a, CW6, para. 171). As the ego so often seeks certainly and simplicity, our comfort with this confusing and emotionally charged muddle may be hard to bear.

This comfort may be further tested if the symbol requires us to question or even acknowledge the very foundations upon which our personality is based, particularly in relation to the ego complex. In a conscious examination of a symbol, we may be asking the ego to question itself, a request which we may then experience as an existential threat. It may be difficult to ask ourselves why we really wear the clothes we wear or move the way we do. It may be completely overwhelming to question the symbols of our racial identity or family role. The unknowable threat of the unconscious and the energy carried by the symbol may terrify the conscious mind, and we may then attempt to ignore or even repress any acknowledgement of the symbol, pushing it back into the unconscious. We may trivialise it or use a veneer of cynical rationalism to dismiss it. The ego works hard to maintain its illusion of control and continuity and generally prefers the contents of the unconscious to stay in the unconscious. This simply locks us into old habits and prevents any meaningful growth. As Jung suggests, 'just seeing and then brushing aside the symbols would... merely re-establish the old neurotic condition and destroy the attempt at a synthesis' (1964, p. 99).

However, if we are able to acknowledge the symbol and to tolerate its challenge to the established order of the psyche, we can then begin to explore the meaning it offers. We can begin to work with it, integrate it, and make different choices for our lives. We can begin to develop what is known as an 'ego-self axis' (Edinger 1960), allowing a stable communication between the rational decision-making of the conscious mind and the intuition, impulse, and potential of the unconscious. It is through the ego-self axis that we can build the confidence to wonder about symbol and the curiosity to explore its possible meanings. A symbol then offers not simply its own meanings but the opportunity to develop a more general capability. In working with a symbol in a single moment of learning, we can begin to strengthen the dialogue between the conscious and unconscious psyche and prepare ourselves for a lifetime of meaningful development, a process of integration known as 'individuation'. This process is inspired by a conscious awareness of symbol, as the transcendent function, and goes to 'the heart of Jung's paradigm' (Horne 1998, p. 25). To support and stimulate this process, helping our clients become more consciously whole, is the essence of a Jungian approach to coaching. Our role is to help the mind enlarge itself through a greater conscious understanding of 'what lies below the surface', and symbol is the foundation of our work. As Jung suggested, 'one creates inner freedom only through the symbol' (Jung 2009, p. 311).

As you reflect on this chapter:

- Pay attention to your immediate surroundings. What possible symbols catch your attention, perhaps as visual images, sounds, or smells?
- What feelings are evoked in you by these symbols? How intensely do you feel them?

References

Barrett L 2023, Considering gender: The other as the archetype of the soul. In L Barrett, *A Jungian approach to coaching: The theory and practice of turning leaders into people*. London: Routledge.

Covington C 1995, No story, no analysis? The role of narrative in interpretation. *Journal of Analytical Psychology* 40(3): 405–417.

Czackis L 2003, Tangele: The history of the Yiddish Tango. *The Jewish Quarterly* 50(1 (189)): 44–52.

Edinger EF 1960, The ego-self paradox. *Journal of Analytical Psychology* 5: 3–18.

Eliot TS 1977, *The complete poems and plays of TS Eliot*. London: Book Club Associates.

Frank AW 1995, *The wounded storyteller: Body, illness, and ethics*. London: The University of Chicago Press.

Henderson J 1990, *The cultural unconscious: Shadow and self*. Wilmette, IL: Chiron Publications.

Horne M 1998, How does the transcendent function? *The San Francisco Jung Institute Library Journal* 17(2): 21–42.

Jung CG 1927, *The structure and dynamics of the psyche*, CW8.

Jung CG 1956, *Symbols of transformation*, CW5.

Jung CG 1964, *Man and his symbols*. Garden City, NY: Doubleday.

Jung CG 1966, *Two essays on analytical psychology*, CW7.

Jung CG 1971a, *Psychological types*, CW6.

Jung CG 1971b, *The spirit in man, art and literature*. CW15.

Jung CG 1977, *The symbolic life*. CW18.

Jung CG 1988, Nietzsche's Zarathustra: Notes of the seminar given in 1934-1939. JL Barret (ed) *Lecture V, June 3, 1936*, pp. 965–982. Princeton, NJ: Princeton University Press.

Jung CG 2009, *The red book (liber novus)*. New York: W. W. Norton & Company.

Laplanche J and Pontalis J-B 1988, *The language of psychoanalysis*. London: Karnac.

Miller JC 2004, *The transcendent function: Jung's model of psychological growth through dialogue with the unconscious*. Albany, NY: State University of New York Press.

Mindell A 1984, *Dreambody: The body's role in revealing the self*. London: Routledge & Kegan Paul.

Mindell A 1988, *City shadows: Psychological interventions in psychiatry*. London: Routledge & Kegan Paul.

Chapter 3

Developing a Symbolic Attitude

A Foundation for Coaching the Unconscious

Whether we choose to notice it or ignore it, the unconscious is ever present. Its influence is derived from the physical experiences of our own bodies, our shared collective and cultural experiences, and the personal experiences of our own lives. It is not a dead repository but an energetic and living system that operates in parallel to the conscious mind. It drives and shapes our behaviour through 'feeling toned complexes', the combinations of images and emotions that form the 'living units of the unconscious psyche' (Jung 1927, CW8, para. 210). Each complex is 'a series of images in the truest sense, not an accidental juxtaposition or sequence, but a structure that is throughout full of meaning and purpose; it is a 'picturing' of vital activities' (Jung 1927, CW8, para. 618). These images, or symbols, provide a 'shorthand' to the psyche, allowing us to respond quickly and instinctively to changes in the world around us.

We cannot directly and consciously influence the unconscious (because it is by definition unconscious), and any attempt at repression is likely to simply increase its affect. Like a pressure cooker, the unconscious will increase its power if we fail to allow it some expression and we will 'act out' the complex uncontrollably. It may possess us, and, for a moment at least, we will lose conscious control of our actions. We can often repress the complex and its influence upon us through willpower, but we cannot remove it with rational thought alone, and 'at the first suitable opportunity it reappears in all its original strength' (Jung 1927, CW8, para. 201).

We can, however, better understand it and make more conscious choices about our responses. We can notice how the unconscious moves us and then choose to move ourselves in a different way. The key to this 'noticing' is the symbol, which can act as a bridge between the inspiration and impulse of the unconscious and the consideration and objective distance of the conscious mind. They are products of the unconscious, but the concrete forms they ultimately take are shaped through our conscious acknowledgement. Symbol has aspects that are both conscious and unconscious, rational and emotional. In noticing and exploring symbol, we are able to develop a deeper understanding of the one through the other. If we can notice symbols as they become visible

DOI: 10.4324/9781003463269-4

or 'constellate', we can begin to make sense of what is happening below the surface of consciousness. We can begin to understand the unconscious forces that drive us, and we can perhaps 'catch ourselves' acting out our impulse and make different choices. In these choices, we gradually become more integrated. We become more consciously aware of the unconscious and, in doing so, allow ourselves to make use of its intuition without being defined by it. This sense of balance sits at the heart of Jungian psychology and provides the foundation of the individuation process. Jung reminds us that

> Conscious and unconscious do not make a whole when one of them is suppressed and injured by the other. If they must contend, let it at least be a fair fight with equal rights on both sides. Both are aspects of life. Consciousness should defend its reason and protect itself, and the chaotic life of the unconscious should be given the chance of having its way to- as much of it as we can stand... This, roughly, is what I mean by the individuation process.
>
> (Jung 1968, CW9i, para. 522–23)

Introducing the Symbolic Attitude

To work with the unconscious, whether in developing ourselves or in supporting the development of others, we must be able to adopt what Jung described as a 'symbolic attitude': 'a definite view of life endowing the occurrence, whether great or small, with a meaning to which a certain deeper value is given than to pure actuality' (1971, CW6, para. 603). Here we can begin to find symbols in many different forms and in often unexpected places, knowing that 'every psychological expression is a symbol if we assume that it states or signifies something more and other than itself' (1971, CW6, para. 817). With a symbolic attitude, we recognise that almost anything can be a symbol if we are moved by it and can make meaning from it. We are simply open to its potential.

To develop a symbolic attitude, we must first be able to access a state of 'primary experience' (Wilner 1987), which provides a raw and fundamental sense of being in life and in the world, without any premature reaching for conscious meaning. We must take on the somewhat paradoxical role of 'participant observers', where we are living our lives and simultaneously observing our lived experience. This may be challenging in a world of activity and overstimulation, where salacious 'clickbait' threatens to overwhelm anything more subtle and where we are urged to decide without any meaningful reflection. If we remain with 'primary experience', our focus is not directed by conscious goals, and we do not move too quickly to describing our impressions, making associations, or moving to interpretation. We allow our observations to exist 'as they are', tolerating any ambiguity while taking a gentle note of their emotional intensity and their potential symbolic value. This intensity matters, as symbol is highly subjective, and we can know it only in the way it makes us feel. It is the 'sensuously perceptive expression of an inner experience...revealed in its immanent vital force' (Jung 1992b, p. 59). In developing a symbolic attitude, we are then calibrating ourselves as an instrument through which we can view the world. That calibration is based upon a familiarity with our own inner theatre, as the capacity to notice others is dependent on the capacity to first notice ourselves, and we must

> Never forget that in psychology the means by which you judge and observe the psyche is the psyche itself. Have you ever heard of a hammer beating itself? In psychology the observer is the observed. The psyche is not only the object but also the subject of our science.
>
> (Jung 1977, CW18, para. 277)

It is helpful to consider this 'primary experience' as being made up of three intertwined dimensions:

- Being in world: our ability to notice potential symbols in the world around us.
- Being in body: our ability to notice our own physical state.
- Being in mind: our ability to notice our emotions and the spontaneous creations of fantasy and daydreams.

We can begin in any place, depending on what is most striking to us, and then, as we move between the dimensions, we can notice how they relate to each other and so allow a broader network of potential symbols to emerge.

Being in World

For many people, it often seems easiest to begin with our surroundings, as the observation of the 'other' outside seems to be less threatening to the ego than the possibility of the 'other' inside. Here we may find symbols in all their many forms, that move us, provoke us, and shape our behaviour. These symbols may reveal something of our context but also something of ourselves in that context. We can deepen our awareness of ourselves as we observe ourselves in the world. Sometimes we may encounter rich and stimulating environments where we may be overwhelmed by unfamiliar symbols and images. Here we do not have to invest much time in waiting, as the symbols will find us. In describing his impressions of Nepal, the ecologist and philosopher David Abram writes:

> The air had been filled with smells - whether in the towns, where burning incense combined with the aromas of roasting meats and fruits for trade in the open market, and the stench of organic refuse rotting in the ravines, and sometimes of corpses being cremated by the river...And sounds as well: the chants of aspiring monks and adepts blended with the ringing of prayer bells on near and distant slopes, accompanied by the raucous croaks of ravens, and the sigh of the wind pouring over the passes, and the flapping of prayer flags.
>
> (1996, p. 26)

However, if we invest the time, we may also rediscover symbols in the ordinary and the everyday and in things that for the most part we simply take for granted and that pass unnoticed. Here the air may also be filled with smells, like rain on wet concrete or the fumes from a passing car or the smell of baking bread and fresh pastries. If we pay attention, we may notice the sad-looking toy that has been left by the side of the road or the flower on the name badge of the person who serves our coffee. In the familiar spaces of our offices or perhaps even our own homes, we may rediscover how we are greeted or wonder about the positioning of the clock. Are the voices around us raised or hushed, and what are the topics of conversation? On video calls, we may notice the books or pictures behind participants or their blurred background or perhaps the grey generic squares when their cameras have been turned off. All of these images may be symbolic, carrying an energy which draws our attention to them and speaks to something within us. It may speak to our own unconscious or to something we share with our environment. In our observation, we may start to see a complex interplay of relationships that can only begin to be understood through symbols.

On a development programme that I was involved with, participants were asked to shadow another person for a day and then reflect on the experience of being a 'participant observer', observing both the context and their inner world. They then wrote a detailed account of their experience, describing both what they had seen and what was evoked within them. These papers were then presented to small reflective practice groups, where they discussed the overall themes and the implications. One participant described how she had found the experience infuriating and suggested that her time had been wasted. With visible frustration, she told the group that there had been 'nothing of interest' in her observation of a senior manager in a professional services organisation. She described a fairly generic office space with views over many similar glass-walled buildings in the financial district of her city. The manager had not held any meetings, had made no significant telephone calls, and had answered only a few emails. Instead, she spent most of the day eating cake, playing solitaire on her computer, and staring out of her window. She had kicked off her shoes and put her feet on the desk while chewing a pencil. In the absence of any obvious stimulation, the participant had then channelled her boredom and irritation into the production of a detailed description of her surroundings. This in turn provoked a great deal of discussion in the group, in which she was able to recall more details and more potential symbols, leading to associations with her physiological and psychological responses and the possible hypotheses that could be drawn from them.

Being in Body

We may then build on these observations by noting our physical responses to them. In the felt experience of 'being in body', we may observe our physical state as another possible origin of symbol. Here symbol arises from the psychoid unconscious, the boundary between the psyche and the world, and may have a particularly intense or numinous quality. In a twitching leg, a dry throat, or a nervous laugh, we reveal the foundations upon which our psyche is built, and as we become aware of these foundations, we become aware of the psychological significance of them. In her description of the importance of the body in developmental work, the Jungian analyst Cedrus Monte describes the changes that accompanied her own experience of psychical therapy:

> After a series of treatments, I was structurally and psychologically different, very different. Among many other changes, I stood straighter, naturally, becoming taller by almost one-half inch; Without effort, my head rested differently on my torso; My shoe size changed considerably with my feet widening, allowing greater contact with the ground; And most importantly, I no longer experienced pain, a condition which has remained to this day, decades later.
>
> All the energy used to uphold the structural imbalance and withstand the pain was now released, available to propel me forward into life. I felt the ground beneath me as never before; I could stand more readily on my own two feet. I had the energy and strength to meet the world and was eventually able to develop and promote my own work as an artist. In Jungian terms one might say that the negative complex around which nearly all my libido had been focused was addressed to the extent that I become less regressively bound, constructively aligned with my own individuation process, no longer at such odds with who I was and how I could serve in the world.
>
> (Monte 2010, pp. 150–151)

Our development of a symbolic attitude may then begin in simply noticing the way in which we respond physically and emotionally to the sensations of our own bodies. Here we begin to develop a 'bodily knowing' (Monte 2010, p. 152) upon which we can build a more insightful awareness of ourselves and the world in which we live. The developing of this awareness does not have to be a formal meditation but simply a noticing of our physical experience in the moment as a daily practice. It can be a 'checking in' without ceremony as we are walking to work, sitting with a client, or reading this chapter. We can simply scan our bodies for particular sensations that stand out, and once something striking is located, we can linger there for a moment. Do we feel relaxed or tense, and where is any tension located? How does it feel to inhale or exhale? Does our chest feel tight, or is our breathing easy? What does the sun or the wind feel like on our skin? What can we smell? What can we taste? How could we describe these feelings in the most specific way possible.

We can then connect these feelings with the images from our surroundings and begin to reflect on that connection. This 'bodily knowing' helps move us from the intangible and elusive imagining of the psyche to a more lived experience, where we know the symbol to be real because we have physically felt its presence. Jung emphasises that

When an individual has been swept up into the world of symbolic mysteries, nothing comes of it; Nothing can come of it, unless it has been associated with the earth, unless it has occurred when that individual was in the body... Only if you first return to your body, to your earth, can individuation take place; only then does the thing become true.

(Jung 1998, pp. 1313–1314)

In the case of our 'cake eating professional services manager', the observer described how she found it hard to sit still as she described the experience in the group and suggested that the same had been true in the observation itself. She had felt tense and irritable, and her breathing was constricted, in an apparent contrast to the manager she had observed. In fact, the more the manager had relaxed, the more tense she had felt. The combined symbols of inactivity, solitaire, and self-indulgence had aroused a strong physical reaction within her and evoked something more than the 'nothing' she had first reported. She began to recognise the symbols as symbols because she had 'lived out' their energy as an embodied experience.

Being in Mind

We may also wonder about the feelings and images that arise within us, perhaps provoked by our surroundings or our physical experience or perhaps gradually appearing with their own energy from the unknown depths of our unconscious. In the same way that we may begin to name bodily sensations with increasing acuity, we can begin to name our emotions. We can consider the tone and intensity of the emotion, and as we study ourselves more closely, we may move beyond simple categories to develop more depth and nuance. We may come to understand what we initially describe as anger, as simply an uncomfortable irritation or perhaps a burning resentment. Sadness may become nostalgia, a yearning for a time that has been lost or the despair of melancholia. We can take inspiration from ancient Greece and notice different forms of love, such as the unconditional love of 'agape', the love and loyalty expressed to family and friends as 'philia', the sexual desire of 'eros', or the self-love of 'philautia'. We may wonder whether we experience these emotions as negative or positive and consider the emotions that then arise in our noticing. We can begin to associate our emotions with other emotions, and as we feel anger, we may then experience shame or guilt or perhaps elation as we acknowledge that initial feeling. As with our observation of the body, we can then turn this noticing into an informal and regular practice as part of our day-to-day lives. As we walk to work, sit quietly on a train, or prepare an evening meal, we can reflect on the landscape of our emotional world. We can try to notice a feeling, name it, and then stay with it, allowing more depth and form to emerge.

We can then further develop our understanding by exploring possible associations with other more concrete images that come to mind. These may not be consciously produced but must 'produce themselves' (Jung 1995, p. 207) as a spontaneous communication from the unconscious in our dreams or day-dreams. In visual images, memories of music, or scraps of inner conversations, the unformed symbols of the unconscious begin to constellate, provoking us to look in new ways or in new places for our inspiration. Jung saw fantasy as the way in which we can discard preconceived conscious limitations and create spaces for new thinking and new ways of being. He suggested that

> The psyche creates reality every day. The only expression I can use for this activity is fantasy. Fantasy is just as much feeling as thinking, as much intuition as sensation. There is no psychic function that, through fantasy, is not inextricably bound up with the other psychic functions…Fantasy, therefore, seems to me the clearest expression of the specific activity of the psyche. It is, pre-eminently, the creative activity from which the answers to all answerable questions come; It is the mother of all possibilities, where, like all psychological opposites, the inner and outer worlds are joined together in union.
>
> (1971, CW6, para. 78)

As we allow fantasy to flow freely, we may even begin to access a subtle dream-like state in our waking moments. Provoked by a heightened awareness of symbol and by sudden moments of intuition, we may loosen the conscious boundaries of the ego to allow a direct connection with the unconscious. Jung suggested that the voice of the unconscious is always present as a constant monologue that shapes but remains unacknowledged by the conscious mind, appearing freely in our dreams but vanishing below the surface when we are awake.

> We are quite probably dreaming all the time, but consciousness makes so much noise that we no longer hear the dream.
>
> (Jung 2008, p. 3)

To develop a symbolic attitude, we must then be able to enable an occasional state of mind that lies between waking and sleeping. We must be able to suppress conscious thoughts enough to allow symbol to emerge, while maintaining them enough to be able to notice the symbol in the first place. In these waking dreams, symbols may appear as single irresistible images or as complex and evolving narratives where each symbol finds its context in a nest of other symbols. As Jung suggested, the 'symbol can neither be thought up or found; it becomes…the symbol grows out of itself and is born from the mind' (2009, p. 311). Once we have allowed the symbol to emerge in this way, we can extend our associations to the body, noticing how fantasy is interconnected with physical sensations, or discover associated symbols in the world around us. These symbols may then provide yet more energy and impetus in the meaningful coincidences termed 'synchronicity' (Jung 1927, CW8, para. 827) where we are reminded of the archetypal symbols of the collective unconscious. We may then begin to capture these symbols for later reflection, in doodles, notes, journals, or simply memory, as a consciously cultivated form of daydreaming.

On this foundation, we can then begin to consciously reflect and work with the symbols. We may never be able to define them or completely explain them, but if we pay attention, we can draw on their insights and energy. Through an understanding of symbol, we can deepen our understanding of the complexes upon which our personality is built and we can make more conscious choices about our lives.

Facing the Darkness

However, as we begin to notice the symbols within and around us (in whatever form they begin to appear), we can then face resistance from the rational consciousness of the ego. In describing how people reacted when faced with the emerging awareness of symbol in the body, the Jungian analyst Arnold Mindell observed:

> Sometimes people giggle. Occasionally they say they say they do not understand. Often, they ask that the question be repeated. Frequently they respond by changing the subject. At first there seems to be no logical reason for them to avoid the body problem. They appear willing to focus on the pain; After all they argue and talk about the body problem. Why are they suddenly embarrassed when asked to take it seriously and find out more about it?
>
> (1984, p. 175)

Similarly, I have seen clients shuffle uncomfortably when I point out that they have used the same unusual word repeatedly during our conversation or inform me confidently that they don't dream. Even experienced coaches may become visibly nervous and avoidant when a symbol begins to constellate during supervision, particularly when that symbol seems charged with the archetypal energy of the collective unconscious.

The more energy bound up with the symbol, the more the ego will fear the possibility of being overwhelmed and the harder it will work to silence or diminish the voice of the unconscious. This may seem to be a very reasonable stance given the timeless and powerful nature of the unconscious. The feelings bound up with the symbol may present themselves with the same intensity with which they were first felt, particularly when the symbol is highly archetypal, reminding us of a primal shared human experience that spans generations. All our shame, rage, or terror may then be lived again in full. This may be particularly true when that voice reveals some past trauma, whether personal or cultural, which we have been unable to face and integrate and which may result in our capacity to produce (or even acknowledge) symbol becoming severely limited (Weis 2009). One obvious defence is to reduce our anxiety through intellectualisation as we cling to the illusion of the rational as the only reality. Here the ego can regain a feeling of control by dismissing the idea of symbol as just 'superstitious nonsense' or by insisting that a possible synchronicity is nothing more than an improbable but still random event. We may also rush to a confident but premature interpretation in our attempt to limit the potential scope of a symbol or distract ourselves from its inconvenient implications. Here we can remove its power to transform by pinning it down like a dead butterfly in a glass case. We can insist upon a coldly intellectual understanding which 'tears another life out from its own peculiar course and forces it into something foreign in which it cannot live' (Jung quoted in Woolfson 2013, p. 140).

If the energy of the symbol does overwhelm us, we may become 'inflated' by it. We may be mesmerised by its numinous power and mystical qualities and lose contact with grounded reality altogether. It possesses us and what follows may be a 'disorientation accompanied either by a feeling of immense power and uniqueness or a sense of nonworth' (Samuels et al. 1986, pp. 81–82). Lacking perspective and distance, we then lose the capacity to work consciously with the symbol, which then loses its value as a developmental catalyst. It takes us and drives us, but we cannot learn from it as our response is a reflex and not a conscious choice. In its defences, the ego is simply trying to protect us from this threat, even when that threat may present an opportunity for healing or growth. Jung consistently emphasised the importance of conscious awareness in symbolic work:

> The position of the ego must be maintained as being of equal value to the counter position of the unconscious, and vice versa. This amounts to a very necessary warning: for just as the conscious mind of civilised man has a restrictive effect on the unconscious, so the rediscovered unconscious often has a really dangerous effect on the ego. In the same way that the ego has suppressed the unconscious before, a liberated unconscious can thrust the ego aside and overwhelm it. There is a danger of the ego losing its head, so to speak.
>
> (Jung 1927, CW8, para. 183)

To develop a symbolic attitude, we must then be able to walk the boundary between the ego and the unconscious, becoming increasingly comfortable with our discomfort. We must be able to face the mysterious void of the unconscious without being overwhelmed by it or by our fear of it. The psychoanalyst Wilfred Bion suggested that the development of 'a capacity for tolerating frustration thus enables the psyche to develop thought as a means by which the frustration that is tolerated is itself made more tolerable' (Bion 1993, p. 112). Only in being able to bear the anxiety provoked by the unconscious can we begin to develop our capacity to make conscious meaning from the symbols it produces. As we begin this journey, we can then observe ourselves observing and reflect on our reactions. We can become a participant observer of ourselves and our surroundings. What is our tolerance for symbols and what are the particular emotions that arise within us as we begin to consciously work with them? What do these emotions suggest about us? What images and sources are we prepared to work with and how far is too far? Which emotions or sensations threaten to overwhelm us and what symbols and associations do they provoke? Our inner dialogue opens the way for a new meaning to emerge, a third position which in Jungian psychology is called the transcendent function. This third position is a product of, but not a compromise between, the impulse and intuition of the unconscious and the rational consideration of the conscious mind.

Moving to Meaning

Once we have been able to overcome our initial fear and resistance to symbols and allowed ourselves to notice them, we can then begin to make meaning from them. We can consider how they fit together, with each symbol adding a new perspective and nuance. We can fill in the gaps, creating a living tapestry of associations which gradually constellates into something that we can begin to articulate and reflect upon. It may be useful to draw or name the symbols that have come to mind and mark out the connections between them as a web of associations, creating an image of the whole in mind or on paper. We can then begin to reflect on both the observed nature of the symbol and its possible implications.

In Jungian psychology, we may think of the process of symbolic meaning-making as 'active imagination'. This is not so much a single technique as a natural and spontaneous process (Chodorow 2006) in which we turn our attention towards an inner fantasy world while maintaining a self-reflective, psychological point of view. In active imagination, we are taking care to balance the intuition of the unconscious, with the analytic frame of the conscious mind, allowing for a gentle tension between the two. As Jung suggested, 'the ideal case would be if these two aspects could exist side by side or rhythmically succeed each other; that is… their own alternation of creation and understanding' (1927, CW8, para. 179). Depending on the inclinations and interests of the individual and the form taken by the emerging symbols, we can draw on a range of different approaches in structured or unstructured ways. We may perform or 'dance out' an intuition, paint a spontaneous visual image or speak a word, or enter rich dialogues with inner beings. With each experience, we may begin to develop and extend the symbol, and with each iteration, we may add new associations and discover new meaning.

However we choose to apply active imagination, there are two principal routes available to us: association and amplification. We can consider our personal associations, building upon the symbol or cluster of symbols with new ideas and images of our own, or we can amplify the symbols, exploring them through the archetypal imagery and myths of the collective psyche. In both cases, we must ensure that we do not stray too far from the original symbols or move too quickly to interpretation. Instead, we must circumambulate the image, returning to view it from different angles and perspectives until a meaning begins to emerge. Jung suggests that for the process to be of real value

> Fantasy must be allowed the freest possible play, yet not in such a manner that it leaves the orbit of its object, namely the affect…the whole procedure is a kind of enrichment and clarification of the affect.
>
> (Jung 1927, CW8, p. 167)

This allows us to develop the symbols, with new insights and new material, while maintaining their original energy and intent. This process will be iterative, and we can never go beyond hypotheses, which will evolve as we continue to add new images and associations and build upon our insights. The symbols themselves will never be fully resolved, and each time we return to them, they may offer some new perspectives. Jung provides us with a useful reminder to check any premature impulse we may have to reach a conscious conclusion:

> [The] unconscious psyche…is not directly accessible to observation - otherwise it would not be unconscious - but can only be inferred. Our inferences can never go beyond: 'it is as if….
>
> (1927, CW8, p. 297)

If we then return to our participant observation, the observer began with an association. She remembered her mother chiding her for sitting around doing nothing and warning her about eating too much, as 'fat people were lazy'. She had grown up with the belief that industrious activity was a virtue and that parental approval and attention were dependent upon her ability to work hard. She confessed her fear that, if she did nothing, she would amount to nothing and perhaps would even be nothing. She would end up alone, playing 'solitaire'. When we amplified the image, she was reminded of the film *Cast Away* (Zemekis 2000), in which, following a plane crash, the protagonist is left utterly alone on a remote island and, with no other company, is forced to create an imaginary friend in the form of a volleyball. She found this possibility to be utterly terrifying as it left her without any way to locate herself in life and with no clear direction. This led the group to consider the archetype of the orphan, an image of the primal fear of a defenceless child, whose abandonment is also the precondition for a heroic journey of self-discovery and the emergence of adulthood. The observer admitted that she felt envious of the relaxed composure of the woman she was observing, who seemed happy to just watch the world go by. It was 'as if' during her observation she had become her mother, channelling her frustration and fear that the manager she was observing (who had unconsciously become her daughter) would waste her life, as perhaps her mother had herself. However, in that moment of frustration and potential rejection, there was also opportunity to rediscover herself again and begin a new learning journey. Together we wondered what it would feel like to take on some of quality of stillness, particularly in the context of coaching and consulting. What new inspirations and insights would be available to her if she just observed with no need for activity and outcomes? What would it be like to develop a symbolic attitude?

Reflections and Implications

As we develop a familiarity and a comfort with symbol, we learn to both participate in our lives and observe that participation and in that observation become able to make more conscious choices. Symbol provides an accessible bridge between the unconscious and conscious mind and facilitates a deeper understanding of ourselves. This understanding can be 'felt' at a physical or emotional level and then consciously developed into something more meaningful. This process of noticing, reflection, and conscious elaboration ensures that the unconscious does not overwhelm us, and that symbol can then be used instead as a foundation for new perspectives: the 'third position' of the transcendent function. Jung described this process as the 'constructive method' (1971, CW6, para. 702), where the products of the unconscious are not seen simply as dark repressed memories of the past but also as intuitive clues, hinting at our experience of the present and our possible futures. For this reason, the development of a symbolic attitude is essential to any developmental practice that seeks to go beyond the superficial, as we support ourselves and our clients in a transition to new ways of seeing and being.

However, symbol offers more than a simple catalyst for personal development or even a greater clarity of what lies below the surface in our professional lives. It can make us more deeply aware of the archetypal in the everyday. It can create an ongoing connection with the shared storehouse of images that is the collective unconscious and beyond that to the raw physical experiences of being human. Jung termed this the 'symbolic life' (1977, CW18). Through a deliberate and reflective engagement with symbol, we can access the timeless and transformative power of the numinous. The archetypal images of the collective unconscious provide us with a series of intuitive and inspiring 'templates' which we can use to reimagine how our lives may be and then perhaps recombine our complexes in new ways. Symbols can then take on new associations and provoke subtly different reactions with us. We can begin to reconnect to the everyday magic of life and use this as a resource as we move increasingly closer to the potential of the Self. Jung saw this 'lived approach' to symbol as being essential for our basic mental health. He suggested that, without it, we may feel increasingly unfulfilled, particularly in a world which emphasises the rational to the detriment of the mystic.

Now, we have no symbolic life, and we are all badly in need of the symbolic life. Only the symbolic life can express the need of the soul – the daily need of the soul, mind you! And because people have no such thing, they can never step out of this mill – this awful, grinding, banal life in which they are 'nothing but.' ... Everything is banal, everything is 'nothing but'; and that is the reason why people are neurotic.

(Jung 1977, CW18, para. 627)

Through archetypal symbols, we can be inspired with new possibilities that make us wonder and encourage us to act. It is for this reason that Jung suggested that 'the approach to the numinous is the real therapy and inasmuch as you attain the numinous experiences you are released from the curse of pathology' (1992a, CW2, p. 377).

As you reflect on this chapter, take a walk outside and pay attention to the world around you.

- What symbols do you notice around you?
- How do you feel physically as you notice them? Which parts of your body demand attention?
- How do you feel emotionally? Can you name your emotions (being as specific as possible)?
- What associations come to mind? What fantasies or daydreams?
- How do we respond to this noticing? What does it feel like to work with symbol in this way? How does any possible resistance manifest itself?

References

Abram D 1996, *The spell of the sensuous*. New York: Vintage Books.
Bion WR 1993, *Second thoughts: Selected papers on psychoanalysis*. London: Routledge.
Chodorow J 2006, Active imagination. In R Papadopoulos (ed.) *The handbook of Jungian psychology: Theory, practice and applications*. London: Routledge.
Jung CG 1927, *The structure and dynamics of the psyche*, CW8.
Jung CG 1964, *Civilisation in transition*, CW10.
Jung CG 1968, *The archetypes and the collective unconscious*, CW9i.
Jung CG 1971, *Psychological types*, CW6.
Jung CG 1977, *The symbolic life*, CW18.
Jung CG 1992a, *Experimental researches*, CW2.
Jung CG 1992b, Letter to Kurt Plachte, 10 January 1929. In G Adler and A Jaffe (eds.) *Letters*, vol. I. Princeton, NJ: Princeton University Press.
Jung CG 1995, *Memories, dreams, reflections*. London: Fontana.

Jung CG 1998, *Visions seminar 2: Notes of the seminar given in 1930-1934*. London: Routledge.

Jung CG 2008, *Children's dreams: Notes from a seminar given in 1936-1940*. Princeton, NJ: Princeton University Press.

Jung CG 2009, *The red book: Liber novus*. London: W. W. Norton & Company.

Mindell A 1984, *Dreambody: The body's role in revealing the self*. London: Routledge & Kegan Paul.

Monte C 2010, The body and movement in analysis. In M Stein (ed.) Jungian psychoanalysis: Working in the spirit of C.G. Jung. Chicago, IL: Open Court.

Samuels A, Shorter B, and Plaut F 1986, *A critical dictionary of Jungian analysis*. London: Routledge.

Weis H 2009, Living with symbols. *Spring* 82: 25–30.

Wilner W 1987, Participatory experience: The participant observer paradox. *American Journal of Psychoanalysis* 47: 342–357.

Woolfson T 2013, The question of psychological types: The correspondence of C. G. Jung and Hans Schmid-Guisan, 1915-1916, J Beebe and E Falzeder (eds.). Princeton, NJ: Princeton University Press.

Zemekis R (Director) 2000, Cast Away [Film], 20th Century Fox, DreamWorks Pictures, ImageMovers and Playtone.

Chapter 4

Exchanging Gifts

The Role of Symbol in the Coaching Relationship

Symbols tell us about ourselves. They provide the intangible feelings and sensations of the unconscious with a tangible form that we can begin to make sense of and work with. This form is primarily subjective, as the symbols of the personal unconscious arise from the experiences of our own lives, and they are charged with our own associations. However, if we pay attention, they may also provide us with a glimpse into the inner theatre of others, albeit a glimpse that is still seen and coloured with our own lenses. In noticing how symbol appears in our relationships, we can begin to develop a deeper understanding of others and the forces that shape their behaviour. We may notice symbols that we share or have created together, which may strengthen our relationships and unlock potential. For a coach with a Jungian-inspired practice, symbol is the essential mediating factor for any developmental work.

Introducing the Transference

Jung emphasised that any relationship is a mutual exchange of unconscious feelings, symbols, and associations. We project our unexamined assumptions onto others, and they do the same to us. Our projections are grounded in feeling-toned symbols which gradually arise within us or which we notice in the outer world, and we respond to those symbols in ways that we may not be consciously aware of. The symbol provokes a reaction within us, and we respond without any rational consideration. These symbols may be personal, arising from our own lived experiences, or they may be drawn from the cultural unconscious (Henderson 1990) and the shared history of a community. Here they will still be coloured by the experiences of our own lives, but they will be shaped by the lives of those around us and those who came before us. Symbols may also arise from the collective unconscious, a psychological record of the shared inheritance of humankind and from the instinctual templates known as archetypes. They may take many forms, from physical gestures or words to images, and each will carry emotional energy and associations that will evoke something within us. The symbols will evolve, and new associations or new symbols may emerge.

DOI: 10.4324/9781003463269-5

This exchange of projections is referred to as the transference, 'a general psychological mechanism that carries over subjective contents of any kind into the object' (Jung 1935, CW18, p. 136) which allows the formation of a 'sort of dynamic relationship between the subject and the object' (Jung 1935, CW18, para. 138). It is a deeply empathetic connection where we begin to feel 'with' another (Jung 1971a, CW6, para. 486). Unless we are aware of it, it has the potential to define our relationships in a regressive way, reinforcing old patterns of behaviour and hindering our development. Driven by these projections and the symbols that carry them, our relationships may become replicas of the past, as we may create 'false connections' with one another. We may relate to others not 'as they are' but as our subjective interpretation of the symbols that pass between us suggests that they are. A male authority figure may then be unconsciously seen as a symbolic representation of, for example, our own father, and we will assume that their behaviour and motivations will be the same. We may be influenced by how father figures are seen in our cultures or perhaps even by archetypal images of fearsome tyrants. A male authority figure who in reality may be benign and kindly may then become a symbol of patriarchal repression who destroys confidence and growth, simply because that is what we expect from our internalised images of male authority. We will look for symbols that reinforce our projections and then respond in the same ways as our younger selves responded to our own fathers, perhaps submitting quietly or perhaps resentfully rebelling. The authority figure in question may then be drawn in by our projections, aligning themselves with our expectations. They may become more domineering, and new symbols may then be created which fuel a self-fulfilling cycle of behaviour. Alternatively, they may be repulsed by the projections, and the connection between us may be damaged beyond repair. We may think of this as a 'countertransference', where an emotional response within us is provoked by another without any conscious awareness on either part. Here it is the symbols that arise in the relationships that influence its course and direction, rather than the real personalities of the participants. The transference is a kind of imaginary relationship between us and the symbols we project or transfer from our unconscious onto another person: 'In these imaginary relationships the other person becomes an *image* or *a carrier of symbols*' (Von Franz 1980, p. 6). The more emotionally charged the symbol, the stronger our response. This may be particularly true when faced with archetypal representations which speak to the raw experiences of being human and carry a profound and numinous energy that may threaten to overwhelm our conscious mind and extinguish rational thought altogether.

In psychoanalytic psychology, this displacement of affect onto another person, with its regressive and negative connotations, is the essence of the transference. It is often seen as a form of defence, which ensures that we can recreate familiar situations as a way to avoid the responsibility of facing difficult emotions and the implications of change. From a Jungian perspective, however, transference can be seen in a more progressive way, as a mutual exchange through which symbols are passed between people to be reformed with new meanings (Perry 2008). Here the unconscious is seen not simply as a passive repository of past habits and experiences but as a purposive and living system (Papadopoulos 2006), and the mutual exchange of the transference provides the opportunity to enrich this system through the combination of new symbols and new associations. Jung was in fact quite critical of a purely regressive view of the psyche, suggesting that 'the continual reduction of all projections to their origins... never produces an adapted attitude to life, for it constantly destroys...every attempt to build up a normal human relationship by resolving it back to its elements' (1966, CW16, para. 279). With a progressive stance, we can view the transference not as a relic of the past but as an intuitive attempt to connect with the symbols and associations that will move us forwards. We can be inspired to reimagine ourselves in new ways.

The route to this understanding lies in our noticing and working with the symbols that pass between us. Although they may have subjective origins, the symbols that arise in the transference become entangled as shared and inter-subjective products of the relationship. In this entanglement, new possibilities begin to appear. In a progressive transference, we are not drawn back to the past but directed instead towards a new future. The symbolic associations and projections in our relationship with a male authority figure, for example, may not lock us into familiar patterns of behaviour but instead may offer new ways of thinking about the potential authority within us. This may be particularly the case with archetypal symbols, which provide access to the shared wisdom of the collective unconscious. In these images, we may discover the eternal wisdom of the sage or courage of the warrior. We may discover that these symbols engage our 'transcendent function' which provokes us to combine the things we are with the things we are not yet and moves us forwards in a 'living birth that leads to a new level of being, a new situation' (Jung 1927, CW8, para. 189). The transference then provides a fertile chaos of symbols, which brings risks but from which also emerges a bridge to a new reality.

A Sacred Marriage

To illustrate the significance and complexity of the transference in personal development work, Jung turned to alchemy as a symbol of combination and transformation. In his 'Psychology of the Transference', he used the Rosarium Philosophorum, a series of 14th-century woodcuts, to illustrate the transference and its significance. The images depict a sacred marriage between a king and a queen, a symbol of relationship as the foundation of personal development. Jung illustrated his interpretation of these images with a simple matrix which he described as the 'counter crossing transference relationships of the... marriage quaternio' (Jung 1966, CW16, para. 425). We can adapt this matrix to illustrate the conscious and unconscious exchanges between coach and client (Figure 4.1).

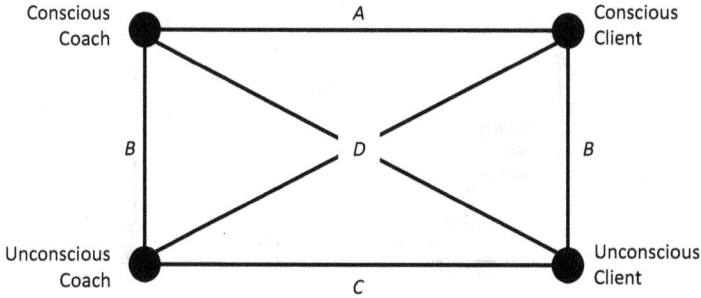

Figure 4.1 The transference quarternio.

The first of these exchanges (A) is a conscious or 'real' conversation, where we are aware of the superficial and observable dimensions of the exchange. Here a client may explain their goals and objectives in concrete and tangible terms, and we may respond with our considered questions or observations. The second exchange (B) is the inner theatre of the coach and the client as individuals and the relationship they have with themselves. In this exchange, feelings and associations begin to arise from the unconscious and symbols begin to constellate. This exchange represents the self-awareness and insight of both parties and the extent to which they are able to work with their respective unconscious in the service of their development. The third exchange (C) happens within the unconscious of both coach and client and is an exchange which may shape our inner theatre and behaviour but remains consciously unacknowledged. It may contain the unformed symbols of the personal unconscious, alongside those of the cultural and collective unconscious, which may be combined in 'feeling toned complexes' carrying numinous, archetypal energy. It is the exchange in which the transference originates. The final exchange (D), forming the matrix between the two, represents both an intuitive and unconscious connection to the other as a real person and a conscious curiosity and interest into what may lie beneath the surface. In this exchange, we can begin to notice the symbols and projections that pass between us and wonder about their possible meanings and implications.

This is a dynamic system where a consciously agreed coaching stance and approach (A) may provoke a reaction within a client (B), which is then projected in the transference onto the coach (C), who is influenced by the projection (B) and responds accordingly (A) in a countertransference to provoke a further reaction, which shows up in their coaching stance (Figure 4.2) to begin the cycle again. The same sequence may also happen the other way around, in the transference projections of the coach onto the client.

In this self-fulfilling cycle of transference and countertransference, both coach and client are guided by the feeling-toned symbols that they create in each other, reinforcing regressive behavioural patterns. Though intended for psychotherapists, Jung's warning is also directly applicable to coaches:

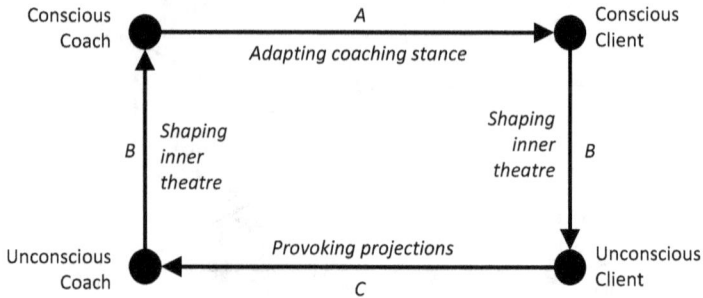

Figure 4.2 A cycle of transference and countertransference.

The patient, by bringing an activated unconscious content to bear upon the doctor, constellates the corresponding unconscious material in him…doctor and patient thus find themselves in a relationship founded on mutual unconsciousness.

(Jung 1966, CW16, para. 364)

If, however, we have been able to develop a symbolic attitude, we may be able to notice and then recognise the potential significance of the symbols that begin to constellate during our conversations (Figure 4.3). We can then develop a more conscious interest in what may lie in our client's unconscious (D). This interest may be noticed by our client, and the sense of connection between us may be strengthened as the client may feel 'seen' and perhaps more understood by us. We can then combine this insight with the symbols arising within us (B) from our own unconscious as a potential indicator of associations that may have been projected into us in the transference (C) from our client. We can notice the countertransference as it arises, and, in this noticing, we can mitigate its effect over us. We can then become more conscious of own possible projections and begin to withdraw them.

We can then begin to work 'with' the transference, adapting our stance and approach to this particular client (A). We can work with the symbols that we

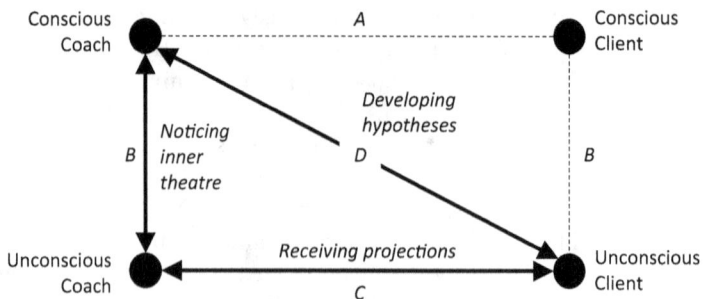

Figure 4.3 Developing self as instrument.

Conscious Coach — *A* Adapting coaching stance → Conscious Client

B — *D* Noticing symbol and creating hypotheses — Shaping inner theatre *B*

Unconscious Coach — *C* — Unconscious Client

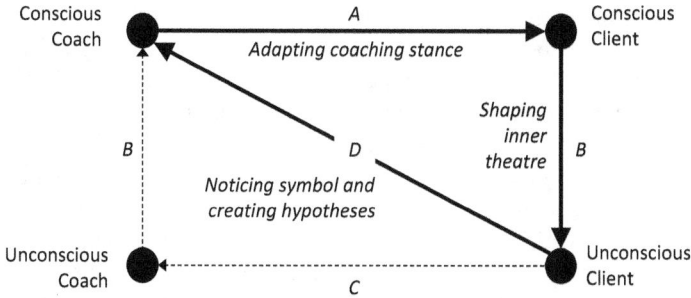

Figure 4.4 Working with the transference.

have noticed, to help them better understand and reshape their own inner the-atre (B) and begin to develop a new sense of self (Figure 4.4). As von Franz has suggested, 'the ego complex is not capable of building itself up' (1996, p. 59) but does so through the symbols that are exchanged in the transference, which provide the focal points and inspiration for the psyche to reorganise itself.

As we become aware of what the client unconsciously needs from us as coaches, and of our own countertransference, we can perhaps then go further and allow ourselves to be affected by the client's projections in a more con-sciously intentional way. Instead of defending ourselves from the client's projec-tions by withdrawing from them into a distant objectivity, we can adapt our coaching stance in a way that is 'felt' by us. Something within us can be acti-vated by our clients, and we can become the symbol they need, entering a coaching relationship that is intersubjective. If the client is seeking, for example, a deeper experience of care, we can begin to feel the impulse to care while main-taining a conscious awareness to avoid being overwhelmed by their projections. As we become more attuned to the client, they may become more receptive to us, becoming aware that we feel what they feel and that we can intuitively pro-vide what they need. A relational matrix then begins to form (Figure 4.5) where the coach and client are consciously aware of their connection and where both

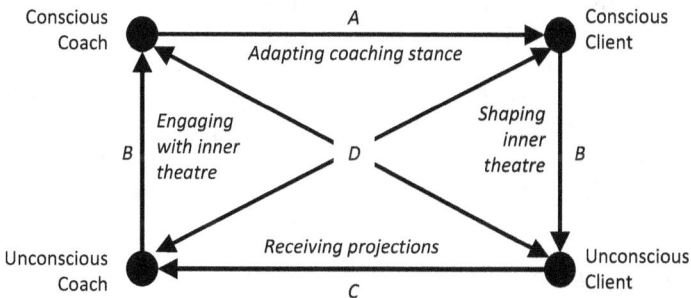

Conscious Coach — *A* Adapting coaching stance → Conscious Client

B Engaging with inner theatre — *D* — Shaping inner theatre *B*

Unconscious Coach — *C* Receiving projections — Unconscious Client

Figure 4.5 Working in the transference.

are potentially changed in the interaction. We may think of this as working 'in' the transference, as both coach and client are to some extent psychologically entangled, with a conscious awareness of that entanglement from the coach and an emergent awareness from the client. The client may not be as consciously competent as the coach in this work, but they can at least begin to work in partnership and, in doing so, begin to 'coach' themselves. If this partnership cannot be formed, then coaching may be experienced as something 'done to' the client rather than 'done with' them. The 'objective' distance between coach and client may then be internalised, casting doubt on their ability to relate to themselves.

This emergent curiosity and deep sense of connection can then be extended beyond the coaching engagement to other relationships. Clients can take their learning from the coaching engagement, out into the 'real world' to build richer and deeper relationships as friends, parents, or leaders. Their own ability to notice others increases, and they begin to withdraw their projections, taking more responsibility for 'what is theirs'. They are better placed to relate to others 'as they are', not as how the client's unconscious needs them to be. It is in this relational matrix of the transference, with the emerging experience of mutual understanding, that development really happens.

> The unrelated human being lacks wholeness, for he can achieve wholeness only through the soul, and the soul cannot exist without his other side which is always found in a 'You'. Wholeness is a combination of I and You, and these show themselves to be parts of a transcendent unity whose nature can only be grasped symbolically.
>
> (1966, CW16, para. 454)

This theme is continued in the images of the Rosarium as the king and queen merge and become one, within a sealed vessel referred to as the 'vas hermeticum'. Here they die, decay, and are reborn. We may imagine this vessel as a safe and secluded 'third area' (Schwartz-Salent 1998) where all possibilities can be considered, and clients can move between the intuition of the unconscious and the reality of their lived experience to consider something new and transcendent.

> As we perceive such shared reality with another person, and as we actually focus on it, allowing it to have its own life, like a third thing in the relationship, something new can occur. The space that we occupy seems to change, and rather than being the subjects, observing this third thing, we begin to feel we are inside it and moved by it... the old forms of relationship die and transform.
>
> (1966, CW16, pp. 5–6)

Coach as Symbol

The first symbol to appear within any coaching relationship, and a starting point for the formation of the transference matrix, is the coach themself.

The coach's reputation or initial impact, combined with the client's conscious or unconscious fantasies of the experience of coaching, will establish a powerful symbol or cluster of symbols that will shape any coaching relationship in its early stages. A client may see the coaching as an opportunity to grow or as an imposition or a suggestion of deficiency and failure. The coaching may have been imposed or sought out. The coach may be an agent of the organisation, working as a spy or a judge or perhaps serving as a status symbol. They may be a soothing mother or a stern father, or they may be a guide through uncharted waters. They may be a magician working with dark arts and mysterious forces or a craftsman whose tools and techniques will secure and hone performance. Each of these images will arise from a transference, bringing affect and evoking a potential countertransference. This may in turn misdirect the coaching as a regressive repetition of the past or provide an opportunity to rework some aspect of the client's unconscious for a more hopeful future.

Noticing and perhaps even discussing these symbols in the early stages of a coaching relationship will provide a sense of what the client needs or at least what their unconscious intuition is suggesting they need. It will provide us with a sense of how we may adapt our approach so that the imagination of the client can 'play' with the symbolic image of the coach, who becomes 'the equivalent of the paintings and the dreams' (Fordham 1989, p. 135) that we find in other symbolic work. Here the client receives the response they unconsciously need to move forwards, not the one that previous experiences have led them to expect. The coach as an object may then become a vehicle for the transcendent function, facilitating 'a transition from one psychological attitude or condition to another' (Samuels et al., 1986, p. 150). In the way in which we respond to a client, we may provide new symbolic interpretations of their projections, 'modelling' the transcendent function for them (Miller 2004, p. 20) and carrying 'unrealized potentials of psychological transformation' (Joseph 1997, p. 153). The client may expect to be directed by a stern and powerful father figure, but their unconscious may be reaching towards a more gentle and playful form of authority which the coach may then offer as an alternative. How we then behave will then have a material impact upon the outcomes of the coaching work. This may be particularly significant when the transference projections are archetypal. Though powerful and energetic, archetypes are themselves unknowable and need to find form in something tangible if they are to be used in support of our development. This tangible form may well be the coach themselves, as we become for our clients the image of the archetypal father, mother, or guide that they need to discover within themselves.

For this reason, Jung suggested that the role of the analyst was central to the analytic relationship (Wiener 2010), and for the same reason, the role of the coach is central to the coaching relationship. Different aspects of our personalities will provide a 'suitable hook' upon which the client can 'hang' their projections, and if we are conscious of these 'hooks', we can use their symbolic forms to provoke and support our work together. In this context, each client may 'meet' a different aspect of the same coach. This is not to suggest that a coach should be inauthentic with each client, but we must be able to use the symbols projected onto us to evoke something within ourselves that our clients can work with. In some small way at least, we need to be what our clients need us to be if we are to create a matrix within which other symbols can be developed. Through the projections of the transference, we can become containers for aspects of the patient's psyche that they are not yet ready to confront while they 'gain distance and the advantage of objectivity' (Perry, 2008, p. 163). This may involve some degree of idealisation where we become a kind of template for the attributes to which our client aspires but which they cannot yet accept in themselves. Provided we are consciously aware of this possibility, we can use it in support of their development and will not be swept up in a countertransference. We can become 'a new object' that is 'not necessarily the incarnation of a former object' (Wiener 2004, p. 168). This is where working 'in' the transference becomes significant, as the coach can allow themselves to deliberately become the symbol that the client needs to show them the way forwards.

We must then begin any coaching assignment not with unexamined and superficial goals but by asking ourselves, what are we to this client, in this place, at this time? A good place to start is by asking the client what they imagine coaching to be and why they may want to work with us. How do they think we can be of help, and how do they want to use us as a coach? They may not have an immediate answer, or at least not one they feel able to articulate clearly, but the symbol must be allowed to constellate in its own time before we can start to work directly with it. Other clients will believe they know what they want and will come with clear objectives, but the symbols that emerge in these early stages may reveal something quite different. We may also decide that these questions will be too challenging or confusing to be asked directly, and we can gently introduce them into early conversations, as we clarify the clients' understanding of the coaching engagement and their underlying intuition. All of their answers may contain symbols with many different meanings and emotional nuances, but if the coach is able to work with them, then both may be able to move gradually towards a constructive and progressive transference. Here the symbol of the coach can set the tone and provide a starting point for the relationship as the client 'clings by means of the transference to the person who seems to provide … a renewal of attitude' (Jung 1927, CW8, para. 146).

Symbols in Relationship

Once we have laid the foundations for our work, we begin to help our clients make conscious meaning from the feelings and symbols that are emerging in our coaching relationship. Jung saw the unconscious and its symbols as a profound source of insight and intuition, which helps us make sense of our lives and find purpose. Our role as coaches is to mediate the emergence of these symbols to provoke new perspectives and growth. As coaches, we support our clients by understanding 'that the transference has as much to do with the...deep drive to move to a new attitude as it does to reductive, early-life experiences' (Miller 2004, p. 20). We are helping our clients to discover what is possible and for this reason, Kast has suggested that

> Facilitating the development of symbols is more important than the process of transference-countertransference itself. Symbols are not only the vehicles for the individuation process, but also refer to life history and future development... they shape the emotions that are connected with complexes, archetypes, and the real relationship.
>
> (2003, p. 107)

Here the symbolic attitude can be seen not simply as a quality of the coach but as a living relational process that is owned by both coach and client. Working with the symbols of the transference is a form of 'lived-through active imagination' (Davidson 1989, p. 188), where both coach and client deliberately engage together with the symbols that arise in the relationship to explore their possible meanings. We do not move swiftly to a superficial and intellectual interpretation of symbol (knowing that may never be possible); instead, we use the symbol as a focal point for a dialogue from which something meaningful and often unexpected can emerge. Symbol can become a common 'language' to express and share ideas that cannot be expressed or shared in any other way. This process begins with the coach's own sensitivity to symbol but with the unfolding awareness of the client in mind.

Bovensiepen (2002) illustrates this idea with a case study describing an emerging symbolic dialogue between himself as a psychotherapist and a young boy. The case study described how the drawing of 'comic book' narratives in a reciprocal exchange during their sessions helped open up new channels for communication and understanding. It allowed the boy to express ideas in a form that could then be developed and exchanged between the two, evolving with each exchange and helping both to make sense of their relationship and their respective worlds. This reciprocal exchange across the transference matrix can be termed a 'reverie' (Bion 1962). In a 'reverie', a coach is able to engage with the unconscious (their own and their client's) to help constellate the symbols of the unconscious so that both coach and client can make meaning from those symbols. We help our clients create a container into which they can project difficult emotions or psychosomatic sensations, so they can take a more tangible and symbolic form. These can be used consciously and deliberately, or unconsciously and intuitively, in the service of development. A reverie is not a clear and sequential narrative or a set of artfully posed questions but a labyrinthine and free-floating dialogue, through which meaning gradually emerges, is lost, and emerges again. It is not a self-conscious, goal-oriented activity but a natural, relational flow which reinforces a sense of connection through the symbols we share. It is a rhythmic back-and-forth movement between layers of meaning, self and other, conscious and unconscious. It is the very essence of the transcendent function, as a gradual symbolic emergence of transformational change. The symbols arising in reverie may gradually become intersubjective, as they are created, shaped, and owned by both parties in the relationship. The meaning made in reverie is a 'we-production' and a 'we-possession' which affects both client and coach.

It is important to stress that reverie may be incompatible with confident and conscious interpretation. A symbol, by definition, 'states or signifies something more and other than itself' (Jung 1971a, CW6, para. 817) and 'remains a perpetual challenge to our thoughts and feelings' (1971b, CW15, para. 119). It contains more possibility than can be revealed by one person. A symbol in a coaching relationship is both subjective and intersubjective and represents aspects of the unconscious of both parties, individually and in combination. Symbols may be associated with collective ideas and experiences but may also have nuances that are unique to each individual and to the dynamics of the relationship within which they appear. They are significant not because we can interpret them with any degree of confidence but because they provide the focal points for a reverie where we work with symbol as an ongoing call to action rather than an easily attained goal. While we may develop some tentative and lightly held hypotheses to move the reverie forwards, this must be without the conceit that we somehow have discovered 'the answer'. Symbols will elude any attempt to pin them down, no matter how gratifying this may feel to us, and if we are to work with them, they must be allowed to exist on their own terms. Our role as coaches is simply to acknowledge the symbols, validating them as relevant within the coaching relationship and then helping meaning to emerge. As Louis Zinkin has suggested, 'the unknowable signified does not need to be known, but it does need to be there' (1998, p. 87).

This may be challenging for a coach who is unfamiliar with the 'unknowable' depths of the unconscious. Often provoked by anxiety and the fear of being overwhelmed, coaches may feel compelled to move quickly to a more finite and manageable but ultimately limiting interpretation of symbols. If a coach is unable to tolerate the uncertainty of the unconscious, they will be unable to engage the client in a reverie and may even project their own fears into the client, where they are amplified. Here the creative potential offered by the unconscious is repressed and the hope of meaningful development becomes limited. It is also possible that, through inexperience and underdevelopment, a coach will be overly confident in their ability to work with the unconscious. They may be propelled towards idealistic outcomes which validate and reinforce their identity as a coach rather than meeting the client 'where they are'. They may move quickly to 'wild' interpretations and, reinforced by their professional authority as a coach, persuade the client to take actions which are distracting or even harmful. Here the 'interpretations often appear as bludgeons designed to enhance one's power at the expense of another's' (Zaleznik 2016, p. 104). If, however, we are able to work sensitively with symbol, reverie can become a gradual movement to a shared awareness. It is the route through which our clients develop a symbolic attitude and a richer relationship with their own unconscious. It is the foundation for individuation.

A coaching client described how much she had changed since she was a child. She found it hard to explain, and I suggested she could always draw a picture if that was easier. She then drew two pictures, the first of which was a young girl with pigtails and a bright red dress, surrounded by trees and flowers. The second was herself as an adult in a tall brown but otherwise featureless rectangular building with small windows. The second image immediately reminded me of a prison, and she agreed that she had the same association. She described how she felt as though she was sitting in the windows of this 'work-prison' watching 'other people live their lives' while she was unable to leave. Her first image was full of joy, and she described how she used to play 'unsupervised' with friends in the woods around her home. She kept the picture and brought it back a few sessions later with some changes. She had made the dress more colourful, adding some polka dots and had included images of her friends. We discussed the importance of the idea of being 'unsupervised', and she associated it with a freedom she did not feel in adult life, being overwhelmed by the responsibilities of motherhood, work, and community obligations. She felt that her life was determined by authority figures, whether her mother-in-law, her manager, or her local priest, and that she had no agency or control. In time, we began to talk about the girl as though she was a real person and a third party in our relationship. She wondered what the 'little girl in the woods' would do or say, and I began to join her in this reverie. We began to discuss the role of authority figures 'in mind', including my own role as her coach. She told me that she had chosen me because I had a reputation for 'rule breaking' and she wanted to 'break rules' again. We discussed what rules she could break and how she could embark upon a series of 'minor transgressions' to rebuild her confidence and begin to play again. She came to the next and final session wearing a bright red floral dress rather than her customary business suit. Her mood was lighter, and she seemed noticeably more confident.

A Neural Coupling

As we become closer to our clients, developing a deeper rapport and connection, we may start to see symbols emerging simultaneously for both parties. We may describe this as a synchronicity, 'a coincidence in time of two or more causally unrelated events which have a similar meaning' (Jung 1927, CW8, para. 849) and which may suggest an underlying systemic order which connects us. In my coaching practice, I have become accustomed to seeing themes repeating in my conversations with different clients, usually arising both within me and in my clients. These themes are almost like ripples, where symbols constellate in waves across different relationships, and they are usually archetypal, arising from the shared associations of the collective unconscious.

Clinical research (Dieckmann 1976) has suggested that archetypal images and associations may be constellated simultaneously in both coach and client and in some cases may be *anticipated* by the coach. This may feel somewhat mystical, even for those who view the psyche through a Jungian lens, but it is a phenomenon that has been strongly supported by recent neuro-biological research. As an understanding or rapport begins to be felt between two individuals, their brain responses may begin to mirror each other and overlap, communication in effect becoming a single activity performed in alignment by two separate brains (Stephens et al. 2010, Hasson et al. 2012, Nummenmaa et al. 2012). This effect is referred to as neural coupling, a direct and physical (but wholly intuitive) communication between individuals which extends beyond rational comprehension to evoke an associative and emotionally toned experience of connection. If I were to tell a story about the glorious smell of a fresh cinnamon bun to someone who likes cinnamon buns as much as I do, not only would they understand the words I was using but the olfactory cortex of their brain would respond as if they too were smelling the bun. Neural coupling is an exchange of symbolic as well as rational meaning, and it extends beyond language to include visual imagery, sounds, and movements.

The most striking aspect of this research is the suggestion that the effect of neural coupling is most pronounced when the communication happens through symbols with meanings that were determined only by the participants themselves. In a number of studies (Galantucci and Garrod 2011, Hasson et al. 2012), pairs of participants played cooperative games online in which they could communicate only using visual symbols. These symbols had no predetermined or established meaning and did not include numbers or letters. To play the games, participants had to develop a symbolic system that was unique to them. It was found that a symbolic system evolved rapidly for the players themselves and became increasingly abstract over time, as they were transmitted through generations of players. However, the symbols were not as easily or intuitively understood by observers who were not actively involved in its creation. It would appear that the symbols that enabled neural coupling could be fully understood only by the people involved in creating them. They were a 'we-production'.

Research has also confirmed Dieckmann's observation that when we establish a close feeling of connection and rapport, we can anticipate the reactions of others. It would appear that in situations where neural coupling has begun to occur, the responses in the listener's brain may actually precede the responses in the speaker's brain (King-Casas B et al. 2005, Stephens et al. 2010). If the speaker is about to talk about the smell of a cinnamon bun, for example, it is the olfactory lobes of the listener's brain that will become active, anticipating the symbol and its effect. These responses suggest that the listeners are unconsciously predicting the speaker's communications, allowing them to then 'fill in the gaps' in any potential misalignment or misunderstanding. Indeed, the more extensive the coupling between a speaker's brain responses and a listener's anticipatory brain responses, the better the comprehension of their communications, whether symbolic or linguistic. The depth of relationship established through neural coupling also determined the extent to which that meaning could be transmitted through speech. The more aligned people feel and the more physically aligned their brains, the more they understand what they are saying to each other.

It appears that it is the *experience of symbolic meaning in relationship* that determines the effectiveness of language and not the other way around. Vocal communication emerges through the interactions between the brains and bodies of signaller and receiver. In the language of Jungian psychology, neurobiological research suggests that the symbols arising from the mutual projections of the transference allow a shared meaning to be made at an unconscious level that then brings us together to create a communion of ideas that we can consciously develop.

Symbols of Relationship

The final symbol to consider in a coaching relationship is the symbol of the relationship itself. We can use the symbols that emerge in a progressive transference to prompt new ways of being, and in the creation of relationship with another, we create the possibility of relationship with ourselves. Instead of projecting responsibility for our reality onto other people or external events, we begin to understand that we also have a responsibility for cocreating that reality. Once we have participated in the creation of a meaningful relationship, we may extend that experience beyond the relationship to participate more fully in the world. This realisation may lead to what Henderson termed the formation of a 'symbolic friendship' (Henderson 1955) where the coach becomes part of the psyche of the client as a 'permanent internal 'friend'. Here we become an 'inner voice' for our clients, to inspire and support creative inner dialogues. As a symbolic 'coach in mind', we can help our clients to develop a symbolic attitude themselves. They may then pay closer attention their own unconscious, making more conscious choices and taking responsibility for their own lives. The coaching relationship simply provides an initial symbolic template which can be internalised and returned to 'in mind' once the engagement has ended. If we can have a meaningful relationship with a coach, we can have a meaningful relationship with ourselves. This realisation is a key step in any development process, and as Jung reminds us:

Everyone who proposes to come to terms with himself must reckon with this basic problem. For, to the degree that he does not admit the validity of the other person, he denies the other within himself the right to exist- and vice versa. The capacity for inner dialogue is a touchstone for outer objectivity.

(Jung 1971a, CW6, para. 187)

Coaching is then not only a developmental process within a safe and secure container but the essential and symbolic focal point and organising principle for all the other symbols that have constellated during the engagement. We even think of it as the transcendent function, as the experience may provide the unifying symbol that suggests a new position beyond our immediate reality (Corbett 1992, Ulanov 1997, Miller 2004).

The coaching relationship may come to represent the client's ability to make meaning for themselves and may be best represented in an alchemical principle known as the 'Axiom of Maria Prophetessa': 'One becomes two, two becomes three, and out of the third comes the one as the fourth' (Jung 1953, CW12, para. 209). The one represents a state of wholeness from which emerges the sense of separation and difference that is two. Here we find ourselves in opposition and conflict, facing often paradoxical situations that we cannot easily resolve. The world around us and within us may feel unfamiliar and threatening, and we are unprepared for it. We begin working with a coach, and we look to them in the transference as the magical 'other' and a guide who can help us return to a state of integration (a regressive transference) or move forwards to a new way of being (a progressive transference). We enter a reverie through which the intuition of the unconscious of both parties can begin to form and reform, guided by symbols. As we begin to accept and tolerate the duality of two, we then allow ourselves to become open to a third position that is both and neither. As Jung suggests:

> This vacillating between the opposites and being tossed back and forth means being contained in the opposites. They become a vessel in which what was previously now one thing and now another floats vibrating, so that the painful suspension between opposites gradually changes into the bilateral activity of the point in the centre' (Jung transformation.
>
> (Jung 1963, CW14, para. 296)

This third position offers a way of seeing a way forward which we had not previously considered and which offers the possibility of a new sense of wholeness and integration, as the one and the fourth. This possibility is the essence of the transcendent function, and that coaching relationship can be seen as the symbol which gives us the hope of finding a way through confusion and anxiety, to feel whole again. For this reason, it has been suggested that the experience of the self 'only comes into existence through interaction with others' (Zinkin 2008, p. 394) and must be 'acquired within a context that includes culture, language and other persons' (Young-Eisendrath and Hall 1991, p. xii). In other words, we cannot develop a sense of self alone but need the presence of others in order to locate and find ourselves. Our relationships with other people provide the symbols we need for the unconscious to provoke and shape our development. The coaching relationship then provides a stable container within which we can begin this process of transformation. It is worth remembering that 'matrix' is the Latin word for womb, and within the matrix of the transference we can be reformed and reborn, like the king and queen of the Rosarium. As the psychologist Jeffrey Miller has suggested:

> When I am able to free myself from the shackles of viewing experience as something happening to me and see it as something that I cocreate, I free myself to see the sacred in the other person. I liberate myself to not only see the third thing (the relationship, the connection, the field) that links me and the other person but also to allow the emergence of the other [within me]... the transcendent function in relationships means living perpetually in the attitude of seeing the mystery in what we used to take for granted.
>
> (2004, p. 133)

Reflections and Implications

When we take a Jungian approach to coaching, we are working with symbols at the very the heart of our practice, noticing them as they arise within us and within our clients. These symbols provide us with a glimpse of the unconscious and allow us to understand what may be happening within our work. This understanding allows us to make conscious decisions to shape our practice, working with each client as an individual in order to help them develop their own self-awareness in support of their own conscious decision making. In doing so, we are helping them to develop a symbolic attitude themselves, becoming less afraid of the unconscious and more intentional in the way in which they engage with its intuition and inspiration. It is the relational matrix of the transference that provides the container within which this awareness can be born.

In the transference, we project our own feelings and expectations onto or into another, and in these projections, symbols begin to surface which may belong to either of us or both of us. These symbols shape how we react and may deepen old patterns of behaviour or provide the templates we need to inspire new ways of being. We are drawn unconsciously into a transference–countertransference exchange, or we notice the symbols and begin to wonder about them. This wondering may not be easy. Not every client may be comfortable working with symbol, even in subtle ways. The voice of the unconscious may be repressed through trauma, the natural defences of the ego or simply through the self-conscious habits of social conditioning, where symbol is easily dismissed as superstitious or indulgent nonsense.

Our role as coaches is then to notice symbols as they constellate in the coaching relationship and 'repurpose them' in the service of development. We can use symbol to help our clients move from a potentially regressive series of projections to a more progressive stance where the symbol attains new associations and new meaning. We can do this directly by acknowledging the symbols and encouraging our clients to explore them or indirectly by adapting our practice to make use of the symbol without bringing the symbol directly to consciousness. Provided we do not rush anxiously to interpretation, we can allow the symbol in one way or another to move us.

As a progressive transference matrix begins to develop, we may find that the coaching relationship itself becomes symbolic. Our process and personal interventions as a coach become less important and serve simply as reminders of the work that we are doing together within the matrix of relationship. Our clients may start to use the matrix, consciously or unconsciously, as its own symbol to provoke and guide a deeper inner journey beyond the boundaries of the coaching engagement. Meeting and taking part in a coaching reverie are then enough to help the client to examine their own inner theatre and to make more conscious choices. They can begin to develop a symbolic attitude, withdrawing their projections and taking more responsibility for their lives. As Wiener has suggested:

> Although Jung held that the symbol-making capacity of the psyche is a natural, archetypal process, many [people] cannot use their imaginative capabilities'. They become blocked and it is only within an authentic relationship where trust can evolve that takes account of transference and countertransference dynamics, that the self begins to emerge and with it, the potential to trust in new relationships and in an internal capacity to make meaning.
>
> (2010, p. 89)

Symbols are indeed the voice of the unconscious, but that voice is at its most articulate when heard in relationship. We just have to be ready to listen.

When you next talk to someone, reflect for a little on

- How do you feel as you talk to them? Do they remind you of anyone?
- What is it about them that creates this association?
- Are there any other images that stand out, such as their clothes or perhaps the words they use? What are your associations with these images?

References

Bion WR 1962, *Learning from experience*. London: Tavistock.

Bovensiepen G 2002, Symbolic attitude and reverie: Problems of symbolization in children and Adolescents. *Journal of Analytical Psychology* 47(2): 241–257.

Corbett L 1992, Therapist mediation of the transcendent function. In M Matton (ed.) *The transcendent function: individual and collective aspects; Proceedings of the Twelfth International Congress for Analytical Psychology, August 23-28*, pp. 402–408. Einsiedeln, Switzerland: Daimon Verlag.

Davidson D 1989, Transference as a form of active imagination. In M Fordham, R Gordon, J Hubback, and K Lambert (eds.) *Technique in Jungian analysis*. London: Karnac.

Dieckmann H 1976, Transference and countertransference: Results of a Berlin research group. *Journal of Analytic Psychology* 21: 25–36.

Fordham M 1989, Notes on the transference. In M Fordham, R Gordon, J Hubback, and K Lambert, (eds.) *Technique in Jungian analysis*. London: Karnac.

Galantucci B and Garrod S 2011, Experimental semiotics: A review. *Frontiers in Human Neuroscience* 17(5): 11.

Hasson U, Ghazanfar AA, Galantucci B, Garrod S, Keysers C 2012, Brain-to-brain coupling: A mechanism for creating and sharing a social world. *Trends in Cognitive Sciences* 16(2): 114–121.

Henderson J 1955, Resolution of the transference in the light of C.G. Jung's psychology. In *Report of the International Congress of Psychotherapy, Zurich 1954*. Bael/New York, Klarger.

Henderson J. 1990, *The cultural unconscious, shadow and self*. Wilmette, IL: Chiron Publications.

Joseph SM 1997, Presence and absence through the mirror of transference: the model of the transcendent function. *Journal of Analytical Psychology* 42(1): 139–156.

Jung CG 1927, *The structure and dynamics of the psyche*. CW8.

Jung CG 1935, *The Tavistock lectures*. CW18.

Jung CG 1953, *Psychology and alchemy*. CW12.

Jung CG 1963, *Mysterium coniunctionis*. CW14.

Jung CG 1966, *The practice of psychotherapy*. CW16.

Jung CG 1971a, *Psychological types*. CW6.

Jung CG 1971b, *The spirit in man, art and literature*. CW15.

Kast V 2003, Transcending the transference. In Withers, R. (ed.) *Controversies in analytical psychology*. Hove, East Sussex: Brunner-Routledge.

King-Casas B, Tomlin D, Anen C, Camerer CF, Quartz SR, Montague PR 2005, Getting to know you: Reputation and trust in a two-person economic exchange. *Science* 308: 78–83.

Miller JC 2004, *The transcendent function: Jung's model of psychological growth through dialogue with the unconscious*. Albany, NY: State University of New York Press.

Nummenmaa L, Glerean E, Viinikainen M, Jääskeläinen IP, Haria R, and Sams M 2012, Emotions promote social interaction by synchronizing brain activity across individuals. *PNAS (Proceedings of the National Academy of Sciences of the United States of America)* June 2012 109(24): 9599–9604.

Papadopoulos RK 2006, Jung's epistemology and methodology. In RK Papadopoulos (ed.) *The handbook of Jungian psychology: Theory, practice, and applications*. Hove, East Sussex: Routledge.

Perry C 2008, Transference and countertransference. In P Young-Eisendrath and T Dawson (eds.), *The Cambridge companion to Jung*. Cambridge, UK: Cambridge University Press.

Samuels A, Shorter B and Plaut F 1986, *A critical dictionary of Jungian analysis*. London: Routledge and Kegan Paul.

Schwartz-Salent N 1998, *The mystery of human relationship: Alchemy and the transformation of self*. New York: Routledge.

Stephens GJ, Silbert LJ, and Hasson U 2010, Speaker-listener neural coupling underlies successful communication. *PNAS (Proceedings of the National Academy of Sciences of the United States of America)* August 2010 107(32): 14425–14430.

Ulanov AB 1997, Transference, the transcendent function and transcendence. *Journal of Analytical Psychology* 42(1): 119–138.

Von Franz M-L 1980, *Projection and re-collection in Jungian psychology: Reflections of the soul*. Peru, IL: Open Court.

Von Franz M-L 1996, *The interpretation of fairy tales*. Boston, MA: Shambhala.

Wiener J 2004, Transference and countertransference. J Cambray and L Carter (eds) *Analytical psychology: Contemporary perspectives in Jungian analysis*. Hove, East Sussex: Routledge.

Wiener J 2010, Working in and with the transference. In M Stein, (ed.) *Jungian psychoanalysis: Working in the spirit of C.G. Jung*. Chicago, IL: Open Court.

Young-Eisendrath P and Hall J 1991, *Jung's self psychology: A constructivist perspective*. New York: Guilford Press.

Zaleznik A 2016, The case for not interpreting unconscious mental life in consulting to organisations. In MFR Kets de Vries, K Korotov, E Florent-Treacy and C Rook, (eds.) Coach and couch: The psychology of making better leaders. Basingstoke, Hampshire: Palgrave Macmillan.

Zinkin L 1998, Paradoxes of the self. In H Zinkin, R Gordon, and J Haynes (eds.) in *Dialogue in the analytic setting*. London: Jessica Kingsley Publishers.

Zinkin L 2008, Your self: Did you find it or did you make it? *Journal of Analytical Psychology* 53(3): 389–406.

Chapter 5

Beginning to Play

A Resolution of the Tension in Developmental Work

Play is the foundation of a Jungian approach to coaching. It is the prerequisite for any meaningful development work as it is through play that we are able to explore what is unknown to us and find the potential that is hidden there. While there are many techniques that may be helpful in supporting play, play itself is not a technique. It is a subjective or intersubjective state of mind and must find its own form. It is a moment of genuine creativity and cannot be commanded or directed without its destruction. We cannot 'play by numbers' or self-consciously design play to deliver predetermined outcomes. In play we must be able to return to the childlike state that allows intuition and creativity to emerge and to guide us. As Jung suggests:

> Every good idea and all creative work are the offspring of the imagination and have their source in ... infantile fantasy. Not the artist alone, but every creative individual whatsoever owes all that is greatest in his life to fantasy. The dynamic principle of fantasy is play, a characteristic also of the child, and as such it appears inconsistent with the principle of serious work. But without this playing with fantasy no creative work has ever yet come to birth. The debt we owe to the play of imagination is incalculable.
>
> (Jung 1971, CW6, para. 93)

Remembering Symbol

We can begin to appreciate the significance of play when we return to the nature of symbol and its role in the development process. A symbol is a 'living thing...an expression for something that cannot be characterised in any other or better way' (Jung 1971, CW6, para. 816) and 'the best possible expression for a complex fact not yet clearly apprehended by consciousness' (Jung 1927, CW8, para. 69). It changes and evolves as we try to engage with it, and we cannot ever succinctly unravel its many possible meanings. It is the mysterious voice of the unconscious, and it speaks with a purpose and intent that always seem to somehow elude us. It is not a 'sign' that can be quickly and easily

DOI: 10.4324/9781003463269-6

interpreted with a single and final definition but the focal point for an evolving accumulation of feelings and associations. Symbol has its own purpose and provokes us to action.

> The vision of the symbol is a pointer to the onward course of life, beckoning with the libido towards a still distant goal...I am speaking, of course, not of symbols that are dead and stiffened by dogma, but of living symbols that rise up from the creative unconscious of the living man.
>
> (Jung 1971, CW6, para. 202)

The developmental value of a symbol lies in its ability to provide an intuitive bridge between the otherwise irreconcilable paradoxes of life. It can bring the energy and insight we need to unlock new perspectives and new ways of being. It has both a rational and non-rational dimension, and we can think of it as a 'vehicle that allows us to move between and create dialogue among those territories that do not otherwise touch one another' (Miller 2004, p. 50). A symbol can inspire us to think very differently about our lives and reimagine the stories of the past, the experiences of the present, and the possibilities of the future. We can call this bridge the 'transcendent function' (Miller 2004, p. 50), and it is an inevitable psychological response to the challenges that accompany any significant transition or change of state. This is a natural process, and if we can begin to tolerate the tension between the unconscious and conscious mind, a symbol will emerge of its own accord. This symbol may be a synthesis of the opposing forces while transcending them both and pointing us towards a new perspective.

Jung suggested that the unconscious and conscious aspects of the psyche have a balancing or 'compensatory' function (Papadopoulos 2006) with each ensuring that the other does not overwhelm us. Without the inspiration of the unconscious, we lose connection with the systems of which we are part and can no longer benefit from their insight and collective wisdom. Without the reflective capacity of the conscious, we can no longer ground ourselves in reality. The conscious mind looks for answers and solutions and creates an objective distance between ourselves and the world. The unconscious reminds us of what is 'felt' and makes fast and fluid connections and associations. Jung believed that our ability to maintain a balance between these two poles defined both our present wellbeing and our development. If we can work with the perpetual tension between these two aspects of the psyche, freely acknowledging our intuitive, emotional life while staying grounded in a consciously considered reality, we will attain a greater sense of wholeness and move more easily towards our potential. We can begin to make better choices for ourselves.

The transcendent function is the activation of a dialogue between the unconscious and the conscious mind, and symbols provide the axis around which the dialogue revolves and from which a new meaning emerges. It is a 'capacity to move back and forth between layers of meaning' (Young-Eisendrath 1992, p. 153), and it is through the symbols of the transcendent function that can we move from 'either/or' to 'both/and'.

> The symbol is the middle way along which the opposites flow together in a new movement, like a watercourse bringing fertility after a long drought.
>
> (Jung 1971, CW6, para. 443)

For anyone who is living through it, the tension that accompanies the transcendent function is not an abstract or intellectual experience. It is numinous and archetypal (Miller 2004, Green 2011) and charged with emotional intensity and confusing imagery. It may offer both hope and fear and threaten to overwhelm us. The conflict associated with the transcendent function often goes to the heart of our identity and our sense of self. It may present itself as the conflict between the ideal of a perfect parent and a perfect career or perhaps between the dream of a meaningful life and the reality of financial security.

I asked a client to tell me about her life. A focal point in her early years was the unresolved tension in her parents' marriage and the unspoken influence they had each had over her. Her father was a gentle and reflective psychotherapist, whose time was spent alternating between patients and research and who had encouraged her to read widely. Her mother had been the principal 'breadwinner' in the family and had challenged the gender norms of her society to forge a high-profile career in finance. Although she had identified most with her father as a child, she had followed her mother's example as she moved through adolescence, studying economics at university to build a career as a finance manager in large multinational organisations. She described how the tension that existed between her parents seemed to have been replicated within her. While she was proud of her career success, she also wanted to rediscover her capacity for a more thoughtful reflective capability. She found herself drawn to a small bookshop-cum-café near her home which had become something of a sanctuary, where she drank coffee and read psychology books. It reminded her of afternoons with her father, and it was to become a transcendent symbol that we often returned to in our conversations, as an image of the balance she needed to restore within. In the years following our work together, she left finance to focus on organisational change and transformation, finally signing up for a master's degree in organisational psychology. She had found a way to integrate the opposing internal images of her parents. The bookshop-cum-café had provided her with a symbol of the transcendent function.

As the alchemical imagery that Jung so often drew upon suggests, something must die for something to be reborn, and the transcendent function promises both death and life. We know that once we fully engage with it, nothing will remain the same. Faced with this possibility, we may turn away in fear, as the conflict may be too troubling, too risky, or simply too inconvenient. It may require more than we are prepared to give, and we may not be ready yet to move on from the current habits and patterns that define us. The struggle between what we are and what we may become may be painful, but it is at least familiar. We may also simply not notice the quiet voice of the unconscious. Lacking a symbolic attitude and an awareness of our inner life and its implications, we may continue to focus on more prosaic and more immediate things until the voice calls again, perhaps a little louder and more urgently. To ignore that 'call to action', however, poses a risk to our psychological wellbeing and development, locking us into patterns which may have outlived their usefulness. A neurotic 'magic circle' forms around us, and we direct our energy away from change and into the defence of the status quo. However, the energy of the unconscious will continue to grow, and one day 'the repressed is going to return' (Moore 2001, p. 95) and the cycle of death and birth will continue.

The one thing we can be certain of is that if we are to move forwards, we are unlikely to find the answers in the things we already know. The formulae we have become used to are unlikely to help us. They are reminders of what we are, not provocations for what we may become and may simply drown out our inner voice. Perhaps they may still offer something to us but not in ways that we can easily predict. As Robert Moore has suggested, 'the archetypal nature of this process is, that before a needed transformation, *no one knows how it will turn out*' (Moore 2001, pp. 84–85). To face our potential and the transcendent function, we have to adapt and evolve. We have to begin to play.

Understanding Play

We can think of play as the way we navigate the tension of the transcendent function, moving between the infinite potential of the unconscious and the finite reality of the conscious mind. Jung suggested that this navigation was synonymous with fantasy, which we may think of not simply as a passing daydream but as a deliberate mediation between our inner and outer worlds, belonging to neither and both: 'It bears no resemblance to the two opposing functions, but stands between them and does justice to both their natures' (Jung 1971, CW6, para. 171). If we are focused only on a rational understanding, we have no access to intuition and the wisdom of the collective unconscious. If we are focused only on the inspiration and images of the unconscious, we have no capacity for reflection and practical meaning-making.

Play must begin with the adoption of a free-floating symbolic attitude where we allow symbols to naturally emerge to conscious awareness, but this alone is not enough. Play is not simply a noticing of symbols but demands that we also interact with them. We must be able to manipulate and rework the symbols that we have noticed, testing their limits, turning them around and upside down, and reforming and combining them to produce something previously unforeseen and unimagined. It is not an introspective mental indulgence but an active and embodied process of experimentation.

The psychoanalyst Donald Winnicott described play as a state of preoccupation and concentration, where we combine ideas from our external reality with images from our internal reality, investing them with new 'meaning and feeling' (1971, p. 69). For Winnicott, play was above all a practical activity with a direction towards a practical (if unknown) outcome. Whatever form it takes, that outcome will bring us a greater sense of agency and conscious choice in the world and the knowledge that we have the capability we need to face life's challenges.

> To control what is outside one has to do things, not simply to think or wish, and doing things takes time. Playing is doing.
>
> (Winnicott 1971, p. 55)

Jung certainly shared this perspective, suggesting that the emergence of the transcendent function and the new ways of seeing and being that come with that can happen only through a felt experience.

> Such an expression cannot be contrived by reason, it can only be created through living.
>
> (Jung 1971, CW6, para. 169)

Winnicott also suggested that play 'involves the body' and the 'manipulation of objects' (1971, p. 69), a perspective that in Jungian terms would place the act of playing deeply in the psychoid unconscious, where the psyche merges with the physical world. Here we can experience symbol at a profoundly archetypal level, creating a direct connection between our sensory experience of the world and our psychological responses. While we may be able to play solely through fantasy and imagination (as adults at least), the interaction with the physical 'not-us' adds a level of depth and intensity that cannot be replicated in mind alone. We may be using our hands to express an emotion or to describe a dream or a feeling, or we may be articulating ideas in new ways, experiencing the sensation of new words and new tones of voice. We may be playing with physical objects or making drawings of the symbols and images we have 'in mind'. In play, the feeling of the pen matters as much as the image it draws. Even digital objects on screen can allow this physical connection with the outside world, as in moving the mouse or the finger, the thought becomes something that is both beyond us and an expression of us. An idea can be worked like paint or clay (Clarke 2023). My client was not dreaming about reading the psychology books that her father loved in the peaceful and reflective space of the café. She was doing it and in that doing was able to more easily reimagine how this inner experience could be integrated with her life in the outer world. She was playing.

Jung used this combination of internal fantasy and external activity to help him make sense of his spilt with Freud. This experience had left him disoriented and confused, and the rational techniques of psychiatry and psychotherapy were unable to help him. In his search for meaning, he returned to his childhood and the inspiration of play.

> Thereupon I said to myself, 'since I know nothing at all, I shall simply do whatever occurs to me'. Thus, I consciously submitted myself to the impulses of the unconscious. The first thing that came to the surface was a childhood memory from perhaps my tenth or eleventh year. At that time, I had had a spell of playing passionately with building blocks. I distinctly recalled how I build little houses and castles, using bottles to form the sides of gates and vaults. Somewhat later I had used ordinary stones, with mud and water. These structures had fascinated me for a long time... As a grown man it seemed impossible to me that I should be able to bridge the distance from the present back to my eleventh year. Yet if I wanted to re-establish contact with that, I had no choice but to return to it and take up once more that child's life with the childish games.... I began accumulating suitable stones, gathering them partly from the lakeshore and partly from the water. And I started building: cottages, a castle, a whole village...I went on with my building game after the noon meal everyday whenever the weather permitted. As soon as I was through eating, I began playing, and continued to do so until the patients arrived; and if I was finished with my work early enough in the evening, I went back to building. In the course of this activity my thoughts clarified, and I was able to grasp the fantasies whose presence in myself I dimly felt... For the building game was only the beginning. It released a stream of fantasies which I later wrote down.
>
> (1995, pp. 197–198)

In his play, Jung was able to suspend his external reality while still maintaining a connection with that external reality. He became simultaneously an eleven-year-old child creating and working with stones and a man observing the child and making meaning from his play. This not only allowed him to deepen his insight into his own experiences but became a lifelong practice. This in turn allowed him to develop the techniques that later became 'active imagination', an approach to working with the unconscious as an aid to development to which we will return in Chapter 7.

In being able to interact with the external world in this way, we can test and extend the limits of our influence and our self-agency. The social scientist Albert Bandura suggested that this capacity 'to exercise control over the nature and quality of one's life is the essence of humanness' (2001, p. 1). With self-agency, we can influence the world rather than simply be passively influenced by it and, in this influence, can more fully feel the archetypal power of the self. We can become the lead actor in our own drama. In play, we can explore the limits of this agency in the real world and consider who we and who we could become. We are not simply imagining how we may act, we are actually acting. In playing with the symbols that constellate through imagination, we begin to discover where those symbols may be pointing and the possible significance they hold for our lives beyond play. This is to suggest not that fantasy in itself cannot be play and that we cannot play entirely 'in mind' but that when this fantasy moves into a sensory and external world, our capacity to play is amplified. This presence of the 'real' provides a tangible and reliable foothold upon which the images of the unconscious can constellate and become truly meaningful. We can then find ways to 'live out' those images in satisfying and, most importantly, realistic ways. Playing may then become an integral part of a more enriched way of life. As Dorothy Davidson has suggested: 'It could even be said that 'the quality of life depends on how far we are able to play out and live what is within us' (Davidson 1979, p. 42).

This is particularly significant when playing within relationship, namely with a coach or a coaching group. If we are playing with someone else, we can draw upon the additional symbols they bring to the relationship and can get immediate feedback on the way we respond to them. We can try out new words or ways of speaking and can see how our developing opinions are received. How do our drawings or stories affect others? In play, we can experience different and perhaps unfamiliar emotions and perhaps learn to tolerate them or even integrate them into our own sense of self. What does it feel like to express anger or to cry? What does it feel like when others do the same? What does it feel like to speak out and lead or to stay silent and follow. Each social interaction can be an opportunity to play with an alchemy of psychological symbols and real-world applications and to see where that leads us.

I begin many leadership programmes with a simple drawing exercise where participants introduce themselves. Rather than taking a more conventional and familiar approach, describing their life or career experiences, they are each asked to spend 20 minutes drawing a picture that illustrates their head, heart, and guts – the rational parts of themselves, their emotional selves, and their deeper more instinctive selves. Each participant is given a piece of flip chart paper, and pens are scattered on the floor in front of the group. They are given no other objects or instructions. The pictures themselves are always interesting, sometimes vivid and colourful, and sometimes timid and self-conscious, with often very different levels of aesthetic quality and symbolic depth. However, the most interesting part of the exercise is the 'gallery tour'. Here the pictures are placed up around the room and each person in turn introduces themselves using the picture and its symbols. The other participants are then invited to ask questions or perhaps even comment on aspects of the picture. The group typically tests what is possible and the limits of trust available, and then the pictures become a focal point to 'play' with the intangible feelings of the unconscious, both individual and group. The coach generally does not intervene, and participants very quickly find a 'level' of what they can share and what they can ask. Some questions are not (or perhaps cannot be) answered, and some observations are 'left hanging' as observations. Some participants may 'project themselves' into each other's pictures. Any attempt at interpretation by anyone other than the participant themselves is, however, gently discouraged to ensure that the participants remain in the state of play for as long as possible. As we come to the end of the 'gallery tour', the coach will then invite participants to wonder about the images and experience as a whole and about what they may say about the group. This helps the group to play with the idea that they are a group, who may share themes and be on the same journey together. The exercise is run again at the end of the programme, often several months later, and at this point we usually find that, as the group has established a feeling of relationship, the pictures are much richer and often aesthetically more interesting. It is as if the ego's self-conscious repression of the unconscious voice has relaxed, and participants have begun to develop a symbolic attitude and an enhanced ability to play.

Freedom to Play

However, even with tried-and-tested exercises like this, we cannot guarantee that our clients will play or in what form that play will emerge. Play finds its roots in the unconscious and as a result it is always spontaneous and unpredictable and cannot be commanded. We cannot ask people to play to deliver predetermined goals, even if (and perhaps especially if) the goal is their own development. If the drawings of the head, heart, and guts exercise are made to impress the coach or other participants, the exercise becomes a self-consciously performative and competitive exercise which for the individuals, and perhaps for the group as a whole, will simply repress the impulses of the unconscious. It is likely to function more as an ego defence, reinforcing established patterns of relationship, than as an opportunity to explore the potential of the self. A directed and self-conscious act will produce an outcome that satisfies the ego in its current state but will do little to evoke or nurture the transcendent function. It is the equivalent of giving a child a teddy bear alongside detailed instructions for use and a reward for following them, an approach which may satisfy the needs of the parent but which would do little to support the development of the child. Play is an emergent process and 'the playing has to be spontaneous and not compliant or acquiescent' (Winnicott 1971, p. 68) if there is to be any possibility of real development. It is the essence of the tension between the unknowable unconscious and the known conscious, and it moves in an ebb and flow between the two, as an impulse becomes a symbol and becomes real and then dissolves back into a new form. Von Franz has suggested that when working with the unconscious we must remember that 'it decides on the kind of play, you cannot decide on it' (2000, p. 100) as the experience of play is highly personal to each of us and to the ideas we need to express. When we begin to play, we 'touch uniqueness' (2000, p. 101). Sometimes we may need to sing, sometimes to draw, and sometimes to speak, and to play freely we must be able to follow our impulse as far as possible, allowing the symbols of the unconscious to constellate in the best possible form.

In play, we remain in this free state, in the middle ground of the transcendent function where a tangible idea is in the process of emerging through symbol. It can be given form, but the form is not fixed as 'this' or 'that' and has not had the life sucked out of it through process or interpretation. Play can be seen in the unpredictable and often controversial creations of many artists, and we can find our own inspirations in our approach to our lives and work. Picasso was known for creating images of bulls, in part as an expression of his Spanish heritage, and in 1942 he came across the handlebars and seat of an old bicycle, discarded on the side of the road. In a moment of playful inspiration, he saw them together as a single image that retained the qualities of both their combined symbolic value and their independent prosaic reality. The Bulls Head sculpture was exhibited at the Salon d'Automne in Paris in 1944 and aroused so much outrage that it was removed from the wall. In a conversation with the photographer Georges Brassai, Picasso suggested:

> Guess how I made the bull's head? One day, in a pile of objects all jumbled up together, I found an old bicycle seat right next to a rusty set of handlebars. In a flash, they joined together in my head. The idea of the Bull's Head came to me before I had a chance to think. All I did was weld them together... [but] if you were only to see the bull's head and not the bicycle seat and handlebars that form it, the sculpture would lose ... its impact.
>
> (Brassai 1999, p. 61)

Jung did not play with stones because a methodology or formal technique told him that it would reveal some aspect of his unconscious. He listened to his unconscious and allowed its voice to be heard through his intuition and his play. Play was an activity leading to its own inevitable and unknown end, and he simply had to participate without a goal in mind for its magic to work.

The Fear of Play

Despite the potential value of play, its unpredictability often evokes anxiety, in both client and coach. Winnicott suggested that play happened in the space between 'me' and 'not me' and that the 'precariousness of play belongs to the fact that it is always on the theoretical line between the subjective and that which is objectively perceived' (1971, p. 68). In play, we are walking a tightrope between the limitless possibility of the imagination and limited reality of the world. The lure of either side can be powerful. The unconscious, after all, can be thrilling and magical, while the conscious mind can be familiar and comforting. If we are to change, we need to let go of something that is part of us to make space for the new, but if we let go of too much, we may find ourselves unprotected and unprepared. We may even make space for something that destroys the very basis of our perceived reality, and fearing loss, we may then crush every possibility that questions that reality. Once we have played, we are no longer the same, and the awareness of loss that comes with that understanding will always create at least some level of anxiety.

As we play, a small part of our conscious sense of self and our place in the world is loosened and falls away in a process we can describe as a 'deintegration'. In 'deintegration', our energy and focus move outwards to those objects that are 'not us' (Fordham 1988, Astor 1995), and this movement may remind us of the existential threat of 'disintegration', where we cease to be. While still part of our psyche, the unconscious is an intense embodiment of 'not us', threatening to overwhelm the controlled illusion of the ego with its feeling-toned symbols and associations. However, if we can face this threat and tolerate the risk of disintegration, we can begin to play and explore those objects before 'reintegrating' our new understanding. Those objects can become part of our conscious self. If we face too much anxiety, we cannot play and instead we will mobilise our defences. We become stuck as we cling neurotically to a fixed view of the world. If we face too little anxiety, we do not need to play, and our creative spark quickly fades and dies. Anxiety is then a necessary and inevitable part of play and helps create not only a new understanding of the world but the knowledge that we can overcome that anxiety (Fordham 1969). In play, we learn to learn.

The fear of 'disintegration' and the threat of play are particularly pronounced in the organisational context in which many coaches and consultants operate. Many (if not most) organisations are defined by the need for tangible goals and outcomes, and this very real challenge is often inflated as a defence against the unpredictable qualities of human systems. Organisations and their leaders often need the illusion of control (Kets De Vries 1984) even though this is little more than a neurotic defence against anxiety. As a result, many clients seem unwilling or unable to make use of symbols and play to support their development. It is possible that this is grounded in some significant early-life trauma that is being repressed (Cambray and Carter 2004), but it is equally likely that play is simply no longer part of their adult social world. We may play as children, but once we are told that play is foolish and childish, the value of imagination and fantasy is diminished and our ability to play recedes into the unconscious and reappears only in permissible contexts or relationships. In Chapter 2, I mentioned the psychologist who could no longer accept that he could find 'magic' in his work, and the same may also be true of anyone who has immersed themselves in an organisational or social role, where they become defined by their responsibilities and their persona. Many societies have 'social prohibitions' against play, which is forbidden, denigrated, or perhaps tightly defined and controlled. Play becomes 'childish' or 'pointless' and is seen as a distraction from 'productivity'. These prohibitions are particularly emphasised in modern organisational life by models of heroic leadership which teach us that problems must be solved rationally, with tangible goals that must be met in predictable and defined ways. The 'dragons' must always be killed and cannot be not 'imagined away' or 'played' with.

Even apparently creative techniques, like sandplay or drawing or journaling, may activate these feelings and limit our ability to play. We may become seduced by our aesthetic ability and produce a piece of art or poetry that demonstrates our developed capability rather than freely expresses the emergent impulses of the unconscious. The technique may become a defence to limit and control the wild impulses of the unconscious, and we may direct symbols in ways that impress ourselves and others and follow paths that we are familiar with. If we are artistically inclined, we may still be able to express ourselves in truly creative ways, in the coaching equivalent of Picasso's Bull's Head. Or as a defence against the unconscious, we may simply produce something already known: Are we drawing ten unique images or the same image ten times? In creative techniques, we may also encounter transferential figures from the past reminding us that we cannot draw, that we are clumsy, or that we are inarticulate. The coach may then become a stern parent or a mocking teacher, and the technique may unwittingly evoke feelings of inadequacy and shame, leading to a repression of the unconscious.

During the head, heart, and guts exercise, some people start to draw immediately in a wild and free-form way. They begin to play. Others observe what is happening around them, waiting to see what they are 'permitted' to do in the group and what 'good looks like'. Others quietly plan their drawing, considering what they want to show to the group and to the facilitator, what is acceptable, and what will create the 'right' impression. Others freeze in terror and create the smallest possible drawing in a single colour with no risk of life and nothing that will allow the unconscious to reveal them. To provide as much support as possible for play, I try not to introduce the exercise in a way that amplifies its seriousness or significance. I remind participants that they are managers and not artists and joke that my expectations of artistic quality are very low indeed. I tell them that I have seen mind maps, geometrical shapes, anatomical images, landscapes and seascapes, graphs, and things that I still don't understand. I tell them to have fun! I then let play develop on its own terms, giving them time and space to draw whatever comes to them. When we debrief in the 'gallery tour', I give equal time and space to every drawing and I try to find something that will help them 'play'.

A Coach Who Can Play

Creating the conditions for play and the permission to play is then in large part dependent on the stance of the coach. Can we be playful? In the transference projections of the coaching relationship, we unconsciously communicate our own feelings about play to our clients. Hopefully, we are prepared to help them face their anxiety and move beyond any social prohibitions, as they begin to play with the symbols that are emerging for them. We can allow them to be spontaneous and to test the limits of play and, in doing so, find their own meaning and their own sense of agency. Alternatively, we may be unprepared and perhaps even threatened by the unpredictability of play. We may then enforce new prohibitions as we cling to our familiar techniques and processes at the cost of our client's ability to express what needs to be expressed and to take that in a direction of their choosing. We may decide that art, conversation, or movement is 'good' for a client, because that is our preferred practice. We can convince ourselves that it 'works' for our clients, but really, we cling to it because it works for us. This is not play, and we risk a client rejecting the work or performing it to please and impress us. It is possible for coaches who are not themselves playful to suck any joy and spontaneity out of play and so destroy the transformational potential of any symbol. In play, we cannot observe as bystanders; we must ourselves be able to play, providing an example for our clients. If we are afraid of the open-ended and exploratory nature of play, we will transfer this fear to our clients. We will suggest to them that if we are afraid of a spontaneous engagement with the symbols of the unconscious, then they should be too.

Winnicott describes a case study which for me has always seemed to be the perfect illustration of play in developmental work, providing a symbol that has shaped and inspired my own practice. He was working with a mother and her five-year-old daughter, helping them both make sense of an emotionally demanding family situation. The initial meeting was intended to begin a consultation with the mother and to develop an open-ended 'play relationship' with her daughter. His approach at the very beginning of his work seemed to set the tone:

> As I opened the front door to let in the mother, an eager little girl presented herself, putting forward a small teddy. I did not look at her mother or at her, but I went straight for the teddy and said: 'What's his name?' She said: 'Just Teddy.'

> (1971, p. 59)

In a direct, spontaneous, and playful engagement with the symbol, he demonstrated to the little girl that she was free to play and crucially that she was free to play with him. He had showed her that he was able to engage with her inner world and so encouraged her to do the same.

The challenge for coaches lies in our ability to engage with the symbols constellating in our clients' relationships and play with them without preconceived goals. Just like our clients, we are watched over by social prohibitions and seek the approval of real or imaginary authority figures. We want to be 'good coaches'. We also may be unfamiliar with the numinous power of the unconscious which may evoke an overwhelming fear of the unknown and the unknowable. These prohibitions and fears may be reinforced by our training which often encourages us to work only within well-defined processes towards well-defined goals. I have found that very few coaches in organisational settings are really comfortable playing, and even when play is mentioned, it is often justified by predetermined goals or outcomes. These, of course, prevent any possibility of play and simply allow us to pretend to engage with the unconscious.

Instead, we must know what it really feels like to play in our lives and our work. We must be familiar with the tension between the unconscious and the conscious mind and have deliberately immersed ourselves in that tension. We must be comfortable with the experience of 'not-knowing', referred to by the poet Keats as a 'negative capability' where we can be 'in uncertainties, myster-ies, doubts, without any irritable reaching after fact and reason' (Rollins 1958, p. 193). We can then step beyond merely tolerating that experience and begin to embrace and work with it. We can begin to play. How we respond to the symbols arising from the unconscious will give our clients the template for their own responses. We may encounter images and ideas that shock us or frighten us, but we must be able to tolerate these feelings and continue our play. The satisfying feeling of wholeness and development that we can call the self is found not in the things we create but in the playful experience of creation itself. If I can adapt Winnicott's advice to psychotherapists, placing it in the context of coaching:

> The general principle seems to me to be valid that [coaching] is done in the overlap of the two play areas, that of the [client] and that of the [coach]. If the [coach] cannot play, then [he/she] is not suitable for the work. If the [client] cannot play, then something needs to be done to enable the [client] to become able to play, after which [coaching] may begin
>
> (1971, p. 72)

Enter the Trickster

The coach may find inspiration for their play in the archetypal energy of the Trickster, who is typically found in myths and folk tales as the embodiment of transformation. Trickster, like all archetypes, is not a tangible entity who can be embodied in a single image but a means of describing a particular energy and a way of being. Trickster provides the energy to play and transform, an energy that evokes 'individuality, satire, irony, magic, indeterminacy, open-end-edness, ambiguity, sexuality, chance, disruption and reconciliation, betrayal and loyalty, closure and disclosure, mediation and unity of opposing forces' (Tannen 2007, p. 7). Trickster brings the capacity to stir repressed or unrealised aspects of the personality, provoking the constellation of symbols and provid-ing the inspiration to play with them. For Jung, Trickster was the essence of 'all conceivable opposites' (1992, CW13, para. 284), an embodiment of both para-dox and its resolution through the transcendent function. He/she, for there are Tricksters of both genders (often simultaneously) in most cultures, is both 'spiritual and material' and the 'process by which material is transformed' (1992, CW13, para. 284).

The primary trickster figure of Ancient Greek myth was Hermes, whose name was derived from the cairns of stones used as boundary markers (Downing 1993, p. 56). He symbolised both the existence of the boundary and the ability of the traveller to make the crossing, as a 'guide of souls and....of passages between realms of existence' (Stein 1983, p. 111). Hermes was the 'connection maker' (Lopez-Pedraza 1989, p. 8), who brought gods and mortals together and helped guide the souls of the deceased to the afterlife. Jung described him as a 'a chthonic god of revelation and also the spirit of quicksilver' (1953, CW12, para. 84), where 'chthonic' refers to a mystical world below the world, in its physical depths, and yet beyond it (Hillman 1979, p. 36). Like all trickster figures, he was a deceptive shapeshifter who was the embodiment of experimentation and play. His indefinable and unbounded qualities led Jung to suggest that he is the catalyst by which an individual may turn 'the meaningless into the meaningful' (1939, CW9i, para. 458). He provides a 'fluidity which delights in movement between the inner and outer worlds as a way of seeking and enjoying the absurd' (Tannen 2007, p. 142) before turning it into something unexpected and yet very real. Miller suggests that the transcendent function is itself a psychological manifestation of Trickster as 'it, like he, allows us to cross and recross boundaries to simultaneously hold multiple levels of consciousness' (Miller 2004, p. 109). Trickster is an 'excellent symbol for the living power of the psyche' (Jung 1953, CW12, para. 94) and 'a powerful change locomotive' (Goren-Bar 2022, p. 112), to whose archetypal and numinous power we need to be coupled if we are to approach our potential. Writing about the symbol of Trickster as the Fool of the tarot deck, Frederic Bagutti suggests:

> To approach The Fool, poetry could eventually be more adequate than science. Indeed, foolish may be the one, eager for rational answers, risking himself to question The Fool. He may quickly be proven himself fool by his questions, while The Fool, revealing the … inconsistencies in human behaviour, proving a wise man by his answers. With The Fool we enter a world of uncertainties, where even moral certainties are being questioned. Chasing The Fool, we have to take the risk to get lost, more than we would be in a Chet Baker's jazz jam… Representing the fundamental creative urge, The Fool holds all potentials, which can take shape according to specific needs.
>
> (2018, pp. 16–17)

As coaches, we must, at least to some degree, embody this Trickster energy and 'with the attitude of play all seriousness must vanish' (Jung 1971, CW6, para. 173). We must be able to notice and play with the symbols that arise in relationships and recognise that we may ourselves be symbols, representing the Trickster and his/her ability to play. Trickster 'makes whole what was previously fragmented and does this by linking up the unconscious world with the ego through the symbol' (Kalshed 1996, p. 197), a linking that may be made both explicitly and symbolically by the coach. For our clients, we may represent the capacity to be with the tenson between conscious and unconscious, moving easily between the two to create something new. We must be as comfortable with nonsense as with sense and be familiar with the range of emotions that is associated with transformation, from joy and laughter to sadness or rage. Above all, Trickster demands that our practice be fluid and adaptable, changing quickly as the situation demands. We must be able to comfort and then provoke, provide structure, and then bring chaos, cross boundaries, take up a role and then discard it. We must be both symbolic and rational with our clients, helping them to constellate the symbolic when they become prematurely goal-oriented and, when they become drawn too deeply into reflection, helping them return to reality. We must be in the moment, working with our clients as they are, engaging them in a reverie that moves easily between the unconscious and the conscious mind. If we become trapped in a single process or method or we employ a fixed range of techniques, then we cannot really play.

However, we must also remember that ultimately the dance of Trickster must lead somewhere if it is to have any meaning or purpose. This presents us with another paradox. If we begin to play with a goal in mind, we cannot be truly playful as 'the essence of play is that it has no meaning and is not useful' (von Franz 2000, p. 103). On the other hand, if our play leads nowhere, the experience will lack the numinous quality that comes with meaningful development, and it will not move us. Here 'the finished creation never heals the underlying lack of sense of self' (Winnicott 1971, p. 73) and is little more than a hobby or a leisure activity. Trickster then laughs at our expense.

Reflections and Implications

To play then, we must be able to maintain the precarious balance between the dreamscapes of the unconscious and the hard reality of our lived existence, moving between the two for as long as it takes for something new to emerge. When playing, we allow ourselves to be in the borderland between what we are and what we are not yet, moving fluidly between the two while remaining simultaneously in both. We must be able to work with the known and the unknowable in perfect balance, trusting that the challenges we face will resolve themselves in their own way and in their own time. The experience of play is an embodiment of the transcendent function, and in playing with its symbols, we discover a new and unexpected way of being.

Jung suggests that we may think of the emergence of symbol through the transcendent function, as a 'play instinct' which 'bears no resemblance to the two opposing functions but stands between them and does justice to both their natures' (1971, CW6, para. 171). To play with symbol is then an archetypal reminder of the unfolding potential of the self and the possibility of transformation. This perspective seems to be shared with Winnicott, who suggests that 'playing is itself a therapy' (1971, p. 67) and 'belongs to being alive' (1971, p. 91). It is then not simply something we do but something we have to do if we are to live at all as the 'creation of something new is not accomplished by the intellect, but by the play instinct acting from inner necessity' (1971, CW6, para. 198). To play, we simply have to give in to a natural impulse, accepting the fear of the unconscious but not allowing it to overwhelm us.

However, while the symbol may be the voice of the unconscious, it 'does not of its own accord step into the breach' (Jung 1971, CW6, para. 113). Our role as coaches is to create the conditions within which the symbol may be constellated and acknowledged and within which play may begin. We can give a client a pen and some instructions to draw a picture, but it is the choices they then make that will define the extent to which the exercise is meaningful. A client may follow instructions dutifully, hoping to impress the coach, or they may sense the coach's own anxiety and repress their own impulse to play and in both cases learn nothing. Alternatively, they may follow their intuition and develop the exercise with a spontaneous improvisation, working with the material at hand in often unpredictable ways. They may fold up the paper and draw on their arm instead! Whatever they choose to do, they must believe that play is possible. They must be able to develop the impulses that emerge within them and experience the sense of agency that comes with that. The symbols that arise in play and the way in which a client engages with them must originate from the client themselves. They will discard some symbols and let others live and in these choices will discover an agency and a meaning that are not limited by predetermined goals and objectives. Play must intuitively find its own path and resolve itself in its own time. There will be progress and regress, disappointments and false starts, and then the excitement of discovery. Most importantly, what has been created may be discovered only in retrospect. We can participate in the client's play, as we are not simply observers, but we cannot set the 'rules'. To find their own meaning, our clients must be free to express what needs to be expressed and then take that in a direction of their own choosing.

> In playing, new behavioural strategies are refined and rehearsed until a better adaption to the world is achieved. Apart from the pure joy of experimenting and expressing oneself, there is always also a purpose in play. Boring games are never played for long. Play demands risks, new challenges, finding one's own limits and trying new variations on things already familiar. This happens all by itself.
>
> (Pattis Zoja 2010 p. 146)

Play will happen when we allow it to happen, and the most important contribution we can make as a coach is to find Winnicott's bear and talk to him.

Consider the following:

- When was the last time you played? Without having any outcomes or rules?
- Look around you for something ordinary and unremarkable and play with it for a while. Don't think about why you are playing, just enjoy the moment. What does the object feel like? What can you do with it?
- When you start to get bored, stop and reflect on what you did. What was evoked within you? How did you feel? Did you have any associations?

References

Astor J 1995, *Michael Fordham: Innovations in analytical psychology*. London: Routledge.

Bagutti F 2018, The corporate freak: An exploratory study of the fool. Master's thesis. *Executive master in consulting and coaching for change*. INSEAD: Fontainebleau.

Bandura A 2001, Social cognitive theory: An agentic perspective. *Annual Review of Psychology* 52: 1–26.

Brassai G 1999, *Conversations with Picasso*. Chicago, IL: University of Chicago.

Cambray J and Carter L 2004, Analytic methods revisited. In J Cambray and L Carter (eds.) *Analytical Psychology: contemporary perspectives in Jungian analysis*. Hove, East Sussex: Routledge.

Clarke BO 2023, Synchronous glitch: The serious play of digital matter. *Journal of Analytical Psychology* 68: 443–447.

Davidson D 1979, Playing and the growth of the imagination. *Journal of Analytical Psychology* 24(1): 31–43.

Downing C 1993, *Gods in our midst*. New York: Crossroad.

Fordham M 1969, *Children as individuals*. London: Hodder & Stoughton.

Fordham M 1988, The infant's reach. *Psychological Perspectives* 21.

Goren-Bar A 2022, *An introduction to Jungian coaching*. Abingdon, Oxon: Routledge.

Green EJ 2011, Jungian analytical play therapy. In CE Schaefer (ed.) *Foundations of play therapy*. Hoboken, NJ: John Wiley & Sons.

Hillman J 1979, *The dream and the underworld*. New York: William Morrow.

Jung CG 1927, The structure and dynamics of the psyche. CW8.

Jung CG 1939, *The archetypes and the collective unconscious*. CW9i.

Jung CG 1953, *Psychology and alchemy*. CW12.

Jung CG 1971, *Psychological types*. CW6.

Jung CG 1992, *Alchemical studies*. CW13.

Jung CG 1995, *Memories, dreams, reflections*. London: Fontana Press.

Kalshed D 1996, *The inner world of trauma: Archetypal defenses of the personal spirit*. Hove, East Sussex: Routledge.

Kets De Vries M 1984, *The neurotic organisation*. San Francisco, CA: Jossey-Bass.

Lopez-Pedraza R 1989, *Hermes and his children*. Einsiedeln, Switzerland: Daimon Verlag.

Miller JC 2004, *The transcendent function: Jung's model of psychological growth through dialogue with the unconscious*. Albany, NY: State University of New York Press.

Moore RL 2001, *The archetype of initiation: sacred space, ritual process and personal transformation*. www.xlibris.com Xlibris Corporation.

Papadopoulos RK 2006, Jung's epistemology and methodology. In RK Papadopoulos (ed.) *The handbook of Jungian psychology: Theory, practice, and applications*. Hove, East Sussex: Routledge.

Pattis Zoja E 2010, Sandplay. In M Stein (ed.) Jungian psychoanalysis: Working in the spirit of C.G. Jung. Chicago, IL: Open Court.

Rollins HE (ed.) 1958, *The letters of John Keats*. Cambridge, UK: Cambridge University Press.

Stein M 1983, In midlife. Chelsea, MI: Spring Publications.

Tannen RS 2007, *The female trickster: The mask that reveals. Post-Jungian and postmodern psychological perspectives on women in contemporary culture*. Hove, East Sussex: Routledge.

Von Franz M-L 2000, *The problem of the puer aeternus*. Toronto: Inner City Books.

Winnicott DW 1971, *Playing and reality*. Abingdon, Oxon: Routledge.

Young-Eisendrath P 1992, Locating the transcendent: Inference, rupture, irony. In MA Matoon (ed.) *The transcendent function: individual and collective aspects; proceedings of the Twelfth International Congress for Analytical Psychology, August 23-28* pp. 151–165. Einsiedeln, Switzerland: Daimon Verlag.

Chapter 6

Set and Setting

The Way Mindset and Context Shape Coaching

When we are working in a Jungian way, we are navigating the permeable and dynamic boundary between the unconscious and the conscious mind. We are helping our clients to form what may be termed a stable ego-self axis (Edinger 1960, p. 9): a deliberate awareness of what lies 'below the surface' and the implications of that for our development. Here we can begin to understand that our ego-consciousness is not the whole of us and does not need to limit our potential. What we believe ourselves to be is not all we are and all we may become. Through the ego-self axis, we begin to engage with the self as the archetype of integration and wholeness. We begin to listen more closely to the voice of the unconscious and pay more attention to its symbols. We begin to develop what we can term a 'symbolic attitude', adopting a 'view of the world which assigns meaning to events, whether great or small, and attaches to this meaning a greater value than bare facts' (Jung 1971a, CW6, para. 899). The rich dialogue that opens up between the unconscious and the conscious mind then ensures that any changes to our personality are resilient and sustainable.

However, this is not easy work. The numinous energy and imagery of the unconscious may threaten to overwhelm us at any time, and the ego will work hard to defend its position. In any meaningful development process, we are walking a path between the safe but lifeless rationality of the conscious mind and the inspiring but chaotic emotions of the unconscious. On this path, we will encounter challenging, often mystical, and sometimes terrifying experiences which can overturn our lives, transforming our sense of self and perhaps even tearing us apart as we try to make sense of them. As coaches, we provide the support our clients need to face these challenges. In particular, we must ensure that our clients are adequately prepared for the inevitable turbulence ahead. We must be able to provide the 'set and setting' for the coaching dialogue, ensuring an inner world (the 'set') that is receptive and an outer world (the 'setting') that is conducive. We must ensure the foundations are in place that allow our clients to notice and engage with the whole of the psyche and its potential.

DOI: 10.4324/9781003463269-7

Psychedelics and Nonordinary States of Consciousness

The term 'set and setting' was introduced in 1961 by the controversial clinical psychologist Timothy Leary (1961), a pioneering advocate for the therapeutic use of psychoactive substances and a class of pharmaceuticals we now commonly call psychedelics. Psychedelics induce what we can describe as a 'nonordinary state of consciousness' (Timmermann et al. 2023) in which we move beyond the often-unnoticed world of 'the everyday' to experience consciousness in new and often unusual ways. We may, for example, perceive time and space differently or feel a deep connection with something beyond us. We may develop an enhanced awareness of symbols appearing in the world around us or in the symbols we ourselves produce in the form of hallucinations or visions. Through these experiences, we may become exposed to new and transformative perspectives, which then provoke a lasting shift in our consciousness, extending beyond the effect of the psychedelic itself. It has been suggested (Frecska et al. 2016) that, during nonordinary states of consciousness, our frame of reference shifts from a 'perceptual-cognitive' state, a conscious awareness of our immediate surroundings, to a 'non-local intuitive' state, where our awareness opens up to encompass a 'field of quantum connections and that is not restricted by space-time constraints' (Frecska et al. 2016, p. 155). In essence, we may begin to see the world through the eyes of the world rather than simply through our own rather limited (and potentially inflated) ego-consciousness. We gain perspective and may find new ways of solving problems when our familiar patterns of thinking are exhausted. In Jungian terms, we could describe this perspective as a direct experience of the psychoid unconscious (Jung 1927, CW8, para. 417–418), a bridge between the psyche and the universe, mediating and influencing the way in which we experience ourselves in the world and the world in us. It is through the psychoid that we can experience physical reality as a single entity, the 'unus mundus' or 'one world' (Stevens 2004), of which we are an integral part. For both Jungian psychology and quantum physics (Zabriskie 2004), this reality reaches beyond time and space and exists beyond the conscious mind.

The term psychedelic was invented by the psychiatrist Humphrey Osmond, in a letter to the author Aldous Huxley, as a combination of the ancient Greek words *psyche* ('mind') and *deloun* ('to manifest'). He suggested that 'to fall in hell or soar angelic, you'll need a pinch of psychedelic' (Dyck 2008). This new term for 'mind manifesting' drugs was then presented by Osmond to the New York Academy of Sciences in 1957 alongside research suggesting that psychedelics can reveal a hidden potential within the human psyche (Osmond 1957). Psychedelics are then 'mind-manifesting' in their capacity to reveal aspects of the psyche that may otherwise remain hidden and may not even belong to us alone. They may form part of our evolutionary inheritance and the collective psychology of humankind and perhaps of all living beings. This capacity has been consistently demonstrated in research, and studies have indicated that psychedelics can support reductions in symptoms of depression or addiction (Carhart-Harris et al. 2016, Davis et al. 2021, Johnson et al. 2014) and can lead to enhanced feelings of wellbeing, improvements in interpersonal relationships, and a sense of 'oneness' in nature (Haijen et al. 2018, Kettner et al. 2019). Through an experience of wholeness and the self, they may also support the reconstruction of a new personal narrative and an increased sense of possibility and agency (Carhart-Harris et al. 2012, Timmermann et al. 2023). It would seem that the nonordinary states of consciousness evoked by psychedelics can provide an immersive reframing of our relationships with ourselves. As Jung suggested, 'the numinous is the real therapy' (Von Franz 1990, p. 177).

However, there are risks, although studies suggest that, beyond the myths of popular culture, these are significantly less than those posed by alcohol and many other controlled substances (Schlag et al. 2022). For the most part, these risks appear to be linked to unprepared individuals and unsafe settings where the effects of psychedelics may have the potential to escalate into dangerous or self-harming behaviour (Johnson et al. 2008). Psychedelics may also evoke unconscious content that cannot be integrated, resulting in confusion and emotional disturbance, particularly in people who may have an underlying psychopathology (Nielson et al. 2021, Barber and Dike 2023) or who are inadequately supported through the experience. In her description of an unsupervised ayahuasca session, the Jungian analyst Deborah Byron notes:

> The event devolved into what felt to me to be like an uncontained psychic meteor shower in the energy field of a group...I witnessed the emergence of unprocessed material...bouncing energetically around a group...The next day after the ceremony, I observed one woman in a state of extreme anxiety, with symptoms that resembled PTSD [post-traumatic stress disorder].
>
> (2023, pp. 159–160)

Introducing Set and Setting

To help mitigate these risks and support more positive outcomes, Leary looked at the conditions surrounding psychedelic experiences and proposed that the chemical composition of a particular psychedelic only partly contributed to the quality of the experience. The drug simply served to enhance other more crucial factors, such as 'internal attitudes, expectations and feelings, as well as the external atmosphere and mood prevailing at the time' (Metzner 1999, p. 165). He referred to these factors as 'set and setting'. We can understand 'set' as the internal psychology of a person, including their underlying personality, their emotional state, and any conscious intentions or expectations. 'Setting' is then anything related to the environment in which the experience takes place, including both the physical context and the psychosocial context. The two concepts are then inextricably intertwined; 'set' shapes how 'setting' is perceived, and 'setting' shapes how 'set' evolves.

As Leary and his colleagues developed their thinking (1964), they considered the different types of backgrounds and expectations (e.g. medical, religious, or intellectual) that may influence the effect of nonordinary states of consciousness. They stressed the importance of psychological preparation and advised people to allocate at least three days for the experience and its integration and to prepare themselves by practicing meditation, reading appropriate books, and engaging in thorough introspection and reflective practice. They explored the use of music, lighting, and food as well as the arrangement of the space. They also considered the significance of the people responsible for guiding participants through the experience, noting that these individuals may have 'a profound effect on the experience, both through the kind of preparation they encourage and through the kind of setting and interpersonal interaction they arrange' (Leary et al. 1963).

Although the specific phrasing of 'set and setting' has been formulated and developed over the last few decades, the concept itself has much deeper roots. In 1860, the French poet Baudelaire published a comprehensive account of the use of hashish, the prepared resin of the psychoactive plant cannabis. He thought the drug provided a 'magnifying mirror' for the mind of the user and stressed that it was a combination of psychological state and environment that would determine whether the experience was positive or not.

> Hashish causes an exaggeration, not only of the individual but also of his circumstances and surroundings; you free yourself of all appointments, all obligations requiring punctuality or precision; you free yourself of thoughts occupied with domestic cares and heartaches. But beware, for cares and anxieties, recollections of observations demanding your attention at a specific time, will toll like a passing bell through your intoxicated thoughts to poison your pleasure. Each care will become a torture and each anxiety a cruel torment. If all of the aforementioned conditions have been met, if the weather is fair and you have found a favourable setting, a variegated landscape or a poetically decorated apartment, and moreover if you might hope for some music, then all is for the better.
>
> (1996, p. 41)

Even before the modern use of psychedelics, the preparation for a nonordinary state of consciousness has been central to the experience. Shamanic rituals usually have a strong performative character in which various elements are carefully brought together to set the stage for the visionary journey of the shaman (Helman 2001, Beyer 2010). They deploy rich symbolism and music, within spaces that are often set aside for repeated use. These may be natural spaces such as caves or rock shelters, or places that are created with ritual in mind. A shaman may descend into an underworld, perhaps through narrow tunnels into darkness, before emerging again in a symbolic rebirth. They may blow smoke, sing, and dance in considered and established ways, sometimes with others providing ceremonial support. Some Samoyed shamanic rituals, for example, include an audience who gather around the shaman during his 'dialogue with the spirits' (Eliade 1972, p. 227) and sing in chorus to support his own chanting. The spaces may also be everyday spaces, like Baudelaire's 'poetically decorated apartment' with a symbolism that can form a bridge between the poles of the mystic and the real, between the unconscious and the conscious mind. During the psychedelic rituals of the Desana people of Brazil, the everyday house used as the space for shamanic rituals becomes a symbol of the cosmos itself, and different entrances assume different meanings (Lewis-Williams and Pearce 2005, p. 65). The religious historian Mircea Eliade notes that, in some cases, the use of the narcotic intoxication may itself be symbolic, as the shaman leaves their body to enter the world of ghosts and spirits. They descend into a psychic underworld, dying to be reborn, and the content of the mystical ecstasy may then matter less than the simple fact that it has happened at all (Eliade 1972, p. 477). These symbolic enhancements would appear to be an intrinsic part of the shaman's craft and an essential contributor to the depth and value of their experience.

Beyond Psychedelics

Set and setting may then play a significant role in shaping our psychology beyond the medium of psychedelics. Intense experiences of nonordinary states of consciousness may be created with very different stimuli as the following examples illustrate, only one of which is induced through psychedelics:

1 'Suddenly I saw a large green eye opening and closing. Also something very vague moving in the dark, like a train entering a tunnel or something similar, not very clear. Then, a landscape - outline of hills - very fluid - moving. A wolf's face grinning... view of a tree from under the ground- seen as if I were lying under the tree looking up through its roots' (Mavromatis 1987, p. 20)
2 'The sun was shining and the shadows of the laths made a zebra-like pattern on the ground and across the seat and back of a garden chair...That chair – shall I ever forget it? Where the shadows fell on the canvas upholstery, stripes of a deep but glowing indigo alternated with stripes of an incandescence so intensely bright it was hard to believe they could be made of anything but blue fire' (Huxley 1994, p. 35)
3 'It looks like a white slanted line in the sky that goes underground...I can go either up or down...if I don't cool down my body will disappear. The hot steam inside me leaves my body, giving me new eyes. The eyes can become any colour. I can change into another form and travel to other places' (Keeney 2003, pp. 105–108)

The first example is a vivid description of 'hypnagogia', the intermediary experience between waking and sleep, when we are neither fully conscious nor fully unconscious. The second is an account of Huxley's own experience with mescalin, and the third is a statement from a San healer from southern Africa, whose experience was evoked through rhythmic dancing, drumming, and hyperventilation. All three are clearly profound experiences with similar intensity and tone but induced in very different ways.

Our perceptions of the world around us, and the world within us, are shaped by many factors which may be physical or psychological and may include fatigue, hunger, discomfort, or particular emotional states such as fear or joy. Even the way we breathe has a significant impact on our psychological state, affecting our perceptions, our cognitive capability, and our sense of wellbeing (Fried and Grimaldi 1993, Fincham et al. 2023). These perceptions may also not be our own and may instead be projected into us through the phenomenon of projective identification. Here we begin to identify with the mental processes of another person, or a group and our minds may take on some of their emotional state as our own. Our bodies then follow, as the emotions trigger physical responses which fuel our psychological state still further in a repeating cycle of affect. Even ideas and images may be transferred between us through the phenomenon of 'neural coupling' or 'neural entrainment' (Hasson et al. 2012) where, under certain conditions, our brains become physically aligned and thought itself becomes a shared activity. Our set and our psychosocial setting may be then very difficult to disentangle, each shaping the other.

Our physical environment may similarly evoke profound psychological changes in perception, including factors like whether we are in a natural or built environment, the prevailing temperature and weather conditions, or the effect of music. The symbols that we encounter in a particular setting may be highly evocative, stirring the numinous archetypal energy of our physical and psychological human inheritance. An interesting example of this may be found in the descent into darkness, often through narrow tunnels, that forms such a prominent part of shamanic visionary journeys and the rites of passage that mark an individual's transition from one state of social being to another (Turner 1969). Here the setting suggests an experience of death and rebirth, a mythical visit to the underworld where we confront shadows and annihilation in order to make space for the new. This is a universal theme in human myth and ritual, appearing across history in many different cultures, and in Jungian psychology this is often referred to as the nekyia, or night journey: 'a descent into the cave of initiation and secret knowledge' (Jung 1971b, CW15, para. 213). Here we confront and integrate aspects of our own unconscious as an essential part of our ongoing development. Part of us dies in order to make space for the new. This 'cunnicular' experience may be an obvious metaphor to symbolise a deeply embedded vestigial memory of the birth experience, either our own or a collective memory. It may also be a neurological phenomenon, as movement through a vortex is frequently reported in nonordinary states of conscious (Lewis-Williams and Pearce 2005, p. 48). Some sacred sites may have been deliberately constructed to create these dark tunnels and perhaps to stimulate this experience.

> The sensory deprivation offered by neolithic tombs is inescapable. If one stays still for long enough the silence and darkness…seep deeper and deeper into one. There is…security but that security seems to derive from an absence of sensation, a settling, palpable calm. Neolithic people may not have entered the tombs in great numbers nor often, but, when they did, sensory deprivation, probably only one of their ways of altering consciousness, awaited them.
>
> (Lewis-Williams and Pearce 2005, p. 208)

These nonordinary states of consciousness not only are the preserve of psychedelics or sensory deprivation but may be evoked by much smaller nuances in the interplay of set and setting. Research has also explored these states in religious or meditative experiences (Oswald et al. 2023, Timmermann et al. 2023) or even simply through mindful experiences of being in nature (Hood 1977). We know that even scents can relax us, or invigorate us, or shape our behaviour as consumers (Rimkute et al. 2016). If we pay attention and begin to develop our sensitivity to the voice of the unconscious, we may begin to access a new level of awareness of the world within us and around us. This is the very essence of a symbolic attitude. As Jung suggested, hallucinations are not 'merely a pathological phenomenon [or perhaps one derived from psychedelics or altered states] but one that occurs also in the sphere of the normal' (1977, CW18, para. 1113). We may experience an epiphany of sorts in the quiet darkness of a tiny church in Venice, the silence of a forest, or even the overwhelming buzz of a casino. A piece of music or the smell of soil after rain may bring back vivid childhood memories and long-forgotten associations and images. Here we can begin to understand the advice of English poet and mystic William Blake:

> To see a World in a Grain of Sand
> *And a Heaven in a Wild Flower*
> *Hold Infinity in the palm of your hand*
> And Eternity in an hour.
>
> (Blake in Raine 1986)

Some years ago, I was working in Kyoto. At the time, I was a practicing Buddhist and wanted to visit one of the many Zen temples in the city. My first feelings were of profound disappointment, as the temple precincts were filled with tourists, chattering and taking photographs, and the zendos, or meditation halls, themselves were all closed. I wandered around for a while until, overwhelmed by the noise, I ducked into a narrow alleyway leading to a leafy courtyard, at the end of which was the open door of a small zendo. The room was empty and silent, with a polished wooden floor. I removed my shoes and entered, bowed as I would do in my home temple, and sat on a meditation cushion with my back to a wall. Within a few minutes of my entering, a black-robed monk also entered. He bowed to me, and I returned his bow as he sat opposite. We then both sat in silence. All I could hear was my own breasting and occasionally the wind in some unseen trees. It was quite literally perfect, and as I counted my breaths in a basic meditation exercise, I completely lost track of time. When I left the room, I realised I had spent nearly an hour there. I now understand that I had entered the place stressed but with a hopeful mindset and the need for a sanctuary that matched my imagined ideal of Kyoto. I wanted to be saved. I had no other plans and nothing to distract me from my discovery. The symbols of the setting had provided me with that sanctuary, from the shady tree in the courtyard, to the smell of incense and old wood, to the gratifying presence of the monk. This was not a meditation in my living room.

Even a gentle loosening of the boundary between the unconscious and the conscious mind may then move us towards a nonordinary state of consciousness. Jung suggested that the experience of hallucination was simply a manifestation of aspects of intuition which was not yet ready to become conscious and, in this sense, is analogous to the constellation of symbol, albeit in a much more intense form. We may then think about nonordinary states of consciousness as simply the unconscious voice, speaking what needs to be spoken, without the repression of the conscious mind. Symbols begin to constellate, and we gradually feel the energy of the archetypal.

> As the word [hallucination] itself indicates, a certain spontaneity attaches to the phenomenon; it is as though the psychic content has a life of its own and forced its way into consciousness by its own strength. This peculiarity probably explains the ease with which the brain wave assumes a hallucinatory character. Common speech is familiar with these transitions from brain wave to hallucination. In the mildest cases we say: 'I thought'; 'it occurred to me' is a little stronger; stronger still is 'it was as though an inner voice said', and finally 'it was as though someone were calling to me', or 'I heard a voice quite distinctly.
>
> (Jung 1977, CW18, para. 1113)

All these experiences can simply be placed on a spectrum of intensity, and their placement is established in the interplay between the mind of the individual, the social context, and the physical environment. Deborah Byron has suggested (2012, 2023) that our consciousness exists across a range of four distinct stages which may be attained with or without the aid of psychedelics. We begin with the *physical* level, representing our everyday experience and immediate reality. This level functions solely in the domain of ego-consciousness. We then move to the *symbolic* level, which occurs in 'dreams and waking states of reverie and flow states involving the creative process' (2023, p. 161) and which provides the developmental bridge between the unconscious and the conscious mind. The third level is the *mythic* level, which we may think of as the archetypal realm of the collective or cultural unconscious and in which many of the symbols that appear in developmental work have their origins. Finally, we may encounter the *energetic* level, where we may directly encounter the archetype of the self and experience a state of oneness with all things. Here our physical reality and sequential time vanish into the state of primordial unified reality that is the 'unus mundus'. Set and setting may influence our experience at each stage or perhaps evoke a new state of mind altogether. We may discover the numinous under the influence of LSD or listening to drums in a deep, dark cave or perhaps simply by doodling on blank page or by letting our mind wander in a reflective space. Our 'psychedelic' may be nothing more than a pencil and paper in a quiet room.

Set and Setting in Coaching

Given the potential breadth of influence that 'set and setting' may then have on meaningful developmental experiences, it feels disappointing then that this valuable provocation has been largely confined to the field of psychedelics and spiritual experiences. While the energetic level may be the domain of psychedelics and altered states, we can imagine coaching as the first stirring of a non-ordinary state of consciousness placed on Bryon's second, symbolic level. Here 'set and setting' can serve as practical frame of reference for coaches who may be working with the unconscious and a reminder that in coaching our clients are not participating in the day-to-day. They are not buying groceries, updating a spreadsheet, or delivering a presentation. Instead, in coaching, they are exploring their hopes and fears. They are noticing themselves and the world around them as if for the first time. The hardness of their reality is for a short while suspended, and our clients can consider 'what if' as they pay attention to the intuition, insights, and symbols of the unconscious.

Through an awareness of 'set and setting', we can more deliberately consider the forces that shape the feeling-toned symbolic space which in turn provide the bridge between psyche and the 'real' world. Here our clients are suspending, at least to some extent, the fixed and familiar boundaries of ego-consciousness and creating space for something new to be integrated. This bridge was referred to by the psychoanalyst Donald Winnicott as a 'potential space' (Winnicott 1971), where 'me' and 'not-me' coexist and the boundaries that separate them become permeable. We can think of potential space as 'a third area of human living, one neither inside the individual nor outside in the world of shared reality....negating the idea of space and separation' (Winnicott 1971, p. 148). It is here that we can begin to play and experiment with 'reality', reimagining 'what is' and 'what could be'. Without secure and dependable potential spaces, our creative potential and our developmental experiences will be impoverished. On this bridge, the 'set and setting' are the symbolic variables that determine the movement of traffic, including the 'vehicles' that are allowed to cross and the speed and direction of their crossing. With an appropriate 'set and setting', we can begin to create a potential space that enables a free flow between the creative possibility of the unconscious and the practical rationality of the conscious mind. We cannot 'make people play', but we can help create a setting within which play becomes possible.

Culture, Context, and Expectations

An obvious place to begin is the simple recognition that coaching takes place not in a vacuum but in a social and cultural context, which may include the groups and organisations to which both coach and client belong. Here we will encounter not simply the day-to-day reality of our lives but the lenses through which we view that reality and the underlying cultural complexes that may then shape our behaviour. A cultural complex is a series of related and emotionally charged associations and assumptions that have arisen from the shared experiences of a group of people (Singer and Kimbles 2004). These experiences may be historical, having happened before any individual in the group was born, but they are lived again in the present. They remind members of the group of who they are and how they should respond to given situations, influencing the behaviour of those members as individuals and as a group. Within any nation, society, or organisation, we may find a number of cultural complexes, all interacting with each other in different ways. They may include complexes linked to religious or racial groups, socio-economic groups or gender, and a sense of national identity itself. The cultural complex will shape how we perceive the world and how we are perceived. It has a significant influence on 'set' as we enter a coaching engagement, and it may evoke strong projections between coach and client, perhaps leading to conflict or collusion. We may not be able to predict these projections, but an awareness of their potential existence may help us notice them and respond as they arise.

Cultural and personal complexes may also colour our expectations of the coaching itself. Both coach and client approach the work with assumptions and fantasies, which will shape their behaviour and their relationship. Is the coach a saviour or a sounding board? Is the coaching a badge of honour or a symbol of failure? Is the coaching a sign of weakness or an opportunity to perform heroically for an approving authority figure? Does the client enter the engagement willingly or unwillingly? The stated outcomes, explicit or assumed, may be a symbol of a regressive expectation or a progressive opportunity, locking us into previous habits or moving us forwards to new ways of being. How this symbol is then interpreted depends on both coach and client and on the way their relationship unfolds. Many coaches are taught to offer 'powerful' or 'transformative questions' and will enter their coaching relationships with this underlying need. Their self-worth as a coach is often dependent on the outcomes they magically evoke, and they will inevitably project these expectations onto their clients. If there is no Damascene moment of transformation, what impact will this have on the coach and therefore on the client? Have both or either of us failed? Our sensitivity to the backdrop that defines us as coaches and that shapes our clients will have significant implications for our work together.

I was asked to coach a client who had just been promoted to a senior role within a global financial services organisation. When I arrived for our chemistry meeting, I could immediately tell that she was close to tears. Rather than talk about the formal outcomes for the assignment, which was to help her drive performance in a failing department, I asked her how she was feeling. She confessed that she was about to resign and in fact had planned to do so after our chemistry meeting. She told me that to take the promotion she had moved to a new function and a new country and now had a new manager who was located elsewhere in the world. She felt isolated and alone, without the support network of friends who had previously sustained her. She also told me that I was the third coach she had seen and apparently the first who had asked her how she was feeling. The other coaches had simply clarified the stated goals with her and explained the process they intended to follow, focusing on the feedback tools and supporting psychometrics they wanted to use. She felt that her manager had suggested the coaching because she was not 'good enough' for the promotion and the inflexibility of the other coaches had seemed to emphasise this. She felt that while she needed support, the coaching had been imposed on her and the coaches were there to monitor her performance. Being able to 'confess' her fears seemed to make our conversation somewhat lighter, and I was able to transition from being a symbol of surveillance and oppression to something more 'human'. We were able to begin to establish trust and the possibility of relationship, a first step to recreating the support network that she felt had been lost.

While we can never fully appreciate the complexity of the backdrop to our work and the effect it has on the mindset of our clients, we can remind ourselves to reflect upon it as a formal part of any engagement. We can develop a symbolic attitude and begin to wonder about how the unconscious shapes our work, before that work has begun. If the client and coach are operating under different mindsets and expectations, we must be able to consider ways in which we can begin to create a mutual understanding and rapport, perhaps simply by asking some simple questions of ourselves and our clients.

Creating the Boundaries

Having reflected on the context, we can turn our attention to the coaching space itself and should perhaps begin with the way in which we cross the threshold, moving from an ordinary state of consciousness to something more conducive to coaching work. This threshold is the symbolic boundary, without which a distinct potential space could not exist and any coaching conversation would be little more than a transactional conversation in the ordinary course of life. Without the existence of the threshold, such a mindset change becomes impossible. We can easily imagine a situation where a client arrives under time pressure, moving from one appointment to coaching and then moving quickly on from coaching to another appointment, often in the same building. Here the coaching does not take place in a potential space, and the symbols of the everyday world encourage us to repress the voice of the unconscious, preventing any possibility for creativity and meaningful development work. It is impossible to help a client wonder about 'what may be' if they are worrying about 'what is'.

The threshold marks out the potential space as somehow 'magical' or 'sacred' and a place where the numinous energy of the unconscious can reveal itself. It tells us that here we can play safely, without any intrusion from the everyday. It reminds us that we can listen to the voice of the unconscious without being overwhelmed by it, as the boundaries of the space will hold us. As Marie-Louise von Franz has suggested:

'I think nobody can really develop…before having first created a temenos, namely, a sacred grove, a hidden place where he/she can play. The first thing to do is find a Robinson Crusoe playground, and then when you have got rid of all onlookers you can begin! As a child, one needed a place and time and no interfering adult audience.

(von Franz 2000, p. 103)

In coaching, our work is to help create this playground and keep it safe from the interference of the everyday, 'adult' world. This space may be physical or imaginal, existing only in our minds, but both are marked in their own way by symbols. These symbols carry associations and evoke the energy of the unconscious, reminding us of the existence of the space as we move from one reality to another. They provoke us to enter with a new state of mind and the beginnings of a nonordinary state of consciousness. The threshold provides an opportunity to pause and look within, before we take a step forwards.

In the busy district of Sheung Wan in Hong Kong, just above the Cat Street antique market, is the Man Mo Temple complex. It was built in the nineteenth century, to honour the God of Literature (Man Cheong) and the God of War (Mo Tai), and it presents a striking contrast to the towering blocks of flats around it. Inside it is exquisitely decorated with ceramic figurines, carvings, and murals, and the air is thick with incense. However, while the temple is open to anyone, you cannot just shuffle in from the street. Its doorstep is a wooden board of around 30 cm in height, which separates the temple from the world, and to enter the temple requires a deliberate step. Once we have taken this step, we know we are no longer in a modern city, but instead we have entered a sacred world that is set apart from the everyday. As coaches, we need to create the same step for our clients, perhaps not with a wooden board but certainly with something noticeable that demands a subtle shift in consciousness.

Something must happen to signal that we have entered potential space and then again signal when we leave it. A supervision client works in a small and rather ordinary modern building behind an industrial estate, which she shares with a number of other development professionals. While her location in itself is not remarkable, her clients have to walk to her through a strange and desolate wasteland of warehouses, giving them a 'step' to cross and a reminder of where they are going and why.

The threshold may also be nothing more than a simple ritual, a symbol held in mind without any self-conscious artifice. Sometimes all we need to do is sit for a moment in silence and ask a client how they are feeling, in the same tone and same words, as if we are ringing a temple bell. A coaching client is a senior leader in a large multinational organisation, and over the two years we have worked together, our sessions always begin in the same way. We meet in her offices, in the meeting rooms set aside for external visitors, and she always books the same room. I always arrive first and sit in the same chair. She enters the room a few minutes later, and after greeting me, she asks me if I want tea. She then makes tea for us both without talking, and she quietly pours each cup, adds milk, and stirs them. She hands me my cup and then sits in the same chair, and we begin. I have seen her working in other meetings where she never makes tea and is rarely silent. It is probably worth noting, in the context of socio-cultural 'set', that she comes from a culture where tea has an important symbolic role in hospitality and provides an excuse for long conversations. These emergent rituals need not be placed under the spotlight of conscious awareness to be analysed and stripped of life; instead, we simply need to notice that they exist and are significant as symbols of the boundary. We just need to allow them to serve their purpose.

Once the boundary has been marked with its symbols, we have to consider who is permitted to cross. A challenge facing coaches working within organisations is that the organisation often attempts to breach these boundaries. The anxiety of what may be happening in these secretive and magical spaces can be overwhelming, and managers often try to find ways to shape what happens within and reassert their control. This, of course, impacts 'set and setting' as participants come to realise that the boundaries of the space are not secure. The tension between the everyday mind and images and intuition of the unconscious may then become overwhelming, and the ego must assert its authority to protect itself. Meaningful development work becomes impossible. When we open ourselves to the unconscious, we relinquish our tried-and-tested defences, leaving us vulnerable and exposed, and it is the predictable boundaries of potential space that keep us safe. Paradoxically, it is the existence of these boundaries that gives us the freedom to engage with symbols and explore how we may begin to use them to discover new possibilities. As Winnicott suggests:

> Where there is trust and reliability is a potential space, one that become
> an infinite area of separation, which the baby, child, adolescent, adult

may creatively fill with playing...in the potential space...there appears the creative playing that arises naturally out of the relaxed state; it is here that there develops a use of symbols that stand at one and the same time for external world phenomenon and for phenomena of the individual person.

(Winnicott 1971, p. 146)

The Symbols of the Space

Once we have acknowledged the boundaries and their significance, we can turn our attention to the arrangement of the coaching space itself and the effect it may have as a 'setting'. We may want to start by considering whether we are meeting in a public space, the client's workspace, a space of our own, or perhaps even online and then reflect on the symbolic value of our choice of venue. This value will be reflected in both the overall space and the particular symbols within the space. Does the space in some way reflect the work we are doing? Do we need to be near to the client's work? Or a more reflective space? A natural environment may be helpful for a client seeking to reflect on their place in the world but may not be helpful with a client who is entering a new organisation or working through a work-related problem. We may want to focus on creating a space that feels comfortable and relaxed or something more formal, depending on the nature of the assignment and our sense of the mindset and personality of the individuals involved.

We could consider some of the more obvious artefacts that are present in the space, that may have a symbolic value for coach and client. In psychotherapy, the couch is such an artefact and has subject to a great deal of commentary and debate. Far more than a simple place to sit, it has become a symbolic focal point onto which a patient can project any number of unconscious phantasies, as a crib or a coffin or even a womb (Lingiardi and Bei 2011). It has passed into the folklore of psychotherapy, and coaching clients working 'beneath the surface' have often jokingly suggested to me that they need a couch, tapping into a cultural symbol and granting themselves permission to play with the unconscious. We may wonder about the way the light falls or the quality of the air and whether the ambient noise supports our conversation or distracts us. On one leadership programme I am involved in, a garish carpet forms a strange centrepiece that seems to evoke a great deal of humour but eventually becomes a reminder of the space and a shared memory that holds alumni together after the programme. These details may even be significant in online meetings, and we may need to consider our backdrop; is it generic, blurred, or overly curated? I have had online clients remark on how 'cosy' my room feels or on my paintings or the various objects I have on my shelves, all of which serve as reminders of the work we are doing together.

As coaches, we may also have our own preferences and our own sense of what constitutes a suitable setting, but it is often revealing to see how little a client is disturbed by something that is disturbing to us, and vice versa. The symbols within potential space are, after all, symbols because of their subjective affect, and both coach and client will experience them in different ways. We cannot then curate symbols in the coaching space for the client to find, intentionally manipulating their inner journey. Instead, we must allow them to discover their own symbols and derive their own meaning from them. Each symbol will take on different meanings for different people and even different meanings for the same people at different times. For this reason, we can imagine the 'setting' of potential space as a 'dynamic matrix' (Eisner 1997), which is adapted and evolved as part of the process of coaching, which clients can make their own, and in that 'making' discover the agency needed to re-enter the world in new ways. Our role as coaches is simply to provide a setting that is supportive and then to be open to our clients' discoveries in that setting, helping then play in whatever way they chose. As the Jungian analyst Ellen Siegelman has suggested, we need to supply 'an atmosphere or environment, a space or place in which the [client] can count on our steadiness, dependability, benign lack of judgement, our relative predictability and our "thereness"' (1990, p. 174).

Reflections and Implications

While our interaction with the unconscious in coaching is certainly not as intense as in psychedelic experiences, it may still feel very removed from our day-to-day lives. As we engage our imagination and creativity, we may encounter provocative archetypal symbols that suggest new ways of being. In this encounter, we may need to let go of familiar habits and defences and step into an unformed and uncertain future. We may discover images and associations that we do not understand but seem to move us with their compelling, numinous energy. We may even confront the events that shaped and defined our ancestors and be forced to reexamine our cultural identity. We are inevitably drawn towards a nonordinary state of consciousness, and we enter what the author Phillip Pullman has termed the 'borderland' of the imagination (2017). Lying between the fertile chaos of the unconscious and the concrete reality of the world, this 'borderland' offers a 'potential space' or a 'temenos' where we can play and begin to make meaning from the symbols that are surfacing there. If we are to make best use of this space, the reminder of 'set and setting' is then an important one, ensuring that, as far as possible, the foundations for a meaningful dialogue are in place. Through an awareness of 'set and setting', we can help our clients fully participate in the emergence of the self as an integrated sense of wholeness. Our coaching can be 'mind manifesting'.

As a coach or consultant:

- How do you help your clients enter the workspace with a suitable mindset?
- What symbols mark the boundaries?
- What tone do these symbols set? For you and your clients?
- What symbols remind your clients of the work you are doing together?
- What tone do these symbols set? For you and your clients?

References

Barber GS and Dike CC 2023, Ethical and practical considerations for the use of psychedelics in psychiatry. *Psychiatric Services* 74(8): 838–846.

Baudelaire C 1996, *Artificial paradises*. Translated by Stacey Diamond. New York: Citadel Press.

Beyer SV 2010, *Singing to the plants: A guide to Mestizo shamanism in the Upper Amazon*. Albuquerque: University of New Mexico Press.

Byron D 2012, *Lessons of the Inca shamans, part I: Piercing the veil*. Bedford, IN: Pine Winds Press.

Byron D 2023, Are the use of psychedelics really necessary? In L Stein and L Corbett (eds.) *Psychedelics and individuation: Essays by Jungian analysts*. Asheville, NC: Chiron.

Carhart-Harris RL, Erritzoe D, Williams T, Stone JM, Reed LJ, Colasanti A, Nutt DJ 2012, Neural correlates of the psychedelic state as determined by fMRI studies with psilocybin. *Proceedings of the National Academy of Sciences of the United States of America* 109(6): 2138–2143.

Carhart-Harris RL, Bolstridge M, Rucker J, Day CMJ, Erritzoe D, Kaelen M, Bloomfield M, 2016, Psilocybin with psychological support for treatment-resistant depression: An open-label feasibility study. *The Lancet Psychiatry* 3(7): 619–627.

Davis AK, Barrett FS, May DG, Cosimano MP, Sepeda ND, Johnson MW, Finan PH and Griffiths RR 2021, Effects of psilocybin-assisted therapy on major depressive disorder: A randomized clinical trial. *JAMA Psychiatry* 78(5): 481–489.

Dyck E 2008, *Psychedelic psychiatry: LSD from Clinic to campus*. Baltimore, MD: Johns Hopkins University Press.

Edinger E 1960, The ego-self paradox. *Journal of Analytical Psychology* 5: 3–18.

Eisner BG 1997, Set, setting, and matrix. *Journal of Psychoactive Drugs* 29(2): 213–216.

Eliade M 1972, *Shamanism: Archaic techniques of ecstasy*. Princeton, NJ: Princeton University Press.

Fincham GW, Strauss C, Montero-Marin J and Cavanagh K 2023, Effect of breathwork on stress and mental health: A meta-analysis of randomised-controlled trials. *Scientific Reports* 13: 432.

Frecska E, Hoppál M and Luna L 2016, Nonlocality and the shamanic state of consciousness. *NeuroQuantology* 14(2): 155–165.

Fried R and Grimaldi J 1993, *The psychology and physiology of breathing: In behavioral medicine, clinical psychology, and psychiatry*. New York: Plenum Publishing Co.

Haijen EC, Kaelen M, Roseman L, Timmermann C, Kettner H, Russ S, Nutt D, Daws RE, Hampshire AD, Lorenz R and Carhart-Harris RL 2018, Predicting responses to psychedelics: A prospective study. *Frontiers in Pharmacology* 9: 897.

Hasson U, Ghazanfar AA, Galantucci B, Garrod S, Keysers C 2012, Brain-to-brain coupling: A mechanism for creating and sharing a social world. *Trends in Cognitive Sciences* 16(2): 114–121.

Helman CG 2001, Placebos and nocebos: The cultural construction of belief. In: D Peters (ed.) Understanding the placebo effect in complementary medicine. Edinburgh: Churchill Livingstone.

Hood RW 1977, Eliciting mystical states of consciousness with semistructured nature experiences. *Journal for the Scientific Study of Religion* 16(2): 155–163.

Huxley A 1994, *The doors of perception*. London: Flamingo.

Johnson MW, Richards WA, Griffiths RR 2008, Human hallucinogen research: Guidelines for safety. *Journal of Psychopharmacology* 22(6): 603–620.

Johnson MW, Garcia-Romeu, A, Cosimano, MP and Griffiths, RR, 2014, Pilot study of the 5-HT2AR agonist psilocybin in the treatment of tobacco addiction. *Journal of Psychopharmacology* 28(11): 983–992.

Jung CG 1927, *The structure and dynamics of the psyche*, CW8.

Jung CG 1971a, *Psychological types*, CW6.

Jung CG 1971b, *The spirit in man, art and literature*, CW15.

Jung CG 1977, *The symbolic life*, CW18.

Keeney B 2003, *Ropes to god: experiencing the Bushman spiritual universe*. Philadelphia, PA: Ringing Rocks Press.

Kettner H, Gandy S, Haijen EC and Carhart-Harris RL 2019. From egoism to ecoism: Psychedelics increase nature relatedness in a state-mediated and context-dependent manner. *International Journal of Environmental Research and Public Health* 16(24): 5147.

Leary T 1961, Drugs, set & suggestibility. Paper presented at *The Annual Meeting of the American Psychological Association, 6 September 1961*.

Leary T, Litwin GH, and Metzner R 1963, Reactions to psilocybin in a supportive environment. *The Journal of Nervous and Mental Disease* 137(6): 561–573.

Leary T, Metzner R and Alpert R 1964, The psychedelic experience: A manual based on the Tibetan Book of the Dead. New York: University Books.

Lewis-Williams D and Pearce D 2005, *Inside the neolithic mind*. London: Thames & Hudson.

Lingiardi V and Bei FD 2011, Questioning the couch: Historical and clinical perspectives. *Psychoanalytic Psychology* 28: 389–404.

Mavromatis A 1987, *Hypnagogia: The unique state of consciousness between wakefulness and sleep*. London: Routledge & Kegan Paul.

Metzner R 1999, From Harvard to Zihuatanejo. In R Forte (ed.) *Timothy Leary: Outside looking in*. Rochester, VT: Part Street Press.

Nielson JL, Megler JD, Cavnar C 2021, A qualitative assessment of risks and benefits of ayahuasca for trauma survivors. In BC Labate and C Cavnar (eds.) *Ayahuasca healing and science*. New York: Springer, Cham.

Osmond H 1957, *The pharmacology of psychotomimetic and psychotherapeutic drugs* 66(3): 418–434.

Oswald V, Vanhaudenhuyse A, Annen J, Martial C, Bicego A, Rousseaux F, Sombrun C, Harel Y, Faymonville M-E, Laureys S, Jerbi K and Gosseries O 2023, Autonomic nervous system modulation during self-induced non-ordinary states of consciousness. *Scientific Reports* 13: 15811.

Pullman P 2017, *Daemon voices: On stories and storytelling*. New York: Alfred A Knopf.

Raine K (ed.) 1986, A choice of Blake's verse. London: Faber & Faber.

Rimkute J, Moraes C and Ferreira C 2016, The effects of scent on consumer behaviour. *International Journal of Consumer Studies* 40(1): 24–34.

Schlag AK, Aday J, Salam I, Neill JC and Nutt DJ 2022, Adverse effects of psychedelics: From anecdotes and misinformation to systematic science. *Journal of Psychopharmacology* 36(3): 258–272.

Siegelman EY 1990, *Metaphor and meaning in psychology*. New York: Guilford Press.

Singer T and Kimbles SL 2004, *The cultural complex: Contemporary Jungian perspectives on psyche and society*. Hove, East Sussex: Routledge.

Stevens A 2004, The archetypes. In R Papadopoulos (ed.), *The handbook of Jungian psychology: Theory, practice, applications*. Hove, East Sussex: Routledge.

Timmermann C, Bauer PR, Gosseries O, Vanhaudenhuyse A, Vollenweider F, Laureys S, Singer T, Antonova E, and Lutz A 2023, A neurophenomenological approach to non-ordinary states of consciousness: Hypnosis, meditation, and psychedelics. *Trends in Cognitive Sciences* 27(2): 139–159.

Turner V 1969, *The ritual process: Structure and antistructure*. Hawthorne, NY: Aldine De Gruyter.

Von Franz M-L 1990, *Psychotherapy*. Boulder, CO: Shambahla Publications.

Von Franz M-L 2000, *The problem of the puer aeternus*. Toronto: Inner City Books.

Winnicott DW 1971, *Playing and reality*. London: Tavistock Publications.

Zabriskie B 2004, Endnotes: Whence and whither. In J Cambray and L Carter (eds.), *Analytical psychology: Contemporary perspectives in Jungian analysis*. Hove, East Sussex: Routledge.

Chapter 7

Tracing the Spiral

An Introduction to the Principles of Active Imagination

Working with symbols to understand the voice of the unconscious lies at the very heart of Jungian psychology. Jung noticed that the symbols produced by the unconscious can be used deliberately to deepen our understanding of the unconscious forces that drive us. Once we can begin to understand the significance of symbols and the wellspring of intuition that they reveal, we can make different choices and consider new ways of being. Being able to consciously and intentionally work with symbols allows us to explore developmental paths that we had previously not imagined. It allows an activation of what is termed the 'transcendent function' (Samuels et al., 1986, p. 150), an integration between the conflicting forces of real and the imaginal, the rational and the intuitive. Through the symbols arising as part of the transcendent function, we can approach the potential of the archetypal self and the possibility of a more integrated and a more soulful way of being. Symbols are so profoundly embedded in the unconscious that they provide us with what James Hillman has termed a 'royal road to soul making' (Hillman 1975, p. 23), and for Hillman this requires a life that is filled with imagination:

> To live psychologically means to imagine things; To be in touch with soul means to live in sensuous connection with fantasy. To be in soul is to experience the fantasy of all realities and the basic reality of fantasy.
>
> (Hillman 1975, p. 23)

To understand how to work with symbols, we must understand 'active imagination', a deliberate engagement with the unconscious that Murray Stein has described as one of the 'four pillars of analytical psychology' (2000). It is very different from daydreaming or passive fantasy, or even the spontaneous experimentation of play, as it creates an intentional bridge between the intuitive impulses of the unconscious and the self-awareness of the conscious mind. In active imagination, we work directly with symbols to uncover enough meaning to allow us to move towards real, if unknown, outcomes. Jung proposes that

DOI: 10.4324/9781003463269-8

[Active imagination] is a method…of introspection for observing the stream of interior images. One concentrates one's attention on some impressive but unintelligible dream image, or on a spontaneous visual impression, and observes the changes taking place in it.

(Jung 1969b, CW9i, para. 190)

It is grounded in Jung's suggestion that the psyche has a teleological or purposive function, where the unconscious is not simply a 'storage unit' for the memories of the past but a living and progressive system. It draws upon a font of collective wisdom to prompt the unconscious mind to keep developing, intuitively suggesting new ways of thinking about the present and the future. The unconscious has a symbolic voice, loaded with intent and emotion, and active imagination compels us to listen intently to that voice and to follow its lead.

Origins

The origins of active imagination can be found in Jung's own inner journey, as he attempted to make sense of the traumatic breakdown of his relationship with Freud. A number of troubling dreams provoked him to begin a conscious exploration of his inner world, and he began by returning intuitively to a childhood game, where he built 'cottages, a castle, a whole village' (Jung 1995, p. 198) on the lake shore near his home. This game released a stream of vivid fantasies and images, into which he began to deliberately immerse himself. He encountered aspects of his unconscious as people, with whom he initiated a conscious dialogue, and with each dialogue he was confronted by new perspectives and new symbols. He then recorded his experiences and began to illustrate them in a series of journals that became 'The Red Book' (Jung 2009). He was aware of the dangers of a deep immersion in the products of the unconscious but also saw this as an essential step in his own development. He realised that if he was to move towards the potential of the self, a confrontation with the unconscious was inevitable and worth the risk.

It is, of course, ironical that I, a psychiatrist, should at almost step of my experiment have run into the same psychic material which is the stuff of psychosis and is found in the insane. This is the fund of unconscious images which fatally confuses the mental patient. But it is also the matrix of a mythopoetic imagination which has vanished from our rational age. Though such imagination is present everywhere, it is both taboo and dreaded, so that it even appears to be a risky experiment or a questionable adventure to entrust oneself to the uncertain path that leads into the depths of the unconscious… Unpopular, ambiguous, and dangerous, it is a voice of discovery to the other pole of the world.

(Jung 1995, p. 213)

Crucially, it was this exploration of active imagination as a way to the integration of the psyche that led to the formulation of many, or perhaps even most, of the basic concepts of Jungian psychology.

> The years when I was pursuing my inner images were the most important in my life- in them everything essential was decided. It all began then...It was the *prima materia* for a lifetime's work.
>
> (Jung 1995, p. 225)

An Introduction

We can think of active imagination as 'a process of dreaming with open eyes' (Samuels et al., 1986, p. 9). However, it is a difficult process to pin down with simple definitions and techniques, as it takes as many forms as the symbols that it works with. How we approach active imagination will depend on where the unconscious leads us and what it is trying to express. It is a 'channel for "messages" from the unconscious by any means' (Samuels et al., 1986, p. 12) and may involve modelling, writing, painting, talking, or movement. It is a state of being rather than a single, replicable 'technique'. We may intuitively find ourselves moving forwards and backwards, revisiting emerging symbols and gaining new perspective and understanding with each iteration. As Jung has suggested, in active imagination 'there is no linear evolution; there is only a circumambulation of the self' (1995, p. 222).

Whatever 'means' we choose, active imagination will demand that we suspend reality to engage with the unconscious while maintaining a conscious and reflective awareness of our experience. In her extraordinary study of active imagination, *The Old Wise Woman*, the Jungian analyst Rix Weaver suggests.

> It is as if imagination begins to stir and a dream of the unconscious begins to unfold. Generally, the ego is included in the drama, moving through the scene or asking questions. So, with an attitude that acknowledges the reality of the psyche, a conversation begins between unconscious and conscious, and thus one enters the dialectic method which allows the psyche freedom of expression.
>
> (Weaver 1964, p. 4)

Active imagination demands that we are able to maintain a balance between two conflicting forces within the psyche. The first is the aesthetic tendency towards artistic elaboration and the mystical possibility of the unconscious. The second is the scientific tendency towards intellectual understanding and the rational finality of the conscious. In active imagination, we must walk the path between the unconscious and the conscious mind without falling too much into the grip of either. If we are persuaded by the unconscious, we may become intoxicated with magical symbols and our capacity to produce them. We may lose sight of reality and become inflated with archetypal energy. If the conscious mind becomes dominant, we may prematurely silence the unconscious and lose the opportunity to explore new ideas and perspectives. We may become stuck in the familiar known, unable to progress. If we are able to walk this middle path, we may be inspired by the unconscious and, at the same time, remain grounded in the real world.

Jung's original method had two parts, 'letting the unconscious come up' and then 'coming to terms with the unconscious' (Chodorow 2006, p. 224). However, his formulation has since been further developed, typically into four stages with some variations (von Franz 1980, Dallett 1982, Salman 2010), and I would frame my own interpretation as follows.

Stage 1: Noticing

Active imagination usually begins with a level of psychological disturbance or discomfort. We can imagine it as an emotionally charged provocation from the unconscious, which demands our attention and carries the emotional energy needed to prompt action. We have a mental itch that we need to scratch. This provocation is where we must start, and as Jung suggests:

> He must make the emotional state the basis or starting point of the procedure. He must make himself as conscious as possible of the mood he is in, sinking himself in it without reserve and noting down on paper all the fantasies and other associations that come up. Fantasy must be allowed the freest possible play, yet not in such a manner that it leaves the orbit of its object, namely the affect... The whole procedure is a kind of enrichment and clarification of the affect.
>
> (Jung 1969a, CW8, para. 167)

We should then begin by establishing a 'set and setting' that support the development of a 'nonordinary state of consciousness', a state of mind that has more in common with a gentle meditative trance or a moment of waking from a dream than with the conscious awareness of the day-to-day. We can remove any distractions and immerse ourselves in both our inner and outer worlds 'as they are', allowing the emergent symbols to appear in any form that they chose to adopt and with whatever energy that is associated with them. The voice of the unconscious will speak to us in whatever language it chooses, and we simply have to listen and follow its lead. This may be challenging as the ego will often work against its own need to judge and devalue the symbols and that arise and even the process itself. It may also develop an 'aesthetic tendency' and attempt to focus on the quality of the image as a piece of artistic expression, ignoring the message it contains (von Franz 1980).

The role of the coach may be essential here in providing the possibility of a safe container within which the client can begin to confront the unconscious. While some Jungians (Bonasera 2024) have suggested that active imagination is a journey we must take alone, this seems to deny the significance of relationship as an intrinsic part of individuation. Andrew Samuels notes that the analyst, and by extension the coach, can be a 'representative of the observing ego' (Samuels 1985, p. 202), providing a relational space within which our clients can drop their conscious defences for a while and begin to play. The coaching relationship itself may even become an essential part of the process, and the projections and symbolism within the relationship and of the relationship may provide 'a lived through active imagination' (Davidson 1966, p. 136). The dialogue with the coach can often be the first stage of a richer inner dialogue for the client, and emergent symbols can be explored and tested within the safety of the coaching space.

We can then start to notice the appearance of symbol. Here we must be able to adopt a symbolic attitude, where we are prepared 'for almost anything to become an image' and where we are ready to 'bring out the symbolic potential in such images' (Hubback 1969, p. 39). We must be able to access a gentle state of free-floating awareness where images and ideas can 'wash over us' without our clinging to them and prematurely attempting to 'fix' a particular meaning. These symbols may appear spontaneously in different ways for different people. We may hear an inner voice, notice strong visual images, or experience overwhelming physical sensations that inspire us to dance or to run. For some people, particularly those who may be less familiar or comfortable with the unconscious, we may tell stories, particularly stories about other people which help to reveal aspects of the tellers' own unconscious that have remained hidden. Each of us will begin to notice the emergence of the unconscious in different ways. As Jung suggests:

> Switch off your noisy consciousness and listen quietly inwards and look at the images that appear before your inner eye or hearken to the words which the muscles of your speech apparatus are trying to form. Write down what then comes without criticism. Images should be drawn or painted assiduously no matter whether you can do it or not. Once you have got at least fragments of these contents, then you may meditate on them afterwards. Don't criticise anything away! If any questions rise, put them to the unconscious again the next day. Don't be content with your own explanations no matter how intelligent they are… The important thing is to let the unconscious take the lead. You must always be convinced that you have mere after-knowledge and nothing else. In this case the unconscious really does know better.
>
> (2015, p. 83)

It is important to reemphasise at this stage that the symbol must be allowed to point the way, and we cannot predetermine how the unconscious will manifest.

We may have decided that we will approach active imagination through a particular and often familiar exercise, something that makes us feel comfortable, but the unconscious may have different ideas. Part of the stage of Noticing is noticing not simply the symbols that begin to constellate but also their form, which may itself be symbolic. If we have an urge to move for example, it is possible that both the movements and the urge itself are symbols which we can begin to explore. Weaver suggests that the ego must be able to participate in a 'meaningful' way, where 'meaningful' is an entirely subjective feeling representing the needs of the unconscious: 'Only the person who has done the work is the final judge of what is meaningful' (1964, p. 18).

Stage 2: Focusing

As symbols constellate, we can then begin to narrow our focus and take a more deliberately conscious position. We can pay particular attention to those symbols which intuitively seem to be most significant and which carry the most energy. It is this deliberate attention that differentiates active imagination from daydreaming or fantasy as here we are not simply allowing a symbol to 'be'; we are beginning to work with it in the service of our development. We can begin to record the images, holding them in mind but also noting down our impressions, making drawings, or perhaps working with any material that can be adapted to capture the essence of the symbol. This process may be quite challenging at first, as some images may be obscure or only half-formed, and others lost in a dense and dynamic web of other symbols and associations. We may also feel a little self-conscious as we move from the imaginal to the concrete, suspending the reality of our day-to-day lives as we do so. The experience of the unconscious is often overwhelming, and even when we are familiar with it, we may reflexively respond with the predictable scepticism that defines the modern mind and reject the possibility offered by a symbolic attitude as 'childish', 'mystical', or 'deluded'. We may prefer an 'evidence based' approach, where the 'evidence' is supplied by an approving other rather than the experience of our own unconscious. Jung suggests:

> Each time the fantasy material is to be produced, the activity of consciousness must be switched off again. In most cases the results of these efforts are not very encouraging at first. Usually, they consist of tenuous webs of fantasy that give no clear indication of their origin or their goal. For many people it is easiest to write them down; Others visualise them, and others again draw or paint them with or without visualisation. If there is a high degree of conscious cramp, often only the hands are capable of fantasy; They model or draw figures that are sometimes quite foreign to the conscious mind. These exercises must be continued until the cramp in the conscious mind is relaxed, in other words, until one can let things happen, which is the

next goal of the exercise. In this way a new attitude is created, an attitude that accepts the irrational and incomprehensible simply because it is happening.

(1968, CW13, para. 21–23)

Stage 3: Conversing

Having located and clarified the symbol or symbols that we wish to focus upon, we can begin to enter a 'conversation' with them, a term that suggests a repeating and mutual exchange between the symbol and ourselves. In 'conversation', we can pay attention to the symbol, work with it, and then pay attention again until some meaning slowly emerges. This is a gradual and repetitive stage.

The way in which we approach this 'conversation' depends on ourselves and our clients and on the strange alchemy of our relationship. It may quite literally be a conversation, perhaps with the coach or perhaps alone or with an inner voice. For some, it may be drawing, or a reflection on tarot cards, or through playing music, or a conscious engagement with dream material, watching our dreams unfold over days, weeks, or years. We cannot plan ahead but must be guided by our intuition and by the symbols themselves, using 'what works' in the moment. If a symbol needs to be spoken, then forcing it into a drawing will simply diminish its possible meaning. We can use three broad techniques to help us in this 'conversation': association, amplification, and personification.

With association, we may be reminded of other symbols or feelings from our own experience, allowing different perspectives to emerge. These reminders may be directly associated or, more usually, connected in often unexpected and indirect ways. We may, for example, discover the symbol of a cat and wonder about the cats we have known, perhaps associating to different places we have lived or other times in our lives or perhaps the individual personalities of the cats. The associations may then form a sort of psychological matrix within which a symbol is embedded (Cambray and Carter 2004), allowing us to look at the symbol from different angles and perspectives and achieve a more complete, multidimensional sense of its possible meanings.

Amplification is an extension of association and is a central method within Jungian thinking as it enables us to go beyond the limitations of our own experience and the personal unconscious. By placing the symbol into a broader, collective context, we may be able to identify patterns of meaning that bring the symbol to life.

> It calls on the past, on what is "known' as it has been expressed symbolically in collective and cultural mythology, folklore, traditional symbols, and customs. It amplifies the field of an image from the obscurely personal into the cultural and archetypal.
>
> (Salman 2010, p. 122)

We may, for example, encounter the image of a cat and, rather than simply associate the image with cats from our own experience, may amplify it and begin to wonder about the significance of the cat in myth or folktales. We may wonder about Egyptian cat goddesses or the significance of a witch's familiar. We may reflect on the cat as a symbol in our own culture or perhaps consider scientific research into the physiology, psychology, and behaviour of cats. In this way, we can explore the archetypal essence of the symbol, connecting with the numinous energy of the collective unconscious which gives 'the probing intellect the raw material which is indispensable for its vitality' (Jung 1995, p. 348). As we amplify symbols, we are connecting to the collective inheritance and wisdom upon which our own psyche is built and through which we may find the inspiration to face life in new ways. As Jung suggested, 'even the most individual systems are not absolutely unique... but offer striking unmistakable analogies with other systems' (1960, CW3, para. 413), and through the inspiration of the archetypal symbols of the collective unconscious, we bring our own experiences to life by building on the experiences of our ancestors. While we may, of course, simply use an internet search engine to support this approach, it may also be worthwhile reflecting on Jung's advice to 'know as much as possible about primitive psychology, mythology, archaeology, and comparative religion because these fields offer... invaluable analogies with which to enrich associations' (1931, CW16, para. 96).

Finally, we may 'personify' the symbol, imagining it as something 'other' than ourselves with its own life and intention (Weaver 1964, Hannah 1981). We let it 'speak' on its own behalf, and we can attempt to see the world from its unique perspective. We can question it, and it can respond on behalf of the unconscious. We can argue with the symbol, or joke with it, and eventually we may find a place for its wisdom in our conscious mind. In the same way that Jung entered a dialogue with his 'inner feminine', we may ask the symbol of the cat what it has to say to us. It is through personification that we can begin to recognise that our ego consciousness is not the whole of the psyche (Hillman 1975) and that symbols are an expression of our complexes, those unconscious entanglements of associations and energy that form the building blocks of our personalities. We can begin to acknowledge that the symbols we notice represent something that is simultaneously part of us and yet independent of our conscious control. Symbols suggest how things are for the unconscious, and through active imagination, we can discover the intention behind them. Personification is a process of separation and objectivity and paradoxically enables the integration of the unconscious and a movement towards the sense of wholeness that we can call the 'self'. In allowing the unconscious to have a distinct voice of its own, we can enlarge our conscious awareness of what we are and what we may become.

As a coach, I have found it useful to combine all three of these methods, moving between them to create a 'mental map' of the landscape that surrounds a particular symbol or group of symbols. An association may cast light on an amplification which may then be allowed to speak with us in a personification, deepening our understanding. This understanding is not simply of a single symbol but of a dynamic web of meaning which is best represented through that symbol. In active imagination, we are not simplistically interpreting an isolated image but understanding that image in a rich three-dimensional context through our conversation with the unconscious at both a personal and collective level. We are reminded of both our existing sense of self as understood by our ego consciousness and the potential that is open to us through a connection with the collective unconscious. This combination may create a complex web of images and associations. To help me see the 'wood for the trees', the system in the midst of all this symbolism, I often make a note of the most meaningful words or images in a notebook, a large piece of paper, or even on a whiteboard to create an emergent network of ideas. This often becomes a focal point for my coaching, with me and my client updating and adapting the image to provide new perspectives, questions for exploration, or suggestions for further development.

Whichever technique we are drawn towards and whatever method we use to make sense of what is emerging, it is important that we do not move too far from the original symbols that we have chosen as our focus. If we allow ourselves to move too far from the image, we may lose sight of its original intention, and our attention may become fixed on distracting images which are perhaps more convenient or less challenging to our ego consciousness. Instead, we should 'circumambulate' the symbol, moving around it for new perspectives before returning to it to begin again. As the Jungian analyst Barbara Hannah suggests:

> Images must not be allowed to change like a kaleidoscope. If the first image is a bird... left to itself it may turn with lightning rapidity into a lion, a ship on the sea, a scene from a battle, or whatnot. The technique consists of keeping one's attention on the first image and not letting the bird escape until it is explained why it has appeared to us.
>
> (1981, p. 21)

This circling may make active imagination less sequential than these simple stages suggest. In application, it is usually far more labyrinthine and chaotic, moving back and forth between stages, as it fuels itself with a constant supply of new material.

Stage 4: Integrating

As our 'conversation' progresses, we find that a sense of meaning begins to slowly emerge. This is not a final interpretation but a sense of trajectory, pointing the way forwards for further experiments and exploration. We are not looking to pin down the unconscious, as we can never really understand its specific intention and meaning. Any attempt to do so can leave us with an image that has no mystery and lacks the energy and power to move us and change us. Instead, we need to understand it enough to begin to take practical action. Active imagination does not help us locate a final goal or outcome but supports us on an ongoing developmental journey through the expression of 'essential messages about the psyche's emerging relationship with itself' (Salman 2010, p. 129). It is through an appreciation of this emerging relationship that we can equip ourselves to take the next step with a dawning awareness of meaning rather than a forced rush to closure. It is a recognition that the energy of the symbol is an intrinsic part of its value and that to maintain its energy some aspect of the symbol must remain rooted in the unconscious.

> It is much better not to analyse them while they're going on, for then the author of the fantasy becomes self-conscious and knows what it could be about, which inhibits further working of the fantasy.
>
> (Von Franz 1996, p. 107)

We 'know' what the symbol means, and if we attempt a full and absolute interpretation of it, we paradoxically destroy that 'knowing' and its capacity to move us. The symbols that emerge through active imagination are not 'true' in the literal sense but point towards something that we must pay attention to if we are to develop. They have the power to move us, but the future they suggest must ultimately be consciously created by us.

However, it is essential that the dialogue still allow an equal participation from both the unconscious and the conscious mind. We may describe this as an 'ethical' confrontation, where our conscious mind takes the voice of the unconscious seriously and with the respect it deserves. It is this seriousness that allows us to take our next steps into real life, where we can consciously use what we have integrated and can begin the process again.

A Case Study

My client was an experienced coach in his mid 50s with an established reputation. He came to supervision looking to explore ways in which he could develop his practice as he felt stuck and wanted to explore his identity as a coach going forwards. He described himself as feeling a little 'empty and uninspired' and suggested that he was 'starting to bore himself'.

During our first session, it was striking that he spoke very little about coaching and instead began by focusing on a recent walking safari in Africa. In a reverie, he then moved quickly through a number of ideas and associations, describing his fascination with 'way finding' as a 'foundational human skill'. He described his own impulse to walk as both a physical and a psychological imperative. He noted that wildlife can become stuck, travelling and migrating in familiar corridors where they move through the paths of least resistance, but he felt that his own need to walk was somehow different. He did not have an end goal, and the destination was not important to him.

As he talked, I wondered about the archetypal significance of walking, at the level of both the psychoid and the collective unconscious, and I made two immediate associations or perhaps amplifications. The first was with the possible connection between the act of walking and the evolution of intelligence in early hominids. It has been suggested that walking upright changed our perception of distance within our environment, and our hands were also freed up for activities other than walking, which led to changes in brain structure and function (Mithen 1996). Through walking, we could quite literally see more and do more. The second was with the 'songlines' of Aboriginal cultures in Australia. 'Songlines' or 'dreaming tracks' mark the paths which were used by the creator beings as they walked and sang the world into existence and which became oral 'maps' to guide communities as they moved across the landscape. These maps connected the people to the land on which they lived but also to other groups, establishing patterns of relationship.

I shared my thoughts with my client, and he immediately made other associations, speaking about how he was dreaming about pilgrimage and felt a need to go on 'pilgrimage length' walks. We discussed how the essence of pilgrimage was more than simply travelling to a destination but was instead a sacred journey as part of a 'communitas', a special group set aside from society (Turner 1969, Turner 1974). In pilgrimage, we cast aside our existing social roles and travel as equals and, in doing so, rediscover both relationship and identity in new ways. We are reborn in the presence of others. He suggested that that he felt a strong desire for something spiritual and that the idea of walking with others as part of a 'communitas' felt important. Returning to our work together, he felt that he wanted to 'show up and not just be someone's professional'. He wanted to be an 'active participant and an active author'. We wondered whether coaching itself could be a form of songline and whether we were just elders helping our clients to 'sing out' their lives. I was reminded of Jung's suggestion that in developmental work our role is to help our clients locate themselves on a 'lifeline' (1967, CW7, para. 480–502), a narrative which reaches back to a collective past and connects us with a personal future. In being able to consciously discover our lifeline as a guiding myth, we can better understand the intuition of the unconscious at a particular point in time and can then plot the next steps of our journey towards the potential of the self. I wondered about the songline as an archetypal image, reminding my client both of his own need to rediscover his own lifeline and of his work in helping his clients rediscover theirs.

Over the next few sessions, we explored the idea of working with clients through transition, and although our conversations were still superficially symbolic, they had lost the early energy of our first sessions. It felt as though we had strayed too far from the original image and that we had stopped 'walking'.

Then my client came with the news that he had planned a road trip with his son, who had left home the previous year and had been doing leadership training in the US. In what felt like a moment of synchronicity, both father and son seemed to be in a transitional space. The son was becoming a man, distinct and separate from his father, and his father was reshaping both his professional identity as a coach and his parental role. My client suggested that he was 'hoping for a new way of being in relationship' that was less about him 'protecting' his son and more about both of them finding themselves as men. We returned to the symbol of pilgrimage, and he confessed that the destination for the road trip was the campus where he had been to college. He planned on taking his son to visit the places where he lived at this important time in his life, a time when he had just left home and was the same age as his son.

At our next session, he had returned and described a trip that had not unfolded quite as planned. As they left New Orleans, his son started to feel ill, having contracted COVID on the flight. Instead of driving, they rented a small cottage, and he took care of his son – until he became sick and his son then took care of him. This exchange of roles felt levelling and meaningful and supported the development of a bond between them. It felt as though their roles and duty of care had become less like a father and son and more as the reciprocal relationship of one man to another: it may have been a rite of passage for them both. Perhaps not surprisingly, given the archetypal pilgrimage they had embarked upon, arriving at their destination felt much less significant than the journey itself.

This experience seemed to reignite my client's concerns about his practice as a coach. He became even less interested in a more conventional, formulaic approach and more concerned with the nature of relationship and the way in which a narrative unfolded for his clients: 'What is the story you are living?' We returned to his work, and in our subsequent sessions, that theme of the journey kept returning instinctively to our conversations. In one session, he quoted Dante's lament after his exile from Florence: 'I came around and found myself now searching through a dark wood, the right way blurred and lost' (Dante 2012). He suggested that many of the leaders he coached seem to have become lost in the same forest and were forced to 'confront their lostness' if they were to find a new and more meaningful path. They had 'very thin stories' and his role seemed increasingly to 'pull them out and let them expand' into something fuller and more fulfilling. My client suggested that a CEO's journey was one of constant renewal and that each time they seemed to finish a heroic journey, they find themselves at the start of a new one. The experience of the journey mattered more than the destination, and perhaps to support his clients, he needed to have realised that himself.

This symbol then provoked another association, and my client described his return to his ancestral village in Europe. His grandfather had come to America with his children and had always wanted to return but had not been able to do so. His mother's first memory was seeing the Statue of Liberty from the boat they arrived on, and this had reminded her of the Virgin Mary, a symbol of their village. He had recently bought a property in this village, and this purchase felt important to both him and the community. It was a 'coming home' and a 'renewal' which offered hope for the future. He wondered whether 'you need to come home to be more of yourself'.

In a further synchronicity' as I was writing this chapter, my client sent me a message about his younger son who was at university in the US. He had recently visited his son to watch him play football, a game my client had played to a high level, and the journey had also felt significant, as another rite of passage and a transmission between father and son. The most interesting detail, however, was the chance discovery that his son's university was located at the source of the Mississippi river, the same river that flowed into New Orleans and marked the beginning of the journey he had taken with his elder son.

Risks

Active Imagination can open up a powerful dialogue with the unconscious which can reveal its intent and provide the energy to spark profound personal change. However, it also brings risks. Jung suggested three that seem significant (Samuels et al., 1986) and worth remembering.

The first of these risks is that we may become attracted to images that lock us into existing habits instead of suggesting new perspectives. These images may be familiar symbols guiding us along well-trodden paths or associations to new images that progressively lead us away from the original intention of the unconscious. These new images may serve as a defence, avoiding some aspect of the unconscious that the ego finds threatening or inconvenient. A symbol may relay an unconscious intuition that we need a new way of seeing the world but may also remind us of why we see the world the way we do, entrenching our current position. The second risk is that we become overly interested in the aesthetic quality of the images we produce, in the beauty of our drawing or the fluency of our words and lose sight of their intent. We may then become consumed by an unrealistic and narcissistic self-belief or perhaps judge ourselves by collective standards. We may want to meet the real or imagined standards of our coach or of others in our group, aspiring to be recognised as 'artists' rather than remain anchored to the subjective purpose and value of the image. The third risk is that the archetypal content and numinous energy of the unconscious can be overwhelming. This may provoke strong emotional responses which lead to an inflation. Here we begin to identify with the archetype and become consumed by it. We may amplify the image of a mystic wizard and identify with that image, imagining ourselves as exemplars of transcendent wisdom and authority. For example, as coaches, we may see ourselves as casting 'powerful' spells (or asking 'powerful' questions) to 'transform' our clients rather than recognising that we are just ordinary coaches having (almost) ordinary conversations with ordinary managers about yet another change programme.

To maintain an 'ethical' stance, it is important that the ego not lose itself and that it stay grounded in the 'real'. Active imagination requires a balance where 'the position of the ego must be maintained as being of equal value to the counter-position of the unconscious, and vice versa' (Jung 1969a, CW8, para. 183). We must maintain conscious control of the experience.

Reflections and Implications

While we can present active imagination as having a series of structured steps to guide us, it is really no more than an intuitive way of using symbol as a connecting thread that runs through our psychological development. It is a mindset more than a technique. The application of active imagination develops our 'capacity to acknowledge certainty and uncertainty at the same time' (Weaver 1964, p. 18) and equips us to work methodically and rationally with the mystery and complexity of the unconscious. In active imagination, we are simply using symbol as a medium to create a rich and ongoing inner dialogue, which engages both the material of fantasy and the knowledge of the real world on an equal basis. This dialogue provokes the emergence of the transcendent function as the route to new perspectives and new ways of being at a given point in time. Crucially, the archetypal and numinous foundations of the symbols that often appear also provide the energy and impetus needed to move us forwards, as we discover our souls within our work and our lives.

Through the experience of active imagination, we can become more sensitive to the interactions of the whole psyche as an interrelated system and can begin to work with the unconscious without fear. Once we have developed this capability working alongside a coach or psychotherapist, we can continue the practice alone. Active imagination can then start to become a way of life, and we can wander with confidence through the 'dark forest' of our own mind. This confidence in turn allows us to build a deeper relationship with ourselves and with the other within us, which then enriches our relationships with others beyond us. Active imagination helps us find our place in the collective without sacrificing our agency and individuality. It helps us to build the self-knowledge and confidence we need to individuate, becoming both ourselves and full members of our societies.

He knows it because it has happened out of him. Then he becomes more collective and at the same time more wide and, more whole. He knows himself more fully and knows where things are greater than himself, that he has touched transcendent reality. His little conscious attitude is no longer the only thing. Then if he arrives at some sort of philosophy, it will be his own. It is not borrowed from another... Even though he is a grain of sand in the vast Sahara, he is that grain and his difference is that he has realised his connection with other grains and his importance to the whole, for the Sahara owes its existence to many such grains.

(Jung 1969a, CW8, p. 29)

Find a quiet space where you will not be disturbed and let your mind wander.

- Try to notice any images that come to mind. Make a note of them or perhaps even try to draw them. Do not try to explain them or make sense from them. If this is too challenging (and at first it might be), you could perhaps use a deck of image cards and chose those that feel most compelling.
- Make a note of how the images seem to be connected, perhaps even drawing lines between them.
- Are there any images or clusters of images that seem more energised or significant? Focus on them and notice how you feel when you hold them in mind.
- Do any new associations come to mind? Make a note of them.
- Try amplifying the most striking images. Perhaps search the internet for the image or look for its appearance in myth. If the image is a word, consider the origins of the word. What images come to mind then?
- Try to personify the image. What would it say to you? What emotions would it appear to have? How would you respond? What does it feel like to talk to it?
- Finally consider what questions and ideas you are left with. Do not try to rush to an interpretation but instead find something simple that you can reflect on over the following days and record what seems to surface within you.

References

Bonasera G 2024, Is active imagination the sleeping beauty of analytical psychology? In C Tozzi (ed.) *Active imagination in theory, practice and training: The special legacy of CG Jung.* Abingdon, Oxon: Routledge.

Cambray J and Carter L 2004, Analytic methods revisited. In J Cambray and L Carter (eds.) *Analytical psychology: Contemporary perspectives in Jungian analysis.* Hove, East Sussex: Routledge.

Chodorow J 2006, Active imagination. In R Papadopoulos (ed.) *The handbook of Jungian psychology: theory, practice and applications.* Hove, East Sussex: Routledge.

Dallett J 1982, Active imagination in practice. In M Stein (ed.) *Jungian analysis.* Peru, IL: Open Court.

Dante A 2012, *The divine comedy: Inferno, pugatorio, paradiso.* London: Penguin Classics.

Davidson D 1966, Transference as a form of active imagination. *Journal of Analytical Psychology* 11(2): 135–146.

Hannah B 1981, *Encounters with the soul*. Wilmette, IL: Chiron Publications.

Hillman J 1975, *Revisioning psychology*. New York: HarperCollins.

Hubback J 1969, The symbolic attitude in psychotherapy. *Journal of Analytical Psychology* 14(1): 36–47.

Jung CG 1931, *The practice of psychotherapy*, CW16.

Jung CG 1960, *Psychogenesis of mental disease*, CW3.

Jung CG 1967, *Two essays on analytical psychology*, CW7.

Jung CG 1968, *Alchemical studies*, CW13.

Jung CG 1969a, *Structure and dynamics of the psyche*, CW8.

Jung CG 1969b, *Archetypes and the collective unconscious*, CW9i.

Jung CG 1970, *Mysterium coniunctionis*, CW14.

Jung CG 1995, *Memories, dreams, reflections*. London: Fontana Press.

Jung CG 2009, *The red book: Liber novus*. London: WW Norton and Company.

Jung CG 2015, *Letters, volume one 1906-1950*. Abingdon, Oxon: Routledge.

Mithen S 1996, *The prehistory of the mind: the cognitive origins of art, religion and science*. London: Thames and Hudson.

Salman S 2010, Peregrinations of active imagination. In M Stein (ed.) *Jungian psychoanalysis: Working in the spirit of CG Jung*. Chicago, IL: Open Court.

Samuels A 1985, *Jung and the post-Jungians*. London: Routledge.

Samuels A, Shorter B and Plaut F 1986, *A critical dictionary of Jungian analysis*. London: Routledge.

Stein M 2000, *Four pillars of a Jungian approach to psychotherapy* (audiotapes #448, 2 cassettes) Atlanta, GA: Jung Society of Atlanta. www.jungatlanta.com

Turner V 1969, *The ritual process: Structure and anti-structure*. New York: Aldine de Gruyter.

Turner V 1974, *Dramas, fields and metaphors*. London: Cornell University Press.

von Franz M-L 1980, *Methods of treatment in analytical psychology*. Stuttgart: Verlag Adolf Bonz.

von Franz M-L 1996, *The interpretation of fairy tales*. Boston, MA: Shambhala.

Weaver R 1964, *The old wise woman*. London: Vincent Stuart.

Chapter 8

Coaching with Dreams

Considering the Value of Dreamwork in a Coaching Practice

We all dream. We cannot help ourselves. We may not always be able to remember our dreams, but they are there waiting in the darkness for us, as the raw and inevitable voice of the unconscious. This is a voice that needs to be heard. As a coach, I never set out to work with my clients' dreams, and many of my clients will say they do not dream. Instead, I usually stress that, although I often work with dreams, we will not be doing that in this particular coaching relationship. The next session, my client will bring a dream.

> The dream is a natural phenomenon. It does not spring from a special intention. One cannot explain it with a psychology taken from consciousness. We you're dealing with a particular way of functioning independent of the human ego's will and wishes, intention or aim. It is an unintentional occurrence.
>
> (Jung 2006, p. 2)

The dream reveals that part of the psyche that is emotional and intuitive. It may speak to our personal experiences but may also contain fragments of the systems we belong to. It may reveal some part of the unconscious processes of our families, our organisations, our societies, or even the shared collective inheritance of being human. Its voice is symbolic, and it speaks in often strange and mysterious ways which may baffle or terrify us. Dreams can be numinous and moving, or banal and quickly forgettable. Whatever the nature of the dream, it contains new lenses through which the conscious mind can view the world and the potential for sometimes-profound transformation.

Dreams are often avoided in coaching as being too 'deep' and too difficult, although anxiety felt about dreams usually seems to originate from the coach and not the dreamer. This anxiety may be cultural as well as personal, as in the modern world we are often encouraged from a very young age to dismiss our dreams. We are often afraid of the 'other', as something beyond our conscious control and personified by the fertile chaos of the unconscious. This is the 'monster' under our bed, and it comes to us at night. It may expose us to

DOI: 10.4324/9781003463269-9

emotions we are unfamiliar with or would prefer to ignore. It offers possibility in the mystery and ambiguity that lie beyond the comfort of the known. Although we all dream, the ego will often work hard to distract us, and even the idea of the dream can be challenging.

However, working with dreams as part of a coaching practice can provide a valuable source of insight and a sometimes-unexpected foundation for meaningful development work (Kets De Vries 2014). The dream can provide direct access to the unfiltered psyche and provide insights that would not be available in ordinary conversations.

An Immersive Image of Psyche

When we dream, we feel that we are conscious and that our dream is real. We are asleep and unaware of our surroundings and yet are able to construct a dynamic and interactive world of complex images and emotions from a storehouse that lies almost exclusively within us. The material world has very little immediate and direct impact upon the dream, and there are no objects to which we can be subject. We do not respond to the events of the dream, as we have created those events and their unfolding is inevitable. Although the dream usually develops around the locus of a 'dream self' (D'Agostino A et al. 2013) and 'self-less' dreams would appear to be exceedingly rare (Occhionero et al. 2005), we find ourselves immersed in the experience without knowing that it is a dream. We are swept along by the dream and make no attempt to objectively examine, understand, or pass judgement on the experience.[1] We are aware of the dream without being able to reflect on that awareness until we wake.

For this reason, dreaming is said to reveal the psyche in a very pure and isolated form (Revonsuo 2006). Here, the dream is not simply a product of the psyche but an essential image of the psyche at a given moment. Jung suggested that symbol is 'the best possible explanation for a complex fact not yet apprehended by consciousness' (1969a, CW8, para. 69), and in the symbols of the dream, we are granted direct access to the 'complex fact' of the psyche itself, uncluttered by external influences and the censorship of the conscious mind.

> [The dream] shows the inner truth and reality of… [the person] as it really is: not as I conjecture it to be, and not as he would like it to be, but as it is.
>
> (Jung 1931, CW16, para. 304)

> The dream is a spontaneous self-portrayal, in symbolic form of the actual situation in the unconscious.
>
> (Jung 1969a, CW8, para. 505)

Jung also suggested that the dream may only appear as a dream, because it surfaces when the conscious mind is unguarded and relaxed, namely when we are asleep. The dream may, in fact, be a continual movement of the unconscious which simply passes unnoticed at any other time.

> We are quite probably dreaming all the time, but consciousness makes so much noise that we no longer hear the dream when awake.
>
> (Jung 2009, p. 3)

In this sense, the dream is not something we produce, a passive object to our active subject, at least until our conscious mind starts to domesticate it. It encompasses us and embodies us as a continual and dynamic process that, from time to time, disturbs the peace of the conscious mind. As Jung suggests, it is a process that transcends our conscious mind, shaping us in ways of which we are unaware.

> This is the secret of dreams - that we do not dream, but rather we are dreamt. We are the object of the dream, not its subject.... the dreamed is dreamed to us. We are the objects.
>
> (Jung 2009, p. 159)

Beyond Time and Space

Perhaps not surprisingly, given its unconscious origins, the dream is also free from the predictable linear constraints of time and space that define the fully conscious mind. The unconscious is, after all, not a repository of fixed and immutable past events but an evolving interpretation where and our memories shape the present and in turn are shaped by it (Hupbach A et al. 2008, Kroes and Fernandez 2012). As Renos Papadopoulos has proposed, 'it is not only the past that shapes the present, but also the present that shapes the past' (1996, p. 158). Although our memories 'consolidate' and become more stable over time, they are essentially dynamic with only the emotional intensity associated with them remaining consistent. The dream then draws upon a version of past experience held in the unconscious which is represented through a complex web of images and associations. These have a shared underlying emotional tone but are arranged in new and often unusual combinations and narrative forms which would not be accessible to us in any other context.

Research (Hartman and Brezler 2008) has suggested that people who have recently experienced traumatic events may replay the emotional state of fear in their dreams without replicating explicit images of the events themselves. The emotionally charged waking memories are not portrayed in the dream as a copy of the remembered event but instead are replaced by new images, with only the emotional intensity of the original experience remaining. For example, the image of being 'swept away by a huge tidal wave' has been reported frequently in the dreams of people suffering from extreme trauma, such as fires or assaults (Barrett 1996, Hartmann 2001). The image was not related to the

specific trauma experienced but used by the unconscious to symbolically represent the overwhelming emotional tone of the individuals' subsequent dreams.

The dream is not then based on a pale remembered copy of a concrete and
past reality but instead is a vivid representation of a felt and present reality. It
is seen not from the rational perspective of ego consciousness but from the
associative perspective of the unconscious. Past and present, here and there,
merge and overlap in the dream in a way which may be confusing and other-
worldly when seen as a sequential array of 'real' objects but make perfect sense
when seen as a feeling-toned matrix of symbols.

This quality of wholeness ensures that the dream possesses a quality of time
referred to as 'kairos'. The time of the conscious mind can be described as
chronos, a secular, sequential, and measurable passing of time. Chronos allows
us to locate ourselves and separate each moment into distinct units. It is linear
with no sense of the whole. The time of the unconscious mind and therefore of
the dream is kairos, a blurred moment of all-time, where 'time comes apart a
little' (Jung 2009 p. 9) and the emphasis is on a feeling of the sacred and the
significant. Kairos reminds us that something must happen because an alignment of events has made that happening inevitable. In kairos, any image or
event is systemic and can be understood only as part of the whole. Here we are
exposed to the numinous energy of the archetypal and are reminded of the
primal forces that connect us, through the collective and the psychoid unconscious, to the universal experience of life.

When I play a piece of music for the first time, it is an experience of ego
consciousness. 'I' am playing 'the instrument' and there is a 'piece' of music
that I am trying to replicate. Time moves sequentially as chronos, and I am
clumsily aware of every movement and every note. I know what I have played,
I know what I am trying to play, and I know what I need to play next. With
practice the piece falls into the unconscious and I can begin to 'feel' it as a
whole. The music is playing but I am not aware of the 'I' that is playing it. The
meaning I make from the piece is derived not from the single notes but from the
whole. It is the composer, the instrument, the key, the time and place in which
it was written, the time and place in which it is played, and the musician playing it that provide the meaning. The single notes each have significance, as
without them the piece has no coherence, but it is the whole piece that provides
the sense of context and 'rightness' for each note as it is played. This is kairos
and this is the experience of the dream.

A Tribal Connection

The kaironic quality of the unconscious also suggests that a dream may be not
only personal but collective, reflecting the dreams of the many social systems
to which we belong. The dream may not be ours alone, and we may also be
dreaming the dream of others. Hans Dieckmann ran a research group in Berlin
for three years (1976), studying the images and associations made by analysts

and their clients. Some of these images came from the dreams of both. The group noticed that the symbols that arose in client conversations and in the group began to align over time, reflecting both conscious and unconscious exchanges within this community, a community where not all members had actually met in person. The dream images were not distinct and individual but appeared to be a shared construction arising from relationship.

> The research showed that not only were the associations of patients and analyst related, but also the associative processes within our research group itself were related to the development of the group.
>
> (1976, p. 29)

Tess Castleman has developed this idea further (2004), drawing upon indigenous custom and practice from North America, to suggest a 'tribal' unconscious, an intermediate layer between the personal unconscious and the collective, perhaps as a more intimate aspect of the cultural unconscious (Henderson 1990). Here the dreams within a given community become entangled, bringing members together with a shared and intuitive connection. This entanglement has defined our evolution, as we are a species that has survived only through cooperation, but it seems to have been forgotten to a large extent in contemporary society, which too frequently emphasises individualism over community:

> The dream world does not know we have given up tribal life. Our psyches still operate in the old way; The authors of our dreams pick characters from our connecting tribe to use in our nighttime dramas, which inform us about ourselves, about the persons in whom we dream, and about our relationships.
>
> (Castleman 2004, p. xxv)

W. Gordon Lawrence came to a similar conclusion in his development of the concept of 'social dreaming', where the emphasis is placed on the dreams and not the dreamer and the dream is seen a reflection of the themes and patterns of relationship that define human systems. It is a comment on the 'eco-niche' (Lawrence 2006, p. 109) the dreamer inhabits, mirroring the lived experiences that shape and are shaped by the personal, tribal, or cultural unconscious but also containing fragments of the 'cosmos' (Lawrence 2006, p. 109) and the 'infinite' (Lawrence 2003, p. 11). He describes the dream as a 'fractal' (2007, p. 11), a repeating pattern that echoes the systemic image of the psyche described by Marie-Louise Von Franz (1985) and further developed by the biologist Rupert Sheldrake (Figure 8.1).

Here we can imagine the personal unconscious as being part of a repeating pattern of images and emotions, different from the systems within which it is nested, and yet repeating aspects of them. From this perspective, we can then see the dream as simultaneously an expression of the individual, of their

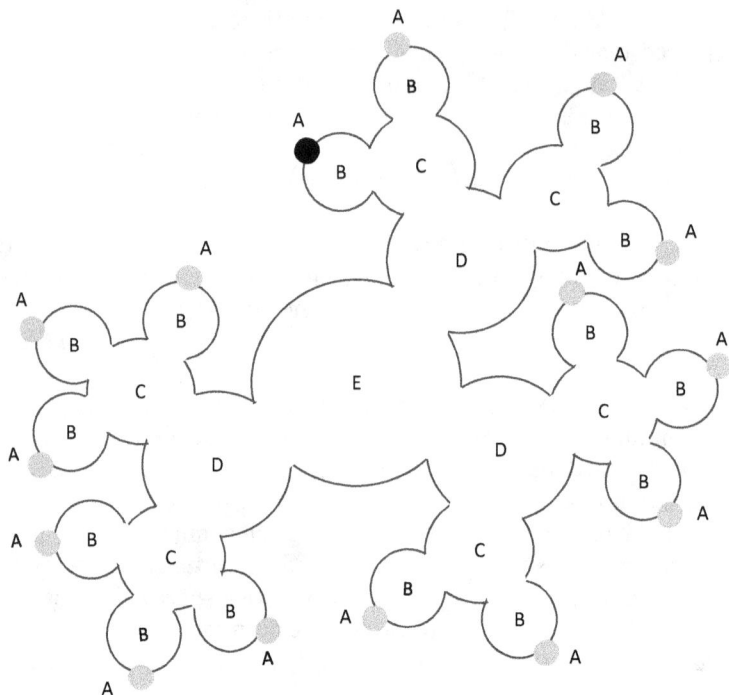

Figure 8.1 A: Ego consciousness, B: personal unconscious, C: group unconscious, D: unconscious of large national units, E: unconscious common to all humanity containing universal archetypal structures. (After Sheldrake 1989.)

communities, and of the inherited origins of humanity and beyond. A dream may then give us insights to ourselves and also to the groups of which we are part, in families, organisations, and societies, and, of course, the coaching relationship. As coaches, we may be part of our clients dreams, and they may be part of ours.

> The dream not only links the information of the past with that of the present, but also links the dreamer who has dreamed with the dreamer who tells and [the person] who listens.
>
> (Nicolò 2014 in Caviglia 2021)

A 'We-Possession'

This has significant implications for coaching, as the dream of a client or indeed of the coach may speak as much to the relationship, as it does to its individual participants. The dream may belong to both, coach and client, reflecting the projections of the transference that pass between us. It may be what we can term a 'we-possession', arising in one person but shared by both. When we pay attention to the dreams in the coaching relationship, we can better understand the relationship we have created together and the implications for coach and client as both individuals and a working partnership. Tess Castleman describes a situation where this principle is well illustrated:

> Years ago, a colleague called to tell me she'd had a dream about me: '
> I dreamed you were trying to steal my silver spoons.' She thought it indicated something terrible about me, so she was calling to warn me that her dream had revealed something secret and awful. I can be secretive, and I certainly am frequently awful, but I don't believe the dream was as literal as she thought...But it unquestionably had a great deal to do with our relationship... In this case, the dreamer projected onto me some aspect that was stealing something precious from her. Stealing can be a metaphor for an unconscious inadequacy, and, in fact, the silver spoons were, for her, a symbolic item of great value, the feminine principle.
> *The dream told her that she feared me, had an unflattering projection on me, and that she had doubts about trusting me. There was also a challenge for me: Did her dream tell me accurately of something I needed to see in myself? I had certainly had a difficult relationship with her, and did not value her age and experience as I might have. I found her a bit controlling, and I am sure I undermined her many times - just like stealing something valuable. I listened to her dream with earnest intent, and that was when our relationship began to improve.*
> (2009, pp. 177–178)

We may then imagine the dream as another form of transference, where the image of the coach or the client and their relationship may be represented within the symbols of the dream.

The Purpose of Dreams

Once we understand what a dream is, we can explore the purpose it serves and the ways in which we can use it in coaching. Jung suggested that a dream has four typical functions, each of which seems to build upon the other in intensity and affect (2006, p. 5):

1 A reaction: An unconscious reaction to a conscious situation in the recent past, where the dream simply reflects something that has recently happened to the dreamer. We may have been frightened by a large dog and that night have a dream about being attacked or threatened.
2 A conflict: A potential conflict between the unconscious and the conscious mind, where some aspect of the unconscious is incompatible with conscious thought. The dreamer may have experienced a challenge to some

shadow aspect of personality (e.g., the expression of an emotion they are uncomfortable with and normally try to repress), and the dream is a reminder of that discomfort. The tension in the psyche may be represented or even provoked in some way by a tension within the dream.

3   A resolution: An attempt by the unconscious to influence or change the conscious mind of the dreamer. Jung suggested that the unconscious attempts to maintain a balance in the psyche and tries to intuitively 'compensate' when some aspect of our personality becomes too dominant. The dream may suggest some form of resolution to an inner conflict, or a new direction through the symbols of the transcendent function (Jung 1969a, CW8) can shape our development. These symbols may suggest a new way of seeing the problem and point the way to a third position, which we had not previously considered. The dream feels meaningful, reminding us of a problem we are facing and offering a potentially transformative solution.

4   An illumination: A representation of something profoundly archetypal, extending far beyond the dreamer to suggest something at the collective level of the unconscious. The dream indicates that significant change may be under way in the world around us and carry a numinous and potentially overwhelming sense of significance. In this dream, we are connected to powerful universal forces which threaten to sweep us before them. It may even provoke a degree of psychological disturbance in its mystery and intensity and is likely to defy any attempt to understand it, except perhaps in retrospect. This is a dream that Jung referred to as a 'great dream' (Jung 2006, p. 5).

In all these cases, the unconscious is attempting to make sense of something which our conscious mind has not fully grasped. In our waking lives, we are facing or beginning to face a reality that we have not yet consciously acknowledged and resolved. This may be a past experience or perhaps something emerging in the present which we are only intuitively aware of. It is a reminder that our conscious mind is only a part, and perhaps a very small part, of the psyche. The dream has the power to inspire us, providing creative insights to problems that the rational mind has been unable or unwilling to provide. The overarching function of the dream is to help us make meaning in a confusing and complex world.

The nineteenth-century German chemist August Kekulé claimed to have pictured the ring structure of benzene after daydreaming of a snake eating its own tail (Rocke 2010), and the quantum physicist Niels Bohr developed the model of the atom based on a dream of sitting on the sun with all the planets moving around him on tiny cords (Portocarrero et al. 2011). Paul McCartney apparently wrote 'Yesterday' following a dream and had to be convinced that the tune was in fact his own original creation (Delano 2003). The dream reveals the working of the unconscious, as it tries to make meaning in the world. It is in this meaning-making function that the dream reveals its importance in coaching and development work. It provides the coach and client with a window into the unconscious and may bring insight and suggest new paths for enquiry.

It was a dream that provided the keystone to Jung's own developmental journey, consolidating his understanding of the self, both as a concept and as a personal revelation. As he emerged from the emotional challenges surrounding his split with Freud, Jung began to realise that the focus of any developmental process was a continual circling of the self as an archetype of centred wholeness and stability. This realisation came to him in a dream, where he found himself to be walking in a dream city that he knew as Liverpool.

> It was night, and winter, and dark, and raining...[I] found a broad square... into which many streets converged... In the centre was a round pool, and in the middle of it a small island. While everything roundabout was obscured by rain, fog, smoke, and dimly lit darkness, the little island blazed with sunlight. On it stood a single tree, a magnolia, in a shower of reddish blossoms. It was as though the tree stood in the sunlight and was at the same time the source of light... They spoke of another Swiss who was living in Liverpool, and expressed surprise that he should have settled there. I was carried away by the beauty of the flowering tree and the sunlit island, and thought, 'I know very well why he has settled here.
>
> (Jung 1995, pp. 223–224)

Jung felt that the damp, grey city represented his own dark depression, and the tree at the centre of the pool offered the hope of resolution. The dream provided both the numinous energy and the symbolism to inspire him and to suggest a way forwards.

> I saw that here the goal had been revealed. One could not go beyond the centre. The centre is the goal, and everything is directed towards that centre. Through this dream I understood that the self is the principle and archetype of orientation and meaning. Therein lies its healing function. For me, this insight signifies an approach to the centre and therefore to the goal. Out of it emerged the first inkling of my personal myth...
>
> ...The dream made it possible for me to take an objective view of the things that filled my being. Without such a vision I might perhaps have lost my orientation and been compelled to abandon my undertaking. But here the meaning had been made clear. When I parted from Freud, I knew that I was plunging into the unknown. Beyond Freud, after all, I knew nothing; But I had taken the step into darkness. When that happens, and then such a dream comes, one feels it as an act of grace.
>
> (Jung 1995, p. 224)

Jung goes on to note that the name of the city itself was a powerful symbol. He reminds us that the liver was seen as the 'seat of life' by many ancient cultures, allowing the dream association of the city of Liverpool to be seen as the source of life itself. The image of the tree is also one he was certainly familiar with, although he does not explore that further in this account. The tree has a central role in shamanism, and its symbolic significance may have its roots in the psychoid unconscious, as a psychosomatic phenomenon. It has been suggested (Lewis-Williams and Pearce 2005) that a feature of an altered state of consciousness is the experience of ascent or descent, and the tree is associated in many cultures across history with a passage between the underworld and the heavens. From the biblical tree of life to the Norse world tree Yggdrasil and the 'philosophical tree' of the alchemists (Jung 1983, CW13, para. 376), the tree has consistently provided a symbol of stability and wholeness, an *axis mundi* (Jung 1983, CW13, p. 162) that supports and holds the cosmos together. It is through the tree that we may access visions of death and rebirth as a continuous passage (Eliade 1958), and in traditional Korean poetry, the magnolia tree in particular was a symbol of weathering hardship to be reborn again. For this reason, it was where the mythical phoenix made its nest (Mullany 2006). Jung frequently cites trees as a powerful archetypal symbol of the self and 'direct embodiments of the incomprehensible meaning of life' (1995, p. 86), even suggesting that its cross-section of rings is itself a mandala (1969b, CW9i, para. 576). In his essay 'On the History and Interpretation of the Tree Symbol' (1983, CW13), he noted:

> Taken on average, the commonest associations to its meaning are growth, life, unfolding of form in a physical and spiritual sense, development, growth from below upwards and from above downwards, the maternal aspect (protection, shade, shelter, nourishing fruits, source of life, solidity, permanence, firm-rootedness, but also being "rooted to the spot"), old age, personality, and finally death and rebirth.
>
> (Jung 1983, CW13, para. 350)

It is then perhaps not surprising that in a dream with a magnolia tree at its centre, he experienced the integrating presence of the archetypal self, which offered him a resolution and enabled him to take the next steps in his own developmental journey. It reminded him that he was ready.

A Starting Point

The most significant thing about the Jung's dream is that, as with all dreams, its value lay in the fact that it was a symbolic experience, rich with associations and charged with feeling. He was moved by it and compelled to wonder about its significance. It demanded his attention. The symbol is, after all, the language of the unconscious, and its role is to channel emotional energy and prompt action.

A sign is always less than the thing it points to, and a symbol is always more than we can understand at first sight. Therefore, we never stop at the sign but go on to the goal it indicates; but we remain with the symbol because it promises more than it reveals.

(CW18, para. 482)

Once the symbol has been interpreted and integrated into the conscious mind, it loses its power and its capacity to provoke and inspire. The challenge we face in working with symbol is how to walk the line between the unconstrained vitality of the unconscious and the reflective capability of the conscious mind: How do we use the symbol to consciously guide us while retaining its capacity to move us? To face this challenge, we must learn to think in ways that are more like the appreciation of art or poetry than the precise instruction of a computer manual. To work with any symbol, but in particular with symbol in dreams, we must keep returning to the dream and deliberately resist the temptation to translate its images into a final concrete form. We must instead circumambulate the dream, exploring and revisiting its images again and again with an open mind.

Focusing on the Details

Having reminded ourselves about the nature of symbol, we can start to pay more attention to how they show up in the dream. This is an important step if we are to avoid the risk of reduction and oversimplification. All symbols will in some way relate to archetypal imagery, as it is the archetype that forms the core of the complex around which the symbols are clustered. Unless we pay attention to the subtle details which mark out this particular symbol as a unique vehicle for meaning, we may lose its essential essence. To say that a dream was about a cat is like saying that the Odyssey is a book about sailing. We need to go further in our noticing. We need to consider what sort of cat. Was it black, marmalade, tabby, or completely hairless? We need to remember how the cat presented itself and how we felt about it. Was it afraid? Were we afraid? Was it hissing or purring? Did we want to stroke it or strike it? We then need to recall its context in the dream and the symbols that seemed to be related to it. We need to remember how it appeared and what it did next. It is also important to notice how the symbols of the dream come together, how they are located in relation to each other, and how they interact. Each symbol is, after all, not disconnected but part of a matrix where each part reveals a little more of the whole. In the dream, nothing exists in isolation.

This detailed noticing may be challenging at first, and it may even be difficult to recall our dreams at all, but if we pay attention, they will come to us. When you wake, instead of getting up immediately just lie at peace for a while and allow the dream to linger. Record the dream immediately in a dream diary if you can and then reflect on the dream during the day, to see what else comes to you, remembering that even the most insignificant detail could, in fact, be significant.

Three Simple Techniques

Armed with a consciously symbolic attitude and a detailed recollection of the dream and its interconnections, we can then deploy the same three simple techniques we may use in an active imagination exercise.

We can begin by associating the symbols of the dream with other images, feelings, and perspectives from the personal experiences of the dreamer. A dream about a cat may remind us of a cat we once knew, which we associated with a particular time or place in our lives. This may lead us to connect the dream with other events and feelings. We may remember past trauma or moments of joy, which are evoked in the shared image. These reminders may be obvious or unexpected, perhaps prompted by the unconscious itself as it continues to feed us with intuitive information. Whatever happens, we must be careful to keep returning to the image. The risk of association is that the ego's fear of the voice of the unconscious or the glittering distractions of other more familiar experiences 'zigzags away from the dream' (Jung 2009, p. 2) and prevents us from focusing on its real intent.

> So the question to the dreamer is: ' what comes to mind about X, what do you think about it? And what else comes to mind about X?' whereas the question in free association is: 'what comes to mind about X? And then? And then?' And so on. In this way, the associations are about other associations instead of about X.
>
> (Jung 2009, p. 2)

We can then continue by *amplifying* the symbols, distilling their essence into a single idea, not as an interpretation but as a feeling or concept that seems to work as a suitable summary. For example, a client brought me the following dream:

> I remember being unable to speak as I tried to shout loudly at a very tall man wearing a black pinstripe suit and shoes with spats, who had the head of an eagle. He was at least twice as tall as me and very imposing. The eagle-head looked at me and made me feel very small and very nervous. I was with the young woman with black hair tied back in a ponytail. She was quite thin and girlish, but laughed at the eagle man, mocking him. It made me less afraid.

Using amplification, we may discover that throughout history the eagle has been a symbol of imperial power, suggesting that the man with the pinstriped suit and the eagle-head could be an image of 'established patriarchal authority'.

The young woman could then be thought of as an aspect of the anima, the unrealised creativity and potential of the unconscious. The dream could then be rephrased as follows:

> I was trying to make the 'established patriarchal authority' hear me but felt afraid. The innocent laughter of the 'unrealised creativity and potential of my unconscious' suggested I should take that authority less seriously, which made me feel braver.

To support the process of amplification, we can also draw upon ancient myths or the symbols of cultural or religious traditions. We can even have a book of symbols (Ronnberg 2022) on hand as an easy reference. In using these images as inspiration, we may begin to approach the archetypal core of the dream and the accumulated experiences of the collective unconscious. We may encounter images of the young hero or the 'Great Mother', reminding us of our own innate courage or our capacity for care. We may meet with their shadows and face the coward or the witch. We may find unusual helpers and strange alchemical images that confuse and mystify us. We will know these images as archetypal from the numinous energy associated with them, and we can allow them to inspire us, knowing that we may be connecting us across time and spaces with the essence of the human condition.

This does not mean, of course, that there is a 'straight line interpretation' between the images of our dreams and the symbols of myth. The personal unconscious may be pointing us in an entirely different direction. However, they may inspire us to make new connections with the images of the collective unconscious, and the shared experiences of humanity. To dream of a cat may not mean we have dreamt of the cat goddess Bastet herself, but from reading about her we may also be prompted to wonder about the combination of fertility, maternal care, and a fierce protective presence in the home, all of which were aspects of the goddess (Monaghan 2010).

Finally, we may consider *personifying* aspects of the dream, allowing us to change perspective and tell the story from the viewpoint of another fragment of our psyche. Everything in the dream is, after all, within us, relating to something that is part of us, and through personification we can allow that part a voice. We can begin to consciously integrate those fragments, recognising that they exist and that they have something to say to us.

A client had a dream where she was being pursued through her house by an unknown person. I asked her to put herself in the place of her assailant and explain why they were attacking her. She replied quickly, 'She won't leave home, and I have to chase her out'. As we explored this response, my client made the connection with her discomfort about leaving her role and striking out on her own. She knew she had reached 'the end of the line' in her work and was bored and frustrated but was afraid of life beyond her familiar role. It would seem that some part of her knew she needed a push.

A combination of these three approaches allows us to consider the symbols of the dream, and its overall narrative, from different angles and perspectives. We can move beyond a confusing linear set of images to something more complete and more multidimensional.

A Rolling Seascape of Dreams

With this sense of the whole dream in mind, we should also remember that, as a dynamic process of the unconscious rather than a static product, dreams may appear in sequences over time and only in observing the sequence can we observe the dream. One dream alone is unlikely to represent a complete picture of the unconscious as it works. Just as the conscious mind may reflect on something for days or weeks, the unconscious will do the same. The symbols of a dream sequence may evolve and change. They may become more or less significant and may be accompanied by new associations that bring nuance or new meanings, like a constantly moving seascape where floating images rise and fall, vanishing from sight or moving to prominence with each new wave.

Questions about a dream may then be answered in subsequent dreams. When we dream or when a client brings a dream to us, we can just 'stay in the question' and, without rushing to closure, can wait and see what happens next. Sometimes if we simply notice the dream, more dreams will emerge and the unconscious finds its own path, without the need for conscious intervention. We can track our dreams over time, perhaps in a dream journal where we can make a detailed record of the dreams, alongside changes that occur in our external environment. Without rushing to an interpretation, we can watch themes evolve and change, making new connections that allow an understanding to surface gradually. We can allow the dream to dream itself onwards, as part of a reverie between the unconscious and the conscious mind. We cannot really map a seascape but can make sense of it only by observing the patterns of its movement.

Interpretation and Emergence

As meaning then begins to emerge from the dream, our main challenge is to resist the comforting finality of interpretation. Interpreting the dream saves us from the anxiety of 'not-knowing' but also limits its possible meaning and its potential to move us. To work with dreams, we need to cultivate what the poet John Keats termed a 'negative capability', where we are able to tolerate 'uncertainties, mysteries, doubts, without any irritable reaching after fact and reason' (Rollins 1958, p. 193). In a state of negative capability, we allow the dream to convey its message gradually.

This is particularly important when working with the dreams of others. The dream is, after all, produced by the unconscious of the dreamer, and even if the dream represents something systemic and shared, we are still viewing it through our own lenses. It is easy to ignore the complex layers of meaning, particularly if the dream contains obviously archetypal imagery which may easily be reduced to something familiar and obvious. Our conscious impressions of the symbol may depend in part on our own knowledge and our own cultural and personal life experiences. It is easy to believe that our immediate interpretation is the only possible interpretation. Jungians are often susceptible to 'archetypal reductionism' (Hall 1983, p. 34) and in particular seem drawn to ancient Greek myth while forgetting that the world has many other mythic narratives and images which do not all conform to that particular cultural template. The dreamer will bring their own context which will shape any archetypal influences and provide additional nuance. Rather than jump quickly to conclusions, it may be easier to simply notice and let the dream reveal its meaning gradually. We can develop lightly held hypothesis to guide our enquiry, but we must be prepared to drop them at a moment's notice when new avenues of exploration open up.

> Symbols mean very much more than can be known at first glance. Their meaning resides in the fact that they compensate an unadapted attitude of consciousness, an attitude that does not fulfil its purpose, and that they would enable it to do this if they were understood. But it becomes impossible to interpret their meaning if they are reduced to something else.
>
> (Jung 1983, CW13, para. 397)

The dream, like the symbols it contains, can never be exhausted, and we will never discover its meaning once and for all. Dreams may not need to be interpreted, simply to be witnessed. In relation to symbolic work more broadly, Louis Zinkin suggests that 'the unknowable signified does not need to be known, but it does need to be there' (1998, p. 87). In other words, we do not need to know for certain what a symbol means, but we do need to be aware of its presence in order to really benefit from it. In recognising and then working with the symbols of the dream, we can carry some part of the dream into our conscious lives. The unconscious is 'given permission' to continue its work, provoking new ways through which the conscious mind can engage with the world. Research (Dement 1972) has suggested that dreams contain solutions to problems despite the dreamer being unaware of the connection. In one instance, the correct answer to a lateral thinking problem was 'water', a solution that the dreamer failed to connect with the dreams he had recorded in a dream diary. The dreams were of various water-based activities, all of which took place in the rain within his dreams.

When we give the dream space and time, we may also continue to unravel its meaning as new ideas and directions occur to us. However certain we were once about its message, we may discover new complexity in even the simplest symbols. Every one of our hypotheses, even those we feel most convinced of, may evolve or be simply left behind as the dream continues to reveal itself. The dream then becomes a continued source of inspiration where no final interpretation is required in order for it to do its work. As Jung suggested, 'dreams pave the way for life, and they determine you without you understanding their language' (2009, p. 233).

The Black Castle

I was supervising a coach, who was beginning to deepen his practice and to work more with unconscious process. He was very enthusiastic about working in a Jungian-inspired way but at the same time had expressed a degree of ambivalence, wondering how far he could go with his clients, who generally came from more conservative organisations. He brought me one of his own dreams.

> This was a black dream. All the colours were black. There were different shades of black, but everything was black. I was walking around the outside of a castle, and I came to a doorway that had no door but was utterly black inside. It was a wall of blackness which seemed to swallow all the light and offered no clue as to what lay within. At the entrance hovered the image of a cat's skull alongside a geometrical matrix. I knew something frightening lurked within, but although I knew I should be afraid, I was not afraid. At this point I woke up.

My client was confused by the dream, and it preoccupied him for several days, as it felt important. He suggested to me, however, that part of him seemed resistant to developing an understanding, as despite his preoccupation with the dream, he seemed to avoid actually working with it in a more deliberate way. The cat's skull in particular bothered him, as it seemed to represent death in some form. In our supervision, we discussed the dream and identified a number of associations which seemed to be of interest.

First, we considered the blackness and the sense of the absolute unknown. The lack of fear was striking as my client felt cautious but unafraid, as if he was ready to face whatever was inside the castle. Second, we explored the image of the cat's skull, to which he had no immediate personal associations, beyond the connection between the skull and the idea of death. We wondered whether something could be dying in him, but this did not feel meaningful, and so instead we amplified the image by considering the symbol of the cat in myths and folktales. The most striking feature about the cat as a symbol is the level of ambivalence that is associated with it as 'like the serpent, its image oscillates between beneficence and malevolence' (von Franz 1999, p. 55). The cat is a creature of the dark unconscious, associated with unpredictable magic, hidden knowledge, and the feminine principle. For this reason, the cat was often linked with fertility goddesses and later with witches, evoking an egoic fear of the uncontrolled creativity of the 'other'. My client immediately connected this with his own ambivalence about his work and his feelings about the corporate world, where the unconscious is usually unwelcome and of which he was still part. Finally, we considered the matrix, a word which is derived from the Latin for 'womb' and is seen in alchemy as the image of relationship with the self and the vessel from which the soul is reborn (Jung 1931, CW16). In the alchemical matrix, the rational mind becomes entwined with the unconscious, the masculine principle with the feminine, and the soul emerges as a more integrated whole. We then wondered about the dream as a representation of the promise of the unknown unconscious, alongside the ambivalence he felt in working with it as a coach, an ambivalence which also appeared in his reluctance to engage with the dream itself.

The following night, my client had another dream, which we discussed at our next supervision session.

It was my birthday, and I went, with a group of friends and colleagues, to an event in the same castle that I had visited earlier. I don't remember entering but I just knew it was the same place. The inside was a cavernous hall that reminded me of an opera house with all the seats removed. There were large tiers leading to central circular area. A lot of people were partying. Some people were having sex and an older woman tried to have sex with me, but I was disinterested. I wandered off. I passed a man in a white shirt and bowler hat playing a piano near a large absinthe fountain. Most of the people were all younger than me and dressed in a very bohemian way and seemed rather self-absorbed. They were only pretending to enjoy themselves. I began to worry that I would not be able to get a taxi. I wanted to go home very badly, and I was afraid I would be stuck here alone when the party finished. At this point I passed a previous assistant of mine who in real life was funny and rather ditzy, but in the dream was sitting at a desk working while the event went on around her. She was wearing a smart suit and typing on a laptop while surrounded by files. She looked calm and focused. I felt strangely comforted by her and realised that she would be able to help me get a taxi. I decided to stay a while longer and at this point, I woke up.

This dream seemed to offer a glimpse into the interior of the black unknown of the earlier dream. My client associated psychodynamic work with a sense of self-indulgence when immersing himself too deeply in the unconscious. It was exciting to him but at the same time did not feel concrete enough to apply to the immediate and very real challenges facing his clients. He felt that this dream was a warning from the unconscious about its own seductive power, not as something dangerous but as something distracting and self-indulgent. It made conscious and validated his underlying ambivalence about his work. He recognised that he could easily become lost in the pleasure of it all, but that would not really satisfy him. The image of his anima was, however, the defining feature of the dream. The contrast between the loose creativity of his assistant in real life and her structured and reassuring presence in the dream suggested that he was able to find balance. He realised that he could leave the world of the unconscious whenever he wanted to. He knew he would not lose himself. He would be able to participate in depth work and easily return to the world outside. We agreed that this dream could be a movement towards integration and the development of a more complete sense of self, something that would be essential if he was to help his clients do the same.

Reflections and Implications

We all dream, and if we are open to the dream, we will be open to a more complete understanding of ourselves. We will be able to examine the workings of the unconscious without fear and perhaps make use of its intuition to help us take our next steps in life. We may start to resolve inner conflicts with unforeseen solutions, and we may even be able to enrich our understanding of what lies below the surface in the systems around us.

Through the dream, we may be granted insights to our relationships, to our communities and organisations, and perhaps also given access to the great problems and the store of collective wisdom that come with being human. These insights are granted through our awareness of symbol and a capacity to 'hold' ourselves through the inevitable anxiety of 'not knowing' that comes with symbolic work. As we develop this capacity, we in turn develop what we can refer to as a stable 'ego-self' axis (Edinger 1960, p. 9). Here we can extend the reach of the conscious mind by acknowledging the significance of the unconscious, intentionally working to integrate its intuition into our waking lives and moving closer to the potential of the self.

We may even begin to see the dream not as an object that is distinct and separate from us but instead as a way of being that is an integral part of our lives, whether we choose to acknowledge it or not. We can let go of the desire for 'knowing' and instead embrace dreams as part of 'living'. Dreaming is the psyche itself doing its 'soul work' (Hillman 1979, p. 201), and the real challenge is simply to keep the dream working in the soul without reaching too quickly for answers. To help us achieve this, Tess Castleman suggests a simple exercise. When we have reflected on a dream, alone, with another, or in a group, leave at least one question about the dream unanswered and allow the psyche the freedom to intuitively choose its path. We must then place our anxious needs for any final interpretation to one side and follow her advice:

> You who seek insight, work to balance yourselves by appreciating the value of the humble phrase, "I don't know."
>
> (Castleman 2009, p. 192)

If you do not already do so, record your dreams in a journal for a few weeks or months. Don't try to interpret the dreams immediately but let them 'settle' for a while. Then come back to the journal and read it.

- Consider what symbols stand out the most, either individually or as clusters and themes.
- What details can you remember about those symbols?
- What associations do you make when thinking about the symbols? What associations come you when considering them as a group?
- What archetypal images come to mind? Do the symbols remind you of any folktales or stories? What results do you get if you search for them on the internet?
- What does the dream feel like when retold from the perspective of one of its symbols? What new insights seem to emerge from this retelling?

Note

1 The exception may be the experience of lucid dreaming, where the dreamer becomes aware that they are dreaming (LaBerge 1990).

References

Barrett D 1996, *Trauma and dreams*. Cambridge, MA: Harvard University Press.

Castleman T 2004, *Threads, knots, tapestries: How a tribal connection is revealed through dreams and synchronicities*. Einsiedeln, Switzerland: Daimon Verlag.

Castleman T 2009, *Sacred dream circles: A guide to facilitating Jungian dream groups*. Einsiedeln, Switzerland: Daimon Verlag.

Caviglia G 2021, Working on dreams, from neuroscience to psychotherapy. *Research in Psychotherapy* 24(2): 540.

D'Agostino A, Castelnovo A and Scarone S 2013, Dreaming and the neurobiology of self: Recent advances and implications for psychiatry. *Frontiers in Psychology* 4: 680.

Delano J 2003, *The Beatles album*. London: PRC Publishing Ltd.

Dement WC 1972, *Some must watch while some just sleep*. New York: Freeman.

Dieckmann H 1976, Transference and countertransference: Results of a Berlin research group. *Journal of Analytical Psychology* 21: 25–36.

Edinger E 1960, The ego-self paradox. *Journal of Analytical Psychology* 5: 3–18.

Eliade M 1958, *Patterns of comparative religion*. New York: Sheed and Ward.

Hall JA 1983, *Jungian dream interpretation: A handbook of theory*. Toronto: Inner City Books.

Hartmann E 2001, *Dreams and nightmares*. New York: Perseus.

Hartmann E and Brezler T 2008, A systematic change in dreams after 9/11/01. *Sleep* 31(2): 213–218.

Henderson J 1990, *The cultural unconscious, shadow and self.* Wilmette, IL: Chiron Publications.

Hillman J 1979, *The dream and the underworld.* New York: HarperPerennial.

Hupbach A, Hardt O, Gomez R, and Nadel L 2008, The dynamics of memory: Context-dependent updating. *Learning Memory* 15: 574–579.

Jung CG 1931, *The practice of psychotherapy,* CW16.

Jung CG 1969a, *Structure and dynamics of the psyche,* CW8.

Jung CG 1969b, *Archetypes and the collective unconscious,* CW9i.

Jung CG 1983, *Alchemical studies,* CW13.

Jung CG 1995, *Memories, dreams, reflections.* Fontana Press.

Jung CG 2006, *Children's dreams: Notes from a seminar given in 1936-1940.* Princeton, NJ: Princeton University Press.

Jung CG 2009, *The red book.* New York: W. W. Norton & Company.

Kets De Vries MDR 2014, Dream journeys: A new territory for executive coaching. *Consulting Psychology Journal: Practice and Research* 66(2): 77–92.

Kroes MCW and Fernandez G 2012, Dynamic neural systems enable adaptive, flexible memories. *Neuroscience & Biobehavioral Reviews* 36(7): 1646–1666.

LaBerge S 1990, Lucid dreaming: Psychophysiological studies of consciousness during REM sleep. In RR Bootzin, JF Kihlstrom and DL Schacter (eds.), *Sleep and cognition* (pp. 109–126). Washington, DC: American Psychological Association.

Lawrence WG 2003, *Experiences in social dreaming.* London: Karnac.

Lawrence WG 2006, Executive coaching, unconscious thinking, and infinity. In H Brunning (ed.) *Executive coaching: Systems-psychodynamic perspective.* London: Karnac.

Lawrence WG 2007, *Infinite possibilities of social dreaming.* London: Karnac Books.

Lewis-Williams D and Pearce D 2005, *Inside the neolithic mind.* London: Thames & Hudson.

Monaghan P 2010, *Goddesses in world culture.* Westport, CT: Praeger.

Mullany F 2006, *Symbolism in Korean ink brush painting.* Folkestone, Kent: Global Oriental Ltd.

Nicolò AM 2014, Family myths and pathological links. In AM Nicolò, P Benghozi and D Lucarelli (eds.), *Families in transformation: A psychoanalytic approach.* London: Karnac Books.

Occhionero M, Cicogna P, Natale V, Esposito MJ, and Bosinelli M 2005, Representation of self in SWS and REM dreams. *Sleep and Hypnosis* 7: 77–83.

Papadopoulos RK 1996, Archetypal family therapy: Developing a Jungian approach to working with families. In L Dodson and T Gibson (eds.) *Psyche and family.* Wilmette, Il: Chiron.

Portocarrero E, Cranor D, and Bove VM 2011, Pillow-talk: Seamless interface for dream priming, recalling and playback. *Proceedings of the fifth international conference on tangible, embedded, and embodied interaction* (pp. 269–272).

Revonsuo A 2006, *Inner presence: Consciousness as a biological phenomenon.* Cambridge, MA: MIT Press.

Rocke AJ 2010, *Image and reality: Kekulé, Kopp, and the scientific imagination.* Chicago, IL: University of Chicago Press.

Rollins HE 1958, *The letters of John Keats.* Cambridge, UK: Cambridge University Press.

Ronnberg A (ed) 2022, *The book of symbols: Reflections on archetypal images.* London: Taschen.

Sheldrake R 1989, *The presence of the past.* London: Fontana/Collins.

von Franz M-L 1985, The transformed berserk. *ReVision* 8(1): 20.

von Franz M-L 1999, *The cat: A tale of feminine redemption.* Toronto: Inner City Books.

Zinkin L 1998, Paradoxes of the self. In H Zinkin, R Gordon and J Haynes (eds.) *Dialogue in the analytic setting.* London: Jessica Kingsley Publishers.

Chapter 9

Symbol in Culture

Exploring the Significance of Symbol in Communities, Organisations, and Societies

The collective and cultural layers of the psyche are not deep and distant. They are lived and present. Our individual psyche is built upon these layers as a living system and shapes our own lives in often hidden but still highly significant ways. Like us, our collective groups, whether these are families, communities, organisations, and societies, also have complexes which bind us together with feeling-toned symbols. We may not always wonder about these symbols or even consciously recognise them, but they speak to something we share. We are never beyond these systems. They are not abstract concepts but often overwhelming pools of energy that pervade every aspect of our being. We are in these collective systems, and they are in us. We can never be free of them; we can only begin to raise them to a level of conscious awareness and wonder about the effect they have on us. As the novelist David Foster Wallace suggested:

> There are these two young fish swimming along, and they happen to meet an older fish swimming the other way, who nods at them and says, "Morning, boys. How's the water?" And the two young fish swim on for a bit, and then eventually one of them looks over at the other and goes, "What the hell is water?"

> (Wallace 2008)

A Shared Unconscious

Jung proposed that the mind of the individual rests on the collective unconscious, the shared experiences of humanity that transcends time and space. It is in the collective unconscious that archetypes first emerge, providing the organising principles around which complexes can begin to form. In Jungian psychology, complexes are the building blocks of 'personality', which we may think of as a stable but still dynamic and emergent patterns of psychological responses that seem to define us. The complex is made up of networks of associated symbols, clustered around an archetypal core, which directs the flow of libido, the energy of life that moves us to action. The archetype cannot itself

DOI: 10.4324/9781003463269-10

be defined but makes its presence known through familiar imagery and intense, feelings that can be described as numinous. We may experience a mother goddess image as profoundly moving because the symbol of maternal care is an archetypal one. It moves us not simply because of our personal experiences but because all the other humans who have survived beyond birth have had, in some way at least, an experience of care.

However, Jung's original conception of the collective unconscious was very broad, and he seemed to ignore the potential impact of the experiences of particular groups in particular contexts. As we look more closely, we discover that 'much of what Jung called personal was actually culturally conditioned' (Henderson 1990, p. 104) and that 'much of what Jung called collective was cultural' (Adams 1996, p. 40). Our mother goddess images may retain an archetypal core but will also feature cultural dimensions which can only really be understand in the context of the community in which they appear. The image of Mary Magdalene, for example, could be considered an archetypal image of a mother goddess but also represents the dynamic image of women through the eyes of the Catholic Church over many centuries. As a saint, she has represented both a 'beautiful sinner and a great penitent' (Maisch 1998, p. ix), but her image 'in every era is an indicator of the image borne by women at that time' (Maisch 1998, p. ix). We cannot really attempt to understand an image of Mary Magdalene without also attempting to understand the cultural context in which that image appears. To bridge this gap, Joseph Henderson proposed an intermediary layer, which he referred to as the 'cultural unconscious': 'an area of historical memory that lies between the collective unconscious and manifest pattern of the culture...which assists in the formation of myth and ritual and also promotes the process of development in individuals' (1990, p. 102). Our personal unconscious, and the development of our personality over time, is then nested not simply in the collective experiences of humanity but in the historical experiences of our own communities, and the two are interdependent. As Jung suggested:

> The psychology of the individual corresponds to the psychology of the nation. What the nation does is done also by each individual and so long as the individual does it, the nation also does it.
>
> (1967, CW7, p. 4)

The pervasive influence of culture can be explained by the formation of 'cultural complexes', which function in much the same way as personal complexes but with an effect that is felt across a community (Singer and Kimbles 2004). That community may face experiences that may be traumatic or at least create some form of collective emotional response. Feeling-charged symbols then begin to collect around an archetypal core to help members make sense of those experiences and suggest responses which allow the community as a whole to survive and adapt. These symbols then become familiar 'markers' which remind us that we *are* a community and direct the way in which we live and work together. The way in which we, as members of the community, see the world is then coloured by the perspectives of those around us and of those who have come before us. Like the complexes of the personal unconscious, we remain for the most part unaware of their pervasive influence on our lives. As Jung suggested, 'everyone knows nowadays that people "have complexes". What is not so well known, though far more important…is that complexes can have us' (1969, CW8, para. 200).

The Symbols of Culture

The symbols bound up with cultural complexes may appear in many different forms. changing and adapting over time as a reflection of the underlying currents of the cultural unconscious. We may observe these cultural way-points as single symbols or as webs of overlapping images, whose meaning lies in interconnection rather than in a single symbol. Cultural symbols are often profoundly archetypal in nature, reflecting archetypal themes and carrying their numinous energy, but in a way that is specific to the culture in question which cannot really be fully appreciated outside this particular context.

> It is as the archetypal moves through the social, cultural and personal filter of the unconscious that it is filled out into an image or an idea that emerges into consciousness.
>
> (Morgan 2002, p. 579)

These symbols may appear as monuments and iconography, flags and cuisine, films or music, sayings and proverbs. Anything that can serve to hold together the associated emotions of the cultural complex can serve as a symbol. Some may be subtle and fleeting, and others blatant and enduring. Through symbols, we may summon the ghosts of our ancestors, to populate our myths and provide us with a rich supply of gods and heroes, as templates to guide and validate us.

Leaders, whether dead or alive, may have a particularly profound symbolic value (Dirkx 1991), transcending their individuality to become an image of some aspect of a particular culture. They may represent something profoundly archetypal or perhaps something unique to the community within which they emerge. They may become what we may think of as a 'leading idea', providing an emotional and psychological anchor for a community (Zaleznik 1977). The leader as symbol directs the flow of energy within the cultural complex and provides an object for group projections. In South Africa, Nelson Mandela became a symbol of a calm and enduring sense of hope and healing, 'enabling the fantasy of the post-apartheid nation, and holding at bay a whole series of repressed and negated undercurrents' (Hook and Vanheule 2016, p. 1).

He became the 'embodiment of the nation that transcends ideology, party, or group' (Frederickson 1990, p. 8) with an influence that became almost archetypal, extending beyond the cultural boundaries of southern Africa to become a global image of paternal wisdom.

Symbols may cluster together to form narratives and myths, often based upon a central founding myth which connects people directly with the feelings and half-remembered experiences from when a culture first came together. These founding myths are particularly significant as they provide a reassuring reminder of our reason for being. They reinforce the established order of our community and alleviate any existential anxiety, offering shelter from a chaotic and a traumatic past (Gutmann and Toral 2018). These founding myths may then be used to justify past or present actions, relieving the community from any responsibility and perhaps associated feelings of guilt or shame. If a land was given by God to a persecuted people, then the responsibility for the actions of those people ultimately rests with God. The displacement, enslavement, or genocide of the existing inhabitants becomes God's will, and our conscience remains untroubled, provided the founding myth and the cultural complex associated with it remain unchallenged.

Ensuring Compliance

Like all symbols, the symbols of a culture will defy any attempt at a final interpretation, but they will demand our attention and evoke something within us. The more embedded we are in the system, the stronger their influence as they remind us of our role and the shared expectations that others have of us. Whatever form a symbol takes, we will know it from its affect. Cultural symbols have the power to shape an entire society over long periods of time. They may evoke a wide range of intense and overwhelming emotions or simply provide a subtle and pervasive sense of place. This energy can move us forwards, bringing communities together and urging change, or it can act as a repressive force, locking us into neurotic patterns of historical behaviour. They will guide our feelings and actions, even as visitors to the system, and they will shape how we see those within the community and those beyond its boundaries. The cultural complex provides a simplistic and formulaic schema that keeps us locked into familiar historical patterns, reminding us of who are and of who we are not.

> Like individual complexes, cultural complexes tend to be repetitive, autonomous, resist consciousness, and collect experience that confirms their historical point of view. Cultural complexes also tend to be bipolar, so that when they are activated the group ego becomes identified with one part of the unconscious complex, while the other part is projected out onto the suitable hook of another group.
>
> (Singer 2002, p. 15)

In his seminal work on organisational culture, the psychologist Ed Shein suggested that one of the features of all cultures is that their rules are 'taught to new members as the correct way to perceive, think, and feel' (1990, p. 111) in relation to certain challenges. These rules and the ways in which they are 'taught' are for the most part profoundly unconscious. It may be assumed that we will simply pay attention to the symbols that surround us and be guided unconsciously by them. Projections and subtle signs of approval or disapproval will ensure that we stay in line, and we may start living a life that may not entirely be ours. Any questions or challenge to the assumptions that define the complex will be met with direct and often emotionally charged correction from group members. If we continue to resist, the system may even reject us entirely, expelling us as a warning to 'the other'.

There is an (almost certainly) apocryphal story, which illustrates this rather well. A group of monkeys were placed in a cage, in the middle of which was a ladder leading to a large bunch of bananas. Every time a monkey tried to climb the ladder, all of the monkeys were sprayed with icy water. Eventually, whenever a monkey started to climb the ladder, the other monkeys attacked them to prevent them from climbing, until none of the monkeys would go near the ladder. One by one, the monkeys were removed from the cage and replaced. Each time a new monkey joined and approached the ladder, the other monkeys would attack them in fear and rage. At first, they remembered the water, but in time, when all of the original monkeys had gone, they only knew not to climb the ladder. If the monkeys had language, we could imagine the ladder becoming a symbol of disaster and of the potential wrath of a monkey god. We could imagine myths being told around monkey campfires, of fools who had attempted to rise above their station to reach the sacred fruit and of the heroes who had averted disaster by stopping them. This is a cultural complex.

A Divided Kingdom

Attracted by rich natural resources and a benign climate, the British Isles have seen repeated patterns of migration throughout history, with a constant stream of new peoples, bringing new cultural norms and from time to time, new ruling dynasties. Some of these migrants came as invaders, others were attracted by economic opportunities, and others were fleeing persecution. One particularly traumatic event that has come to define English history is the Norman invasion of 1066, when the entire ruling class of the country was replaced by a Franco-Norman warrior class in a series of brutal purges, and over 100,000 people died of starvation alone in a devastating military campaign known as the 'harrying of the north' (Morris 2012, p. 228). A contemporary writer lamented that 'England has become the dwelling place of foreigners and a playground for lords of alien blood' (William of Malmsbury in Morris 2012, p. 346). Our language has been enriched by 'loan words' that reflect our changing populations, and for much of our history, our monarchs have not even spoken English as a first language. Modern English is based on a creole of English, French, and Scandinavian, and new words have been added with each wave of migration. Even our national cuisine is borrowed from those who came to settle here; the quintessential fish-and-chip supper arrived with Spanish and Portuguese Jews arriving in the 18th and 19th centuries (Roden 1996, Panayi 2014), and more recently the nationwide adoption of chicken tikka masala was inspired by Bangladeshi migrants in the 1960s (Buettner 2009). These repeated migrations have given us a history of conflict and fragmentation and a somewhat confused relationship towards 'the other'. We are the children of natives, refugees, and conquerors, and we readily accept new arrivals while viewing them with suspicion and fear. An unresolved state of an uncertain identity has been our trauma, and it has fuelled a cultural complex of ambivalence.

Even as colonisers, we seemed ambivalent, and the British Empire was created and sustained 'through a mixture of deception...and an even greater self-deception' (Cashford 2016, p. 54). The celebrated English poet and author Rudyard Kipling wrote a poem called 'The White Man's Burden' where the 'heavy harness' of colonisation was placed on the colonizers, not the colonised, suggesting a reluctant moral imperative to civilise the 'other'.

Take up the White Man's burden—
The savage wars of peace—
Fill full the mouth of Famine
And bid the sickness cease...
...By all ye cry or whisper,
By all ye leave or do,
The silent, sullen peoples
shall weigh your Gods and you.

(Kipling 2020, p. 20)

We may imagine this as a repression of the shadow of colonisation and a denial of its trauma, by a people who themselves had been persecuted through conquest and who had historically welcomed the persecuted. Our ambivalence ensured that we felt uncomfortable in taking up the mantle of empire, with its connotations of oppression, even when our actions suggested otherwise. We may wonder, for example, how it felt to be a Scottish or Irish soldier enforcing imperial rule, when our own parents or grandparents themselves may have been subject to persecution under the same flag. This ambivalence extends to our relationship with our foods, and while politicians have championed chicken tikka masala as a national dish, there is still a perception that food from certain migrant communities lacks cultural depth or value (Buettner 2009, Throup 2021). We project the emotions bound up with our cultural complex onto those communities, eating their food and hating that we enjoy it.

This cultural complex was recently and very visibly enacted upon a group of migrants, who arrived from British colonies in the 1950s and 1960s and who had been granted a legal right to live and work in the United Kingdom. The 'Windrush Generation', named after the ship that brought many of them to these shores, were encouraged to migrate to help fill labour shortages and provide a foundation for post-war economic recovery. Having spent decades in the UK and believing they had a legal right to remain, many were deported under a government policy which deliberately created a 'hostile environment' for migrants. This policy was ironically and very visibly championed by a number of leading politicians, who themselves were migrants to the UK or whose parents were migrants and who seemed to demonise those who had followed the same path. Even the word migrant has become somewhat pejorative, extending beyond its meaning of a person who moves from one place to another, to suggest a threatening and invasive intent.

The flag of the United Kingdom, the Union Flag, has to some extent arisen from this cultural complex as a symbol which carries some hope of integration and an end to conflict. The flag began its life in 1606 as a merger of the English and Scottish flags to mark the ascension of King James I and the union of England and Scotland, a union that was unsurprisingly not universally popular. Describing the Treaty of Union, which formally brought England and Scotland together, the Scottish poet Robert Burns wrote: 'We're bought and sold for English gold, such a parcel of rogues in a nation' (Burns 2015, p. 313). In 1801, the flag also incorporated the cross of St Patrick, representing Ireland, and as the British Empire expanded, bringing a time of prosperity, the flag seemed to represent a single people under a single flag.

However, our cultural complex remined unresolved, and as the empire collapsed, reminding us again of the trauma of fragmentation, our ambivalence towards the 'other' has again begun to surface. This in turn has revived a focus on the Union Flag as a symbol of possible redemption. In the recent Brexit vote, it became the central image and a rallying cry for Britons to unite against the threat of oppression by the European 'other', and since Brexit, it has been used as a backdrop by political parties across the spectrum as a symbol of unity. However, the Brexit vote was itself divisive, and paradoxically the Union Flag is now also seen by many as a reminder of that division, with connotations of isolationism and nationalist extremism. A flag which expanded our sense of community may now be seen as limiting it. The associations we make with our symbols continue to evolve, but the complex of ambivalence towards the 'other' is still very much alive. As Britons, we are, of course, the 'other' as the complex is within us, and we remain at war with ourselves.

Going Beyond Nations

In Jungian psychology, attention has focused for the most part on the cultural unconscious as a national-level phenomenon, but the concept may equally apply to any group of people of any size that comes together with an enduring sense of identity. In recent decades, there has been increasing interest in the idea that established groups of any size, whether families, tribes, religions, political groups, and commercial organisations, may also have a cultural unconscious, with associated complexes that define and shape behaviour within those groups (Papadopoulos 1996, Corlett and Pearson 2003, Ferreira 2021, Barrett 2023). Any organisation may have complexes, as may distinct operating units or functions within those organisations, which help their members derive a sense of togetherness and continuity as 'collective structures of meaning' (Papadopoulos 1996, p. 136). These complexes are also organised around an archetypal core which provides the organising principle and energy to align and shape the collective behaviour of these organisations. We may even think of the organisation as an archetypal image of the self, offering a feeling of togetherness and integration.

Like national cultures, organisational cultures may be shaped by a broad range of factors which may be specific to that organisation, including the original purpose of the organisation, the working practices which have shaped it, or the impact of commercial successes and failures. These factors may also be more general, reflecting the nature and practices of a particular industry. We may wonder about the complexes within an organisation that was set up to alleviate poverty or one that has used or continues to use slave labour or has been involved in genocide. We could reflect on the collective psychological impact of a company that has grown without setbacks through acquisition or one which has faced shame at a national level as a result of catastrophic financial misconduct. What complexes may exist in companies which sell arms, cigarettes, or toys or which cause significant environmental pollution? Some companies may be family-owned and may embody historical family dynamics. Any collective emotional experience that is bound up with the organisation and its shared sense of self may begin to form a cultural complex, which in turn will be represented with unique symbols.

As employees or associates of these organisations, we may then find ourselves subject to more than one complex, reflecting our membership in more than one community. We may be part of a distinct religious or political group, living within a particular national culture, and at the same time find ourselves working within a large multinational company with its own history and cultural norms. Each of our communities will have its own complexes and its own demands, and we will introject the unconscious energy and images of each. They may serve to reinforce our own behaviour or fuel an internal tension with questions about our possible identity.

We may be aware of the myths that are told about the organisation and may even notice particular imagery, but we are typically unaware of the underlying energy that binds them together and the impact they have on us. We may not notice how we are changed by them as they are simply the water in which we swim. Jung referred to this as a 'participation mystique', a psychological connection where 'the subject cannot clearly distinguish himself from the object but is bound to it by a direct relationship which amounts to partial identity'

(1971, CW6, para. 781). In a participation mystique, we become one with the organisation, identifying viscerally with its norms and behaviours, without question or doubt. In doing so, we reinforce the cultural complex, which becomes stronger and begins to attract more people like us. If we need a father figure, we may unconsciously look for organisations which provide suitable leaders and a clear sense of hierarchy, rather than demanding a more psychologically mature approach to individual responsibility. Over time, these organisations will become increasingly patriarchal, and any attempt to challenge the symbolic father figures who represent the complex will be resisted. The cultural complexes may then become indistinguishable from our own, and we may find ourselves comfortably at home, or they may provoke an unbearable level of existential angst as we struggle to fit. In this case, we may reject the organisation, or it may reject us.

Beginning to Notice

If we, as coaches and consultants, are to notice the symbols of the cultural complex, a good place to begin is the experience of entry to the organisation, as we cross its boundaries. Here we can see the organisation with fresh eyes and a clear mind, before we have become immersed and its symbols have become familiar and taken for granted. We may reflect on how we are received by the organisation and how its boundaries are guarded. Is it welcoming or distrustful? What symbols mark the boundaries and announce the culture within? We may also want to consider how the entry makes us feel and wonder about the projections that are passed between us and the organisation (Barrett 2021). What are we as symbols?

Our starting point may even simply be the buildings themselves, the organisational equivalent to the geography of the tribe or the nation-state. The symbols we encounter will provide us with a forewarning of the unconscious forces that shape the organisation and the behaviour of the people within it and the way in which its culture will shape us.

> As we enter the system, we become part of it. We exert influence upon it which may be intentional or simply because we are present. The underlying forces within the [social] arena also exert influence upon us ... we both change the system and are changed by it.
>
> (Barrett 2021, p. 147)

An airline that had been in a slow decline following a decade of underinvestment had asked for a proposal to encourage innovation and collaboration in its senior management population. As I entered the building, I noticed that the main revolving door was jammed, and I had to enter through a side door, the glass of which was noticeably opaque with dirt. Inside we discovered a tiny reception desk set in a wall on one side, reminding me of a small, fast-food kiosk. A rather sad-looking woman sat alone at the desk, wearing the company's old-fashioned uniform and thick make-up. I was asked to wait on an old chair near a large but empty water feature, which was surrounded by wilted plants. When I met with the HR team to discuss the proposal, I felt a sense of real anxiety, particularly when I introduced the idea that a key feature of the proposal was an unstructured approach to dialogue through which managers could surface and develop ideas together. It was made clear to me that this felt far too volatile and disorienting to consider. The symbols of the boundary had already suggested that the creative life of the organisation had run dry. They had become stuck, and the very idea of psychological movement was utterly terrifying. The meeting simply confirmed my initial impressions.

Words and Stories

Once we have begun to pay attention to the obvious physical symbols of the organisation, we may want to focus on its language and the myths that are told and retold. We may discover the language as a symbol that reveals the underlying complex in striking or unusual words or repetitive metaphors and phrases. Jung recognised the significance of words as having symbolic value in his early research using the Word Association Test, where participants are presented with a series of words and asked to respond with the first thing that comes to mind. These words, along with the reaction times and any other associated physical responses, are recorded and analysed to help understand the complexes that shape personality and behaviour. Jung discovered that, while the test is carried out with individuals, it also revealed clusters of symbols in family systems and most significantly shared complexes that created a unique 'culture' in that family (Papadopoulos 1996, p. 131). As Jung suggested, 'the daughter shares her mother's way of thinking, not only in her ideas but also in her form of expression' (Jung 1973, CW2, para. 1005).

While little or no research appears to have been done to explore the potential of the Word Association Test in organisations, it seems reasonable to assume that the symbolic value of words is as present and as influential as it is in family systems. The members of an organisation are likely to use repetitive words, jargon, phrases, and metaphors as symbols to express the underlying cultural complex and reinforce expected behaviours. While consulting an investment bank, I was struck by the frequent use of the language of war. People referred to 'battle lines being drawn', to the 'collateral damage' of decisions, or to spending time 'in the trenches'. The language seemed to evoke an almost heroic sense of suffering and to remind employees of the need to win at all costs. The bank had a culture of long hours and hard work and emphasised the value of the 'survival of the fittest'. One manager mentioned to me in passing that one of their new graduate entrants had simply walked out that morning and not returned, leaving his jacket on the back of his chair. The manager seemed almost elated as he told me that 'I just broke a graduate'.

Language reminds us of who are we are and, by extension, of the boundaries that separate us from who we are not. The symbols of language may carry subtle messages about status and social value, placing people within structures and hierarchies that may be invisible but which will define their role and the limits of their agency. The sociologist Pierre Bourdieu refers to this process as *symbolic violence*, where subjugation occurs symbolically through language norms (1991). In a European subsidiary of an American corporation, the words 'New York' were frequently deployed as a mysterious symbol of power and control, settling conflicts and signifying submission. People were told that 'New York' wanted a particular outcome or had forbidden a particular course of action. However, it was clear to me as an outsider that when the term was used it was usually symbolic and rarely referred to an actual decision by an actual individual. When asked, 'Who in New York?', people rarely had an answer. It was a representative of a cultural complex formed through the trauma of acquisition in the previous decade and reminded members of the organisation that they were at the mercy of a distant and faceless entity. For some this became a source of power and authority, and for others a source of comfort and relief, as it absolved them from any sense of personal accountability. It was the organisational equivalent of 'It is God's will'.

If we listen carefully, we may discover the myths and legends that describe the idealised exploits of heroes or the cautionary tales of outcasts that provide the templates and examples to follow or avoid. These myths may be consciously told, even though their underlying meaning may remain symbolic, or they remain below consciousness, forming 'phantom narratives' (Kimbles 2014) which we are unaware of but are still influenced by. These 'phantom narratives' provide a way of structuring our responses to a cultural complex that allows us to avoid 'the unbearable, the too muchness, the untranslatable' (Kimbles 2014, p. 17) experience of facing the emotions bound up in the complex but that ensures that our behaviour is still aligned. I was working with a large commercial bank which prior to the global financial crisis of 2008 had been widely praised for their bold and aggressive culture. However, this culture had caused them to overreach, taking ill-considered risks which resulted in near bankruptcy and the collapse of their market capitalisation. I had been asked to provide a comprehensive career development framework to support leadership talent, but each time I discussed proposals, the scope was reduced for reasons that were not clearly articulated. Eventually I was asked to provide little more than a short script that managers could use if they wanted. The organisation seemed to be terrified of the ghosts of its past, and any decision that led to any action that went beyond the status quo was to be avoided. Safety lay in everyone keeping their heads down and doing nothing.

The significance of language is often brought home to us when working in or with a language that is not our native tongue. Here we are forced to examine the meaning of the words we use and often discover difference and nuance that we had not previously considered. This sometimes reveals the symbolic aspects of words that we had previously overlooked. One of the most striking aspects of international consulting is that although we work in English (my native tongue), I often work with groups drawn from many different linguistic backgrounds. Sometimes, aware of our inability to communicate clearly, we need to explain words to each other or draw on other languages to explain and elaborate, leading to the emergence of previously hidden assumptions and meanings. I have used this simple insight in my work with native English speakers to explore the meaning of words they use frequently, and often we discover that words are not as commonplace as we had previously imagined. I saw a similar but more pronounced effect during my own studies of infant development, where my tutor would frequently use 'made up words' as the best possible illustration of a babies state of mind. For example, during the weaning stage, where the baby is separating psychologically from the mother and developing a sense of self, my tutor referred to the mother as a 'coming-and-going-person', bringing to life the idea of absence and presence as it may be experienced by a baby. In organisations, jargon may serve the same purpose, being essentially meaningless to outsiders but revealing a meaning that is both conscious and unconscious to the initiated. It can be useful for us to remember that every time we enter a new culture, we are speaking a foreign language.

Self as Instrument

We may also begin to notice how this organisation makes us feel and how our own behaviour is affected by it. Using our 'self as instrument' (van de Loo and Lehman 2016), we can reflect on what is being projected into us from the organisation, deepening our understanding of the unconscious processes within that organisation and becoming more conscious of the influence it may have on us. The feelings evoked in us and the associated symbols that begin to surface may not, after all, belong to us alone and may also represent the cultural complexes that are beginning to act upon us and influence our behaviour. As we develop sensitivity to our own state, we may begin to consider our feelings and the symbols that catch our attention as simultaneously representative some part of our own unconscious and also perhaps of the cultural unconscious of the community, organisation, or society within which we now find ourselves.

The new head office of an organisation that had recently been bailed out by private investors had a large glass atrium, in the centre of which was a cafeteria. I was proudly told by senior leaders that the cafeteria had been designed to encourage collaboration, as people could eat together and meet informally. It was striking that the lack of collaboration was the reason I had been asked to work with the company, and this symbol of the atrium seemed at odds with a culture that was siloed and perhaps even antagonistic. I sat in the cafeteria over a few days at different times, and I was struck by how empty it was. People would come down from their offices, collect their sandwiches, and quickly scurry back to their desks on the floors above. The most striking feeling was of being watched by unseen eyes in the glass offices that surrounded the atrium and in particular in the executive offices on the top floor. I felt exposed and vulnerable and had the association of being in a Panopticon, a design for a prison proposed by the philosopher Jeremy Bentham (Sprigge and Burns 2017). Here prisoners are watched at all times by an unseen guard, and because the prisoners do not know whether they are being observed at a particular moment, they consistently moderate their behaviour. The cafeteria seemed to suggest that the underlying complex was in fact one of paranoia and distrust, where the employees were, in effect, prisoners of controlling and unseen authority figures, perhaps their own leaders and perhaps the faceless investors.

The Shadow of the Ordinary

The offices of a well-known fashion house were beautiful. The reception was white marble and glass, with huge open spaces and nothing that could disturb the clean lines. There were no paintings, sculptures, or plants, and the only images were huge pieces of photographic art, featuring iconic models wearing the latest season's clothes. In the office itself, the desks were made of white semi-opaque glass and were uncluttered. Everything was quiet and calm. No one ate at their desks, and for lunch delicious food was served in the minimalist canteen, in plain but obviously expensive cardboard boxes. Every evening, the desks were completely cleared of paper and personal effects, returning the space to the state of a blank canvas. Employees ostentatiously wore the brand and were ubiquitously good-looking and stylish. An initial impression was of walking uninvited into a futuristic photo shoot for which I was hopelessly unprepared. I was not beautiful enough to be here.

For individuals, the persona is the mask we develop to face the world. It is in itself a complex, with its own feeling-toned symbols, which helps us mediate our relationships. It ensures that we are consistency seen in ways that will guarantee our social success. As the persona forms, those aspects of ourselves that we feel will not support our relationships are rejected and fall into the shadow, the complex which contains those things that we have 'no wish to be ' (Jung 1931, CW16, para. 470). If we, as individuals, overly identify with the persona, we run the risk of living a 'false life' (Casement 2004, p. 100) where we exist only in relation to the perceived approval of others and we lose the capacity to build meaningful relationships, crucially including our relationship with ourselves. This identification may bring considerable short-term social success, but ultimately we lose our sense of self and become stuck in superficial patterns of behaviour (Hudson 1978). Meanwhile, those attributes that have become part of the shadow wait for an opportunity to be heard. We will spend time and effort ensuring that they remain hidden, but the shadow complex carries its own energy and its voice is inevitable. As Jung suggested: 'The more one turns to the light, the greater is the shadow behind one's back' (1995, p. 49).

I wondered then whether in this organisation the cultural complex was intrinsically linked with the persona, arising in part from the industry itself. The daily life of the company required a relentless obsession with image, as if its existence depended entirely upon how it was seen, even behind the scenes. A decade earlier the company had become a representative of tasteless and down-market fast-fashion, facing ridicule from the leading voices in the fashion industry. It had experienced what the cultural historian Paul Fussell has termed 'prole drift' (1985), a highly pejorative term suggesting a social race to the lowest common denominator resulting in the destruction of any intrinsic value and worth. The experience of this trauma seemed to have left a mark as a cultural complex. The importance of beauty seemed to have become a desperate and existential compulsion that extended beyond catwalks, magazines, and boutiques to permeate every corner of the organisation. With this obvious emphasis on persona, it was hard then not to wonder about the shadow. In this place, where was the ugly hiding?

My immediate thoughts lead to the manufacturing process. Often the shadow of an organisation can be found in the caste who are the lowest and who carry the burden of shame and rejection on behalf of others. Other fashion houses have been rocked with scandals around slave labour and sweatshops, but this was not the case here. Products were ethically sourced and made in artisanal workshops that the company was rightfully proud of and presented as another symbol to reinforce their persona. The founding myths of the organisation also revealed very little as these were carefully curated to reinforce the persona and to emphasise the heritage and origins of the brand. They seemed to overwhelm anything more informal.

However, as I looked closer, the symbols revealed a little more. The breakout spaces of the bright atrium, with their perfectly white designer chairs, were usually empty. Overflowing waste bins and cluttered filling cabinets were hidden behind white glass partitions, and the white glass desks seemed to favour style over practicality, as computer mouses did not work well on the reflective surface. Digging deeper, the shadow could be located behind an opaque glass 'wall of the mind', in the company's operating systems, which were chaotic and old-fashioned. They were held together by the company's lowest caste, its head office functions, and any problems relating to them were for the most part simply ignored. It appeared that the shadow of this company was not in the ugly but in the mundane. The messy business of business could not be allowed to disturb the image, as the cultural complex demanded that the mask of aesthetic perfection be maintained. The company was overspending and seemed to have had little conscious awareness of its cash flow and financial exposure. This shadow could never be openly discussed, and organisational myths suggested that people who spoke about it too loudly left shortly afterwards. To be successful in this company, it was important either to ignore the mundane as if it was never there or to silently and discreetly deal with it without needing overt recognition or praise. To challenge the cultural complex of the persona directly was to meet a 'social death', followed shortly by a 'career death'.

Moving to Individuation

However, the symbols that we observe in an organisation need not necessarily be purely regressive, pointing back to an unresolved trauma. Like the symbols that constellate for individuals, they may also be progressive, pointing forwards to a possible redemption. They may even be a deliberate attempt by leadership, representing the conscious mind of the organisation, to work with difficult emotions and reshape underlying cultural forces, integrating past and present trauma. We may imagine this as the development of a stable 'ego-self axis' (Edinger 1960) in the organisation, a prerequisite for a healthy culture. For individuals, the 'ego-self axis' represents the willingness to engage with our complexes and the unconscious forces that shape our lives. It is the route through which growth becomes possible, as we begin to consciously examine the unconscious and make more intentional choices about who we are and how we behave in relationships. We are neither isolated and self-absorbed nor over-whelmed by the unconscious expectations and projections of others. In Jungian psychology, we refer to this process as individuation, a conscious move towards wholeness. As Jung suggested, 'the aim of individuation is nothing less than to divest the self of the false wrappings of the PERSONA on the one hand, and the suggestive power of primordial [archetypal] images on the other' (1967, CW7, para. 269).

If we are to overcome traumatic experiences and free ourselves from the complexes that form around them, we cannot ignore and repress them. Instead, we must be able to face and reexperience them (Winnicott 1974, Winnicott 1980) as only then can we begin to make meaning from them and tell our story forwards in new ways. Once we acknowledge that we are wounded, we can begin to heal and can move more confidently towards our potential. This is both true for the individual and true for the systems of which they are part. If a community is able to face and examine the cultural complex, we may be able to limit its hold over us and perhaps even begin to reshape its movement in a more progressive way. To develop the culture of an organisation or a society, we must be able to face the past and consciously work with the symbols of the cultural complex in new ways. Only then can we begin to create the cultures within which we can develop. We can begin to recognise that individuation in the group and of the group are co-dependent.

In the reception area of a mining company, the digital screens showed the number of deaths in mines that year. Significantly, alongside the tally scrolled the names of those who had died, with information about them and their families. These were not statistics but human beings. Employees and visitors were reminded of the dangerous nature of the company's work, reinforcing a vigilance about safety and a duty of care for each other. A conscious decision had been taken by the company's leadership not to repress the inevitable trauma of the industry but to refashion it in a form that encouraged a culture of care and respect.

Reflections and Implications

The same basic principles that define an individual life define the functioning of any human system. We are affected by the challenges we face in world around us, and in our efforts to make sense of these challenges, we learn strategies to cope with them. We learn how to behave and what things to avoid, and we learn to repress our more difficult memories. This learning is stored in the unconscious in complexes, where the original emotions associated with these challenges are bound up with symbols that provide the waypoints to guide and protect us. Communities, organisations, and societies all have complexes, constructed from shared experiences that may be single, profoundly traumatic events or may be simply the outcomes of persistent exposure to a particular context or set of difficulties. Whatever the cause, they provide the templates for behaviour that draw us in and hold us together.

Familiarity with the cultural complex and its images allows us, as coaches and consultants, a more complete awareness of the individuals we may encounter in our work. We can place them in context and begin to appreciate the systemic and unconscious forces that have shaped them. We can also become more aware of the way in which those forces act upon us and the way in which our own our cultural complexes then drive our responses. Without this understanding, our work will always be incomplete as each of us exists in a context, past and present, which shapes and guides behaviour. As the psychoanalyst Wilfred Bion suggested, 'you cannot understand a recluse living in isolation unless you inform yourself about the group of which he is a member' (1961, p. 133).

It is through symbols that this understanding becomes possible, as they allow us to develop hypotheses about the underlying structure and dynamics of the unconscious which we can then use to help our clients develop their own awareness. We can help them better acknowledge what may be happening below the surface and why and in this acknowledgement begin to reimagine the past in more progressive ways. We can begin to reform the narrative and symbols of the cultural complex as a foundation for growth. We can then use this foundation to work with communities, organisations, or even societies to support a more conscious understanding of collective processes and guide more intentional group or leadership decisions. We can then help individuals take responsibility for the cultures in which they live and work, creating a virtuous cycle where they can contribute to the development of the conditions needed to better support their own development. We can help create human systems which are nurturing and therapeutic.

Visit a building that represents an organisation, perhaps a company or a government institution:

- Consider what symbols are given the most prominence? How are they displayed?
- What associations do you have with these symbols? Do they have a particular resonance for you?
- What other symbols do you see? Do they seem significant? If so, why?
- How do you feel as you enter this organisation? How do its symbols make you feel?
- What do you not see? What do the symbols that are visible suggest may lie in the shadow?
- What are the possible implications of your reflections if you were to work with this organisation or with people from this organisation?

References

Adams MV 1996, *The multicultural imagination*. London: Routledge.

Barrett L 2021, Entering the system: Organisational consulting and the psychology of the transference. In N O'Brien and J O'Brien (eds.) *The professional practice of Jungian coaching*. London: Routledge.

Barrett L 2023, *A Jungian approach to coaching: Turning leaders into people*. London: Routledge.

Bion WR 1961, *Experiences in groups*. London: Routledge.

Bourdieu P 1991, *Language and symbolic power*. Cambridge, UK: Polity Press.

Buettner E 2009, Chicken tikka masala, flock wallpaper and 'real' home cooking: Assessing Britain's 'Indian' restaurant traditions. *Food and History* 7(2): 203–229.

Burns R 2015, *The complete poems and songs of Robert Burns*. Glasgow: Geddes & Grosset.

Casement A 2004, The shadow. In R Papadopoulos (ed.) *The handbook of Jungian psychology: Theory, practice and applications*. Hove, East Sussex: Routledge.

Cashford J 2016, Britain: Autonomy and insularity in an island race. In J Rasche and T Singer (eds.) *Europe's many souls: Exploring cultural complexes and identities*. New Orleans, LA: Spring Books.

Corlett JG and Pearson CS 2003, *Mapping the organisational psyche: A Jungian theory of organisational dynamics and change*. Gainesville, FL: Center for Applications of Psychological Type.

Dirkx JM 1991, Understanding group transformation. In RD Boyd (ed.) *Personal transformations in small groups: A Jungian perspective*. London: Routledge.

Edinger E 1960, The ego-self paradox. *Journal of Analytical Psychology* 5: 3–18.

Ferreira C 2021, Introducing corporate cultural complex. In N O'Brien and J O'Brien (eds.) *The professional practice of Jungian coaching*. London: Routledge.

Frederickson G 1990, The making of Mandela. *New York Review of Books* Sept 27: 8–9.

Fussell P 1985, *Class: Style and status in the USA*. London: Arrow Books.

Gutmann D and Toral S 2018, Psychoanalytic organizational consulting: The role of the founding trauma. *Psychoanalytic Inquiry* 38(4): 312–327.

Henderson J 1990, *The cultural unconscious, shadow and self*. Wilmette, IL: Chiron Publications.

Hook D and Vanheule S 2016, Revisiting the master-signifier, or, Mandela and repression. *Frontiers in Psychology* 6.

Hudson WC 1978, Persona and defence mechanisms. *Journal of Analytical Psychology* 23: 54–62.

Jung CG 1931, *The practice of psychotherapy*, CW16.

Jung CG 1969, *Structure and dynamics of the psyche*, CW8.

Jung CG 1971, *Psychological types*, CW6.

Jung CG 1973, *Experimental researches*, CW2.

Jung CG 1967, *Two essays on analytical psychology*, CW7.

Jung CG 1995, *Memories, dreams, reflections*. London: Fontana Press.

Kimbles S 2014, *Phantom narratives: The unseen contributions of culture to psyche*. London: Rowman & Littlefield.

Kipling R 2020, *The best of Rudyard Kipling: A collection of essential poetry*. Bristol: Read & Co.

Maisch I 1998, *Between contempt and veneration…Mary Magdalene: The image of a woman through the centuries*. Collegeville, MN: Liturgical Press.

Morgan H 2002, Exploring racism. *Journal of Analytical Psychology* 47(4): 567–581.

Morris M 2012, *The Norman conquest*. London: Penguin.

Panayi P 2014, Fish and chips: A takeaway history. London: Reaktion.

Papadopoulos RK 1996, Archetypal family therapy: Developing a Jungian approach to working with families. In L Dodson and T Gibson (eds.) *Psyche and family*. Wilmette, IL: Chiron.

Roden C 1996, *The book of Jewish food: An odyssey from Samarkand to New York*. New York: Knopf.

Schein E 1990, Organisational culture. *American Psychologist* 45(2): 109–119.

Singer T 2002, The cultural complex and archetypal defences of the collective spirit: Baby Zeus, Elian Gonzalez, Constantine's sword, and other holy wars. *San Francisco Jung Institute Library Journal* 20(4): 4–28.

Singer T and Kimbles S 2004, Emerging theory of cultural complexes. In J Cambray and L Carter (eds.) *Analytical psychology: Contemporary perspectives in Jungian analysis*. Hove, East Sussex: Routledge.

Sprigge TLS and Burns JH 2017, *Correspondence of Jeremy Bentham. Volume 1: 1752 to 1776*. London: UCL Press.

Throup S 2021, *The complex reality of British multiculturalism: A case study of Indian food*. Global History and International Relations. http://hdl.handle.net/2105/60351

van de Loo E and Lehman R 2016, Developing night vision and the night vision paradigm. In E Florent-Treacy, M Kets de Vries, R Lehman and E van de Loo (eds.) *The annals of psychodynamic-systemic practitioner research* 1 Fontainebleau, France: INSEAD.

Wallace DF 2008, https://www.newyorker.com/books/page-turner/this-is-water [accessed 30 January 2025].

Winnicott C 1980, Fear of breakdown: A clinical example. *International Journal of Psychoanalysis* 61: 351–357.

Winnicott DW 1974, Fear of breakdown. *International Review of Psychoanalysis* 1: 103–107.

Zaleznik A 1977, Managers and leaders: Are they different? *Harvard Business Review* 55(3): 67–78.

Chapter 10

Returning to the Unconscious

Exploring Symbol, Soma and an Immersion in the World Around Us

The world of our ancestors was enchanted. It was filled with magical symbols that moved them both psychologically and physically. They were not as burdened by the anxious rational need to analyse and understand and had more space for the mysterious. They lived among the symbols of the world and were able to perceive and integrate them, not simply from the removed objectivity of the conscious mind but as felt experiences. Today, most of us live in a domesticated world, where the wildness that was both beyond us and within us has been tamed. We try to keep a safe and respectable distance from the mysterious, and we work hard to drain the magic from the symbols that surround us. We may repress these symbols, denying that they have the ability to move us in profound ways, or we may turn them into leisure pursuits where we can file them away in safe and predictable boxes. Art or poetry can still terrify us or inspire us, but we know that we can safely return to the mundane when we leave the gallery or close the book. Alternatively, we turn to psychotherapy or coaching and objectively analyse the symbols that surface within us and around us, to make conscious meaning from them. We can adopt a symbolic attitude to notice symbols in our dreams or fantasies and pin them like butterflies on a board. This approach, of course, has value, allowing us to better understand ourselves and to make more conscious choices, but in doing so we empty those symbols of their life energy. They lose the power to transform us, as our separation from the mystery of the outer world leads to a separation from the rich creative potential of our own unconscious. With each conscious thought, we slowly turn living images into empty signs, and with each reminder of the rational authority of the ego, we become less whole and less fully human. Jung felt that this alienation from the natural world had resulted in an impoverishment of our emotional vitality, the force that propels us forwards towards a more integrated experience of the Self. He suggested:

> As scientific understanding has grown, so our world has become dehumanised. Man feels himself isolated in the cosmos…and has lost his emotional unconscious identity with natural phenomena. These have slowly lost their

DOI: 10.4324/9781003463269-11

symbolic implications. Thunder is no longer the voice of an angry God, nor is lightning his avenging missile. No river contains a spirit, no tree is the life principle of a man, no snake the embodiment of wisdom, no mountain cave the home of a great demon. No voices now speak to man from stones, plants, and animals, nor does he speak to them believing they can hear. His contact with nature has gone and with it has gone the profound emotional energy that this symbolic connection supplied.

(Jung 1964, p. 95)

Exploring the Edge of Psyche

However, the psyche is still more than the limited awareness of the conscious mind. As Jung suggested, 'the self is not only the centre but also the whole circumference which embraces both conscious and unconscious' (1968, CW12, p. 444), and that circumference is very broad indeed. Our psyche is built on ancient foundations, and whether we like it or not, we are part of something much larger than ourselves. The shared experiences of humanity place us firmly within a collective psychological context which in turn rests upon a somatic reality and inheritance, a level of the unconscious that Jung termed the 'psychoid' (1969a, CW8, para. 382). The psychoid is an intermediary layer that is neither wholly psychological nor wholly physiological, and it is here that our interactions with the physical world begin to find form in the unconscious. Despite the best efforts of our conscious mind to elevate its significance, our more primal and sensual experience of the world is always present to some degree. As James Hillman reminds us:

Since the 'discovery of the unconscious', every sophisticated theory of personality has to admit that whatever I claim to be "me" has at least a portion of its roots beyond my agency and my awareness. These unconscious roots may be planted in territories far away from anything I may call mine, belonging rather to what Jung called the 'psychoid', partly material, partly psychic, a merging of psyche and matter.

(Hillman 1995, pp. xviii–xix)

Seeing, hearing, and walking upright all shape our underlying assumptions of what is possible and in turn provide a frame that defines and limits our conscious understanding of the world. As Jean Knox has suggested, 'our bodily experience directly creates symbolic meaning and conceptual thought' (Knox 2011, p. 1) and defines our sense of what is possible and what is real. Our opposable thumbs, for example, allow us to literally grasp objects and symbolically 'grasp' ideas. Without them we would experience the world in a very different way. Research has, for example, suggested that both human beings and monkeys with opposable thumbs typically fall for a simple magic trick that does not fool species of monkeys that lack opposable thumbs. Researchers

(Garcia-Pelegrin et al. 2023) used a simple sleight-of-hand trick called a 'French Drop', where an object is displayed in one hand while the other hand reaches over to grab it. The palm of the second hand faces inwards, with the magician's thumb concealed behind their fingers. A human audience knows the thumb is concealed and typically assumes that it has grasped the object. Their attention then follows the second hand, only to find it empty as the magician has simply dropped the object into the palm of the original hand. Tempted by small morsels of food, monkeys were encouraged to guess the hand the food was hidden in and those species of monkeys that had opposable thumbs, assumed, like human audiences, that the hidden thumb had grabbed the item and chose the wrong hand. Those species of monkeys that lacked opposable thumbs did not make that assumption and did not fall for the trick. They could not imagine the possible actions of a thumb that they themselves did not possess. Contemporary neuroscience would suggest that 'the same circuitry that can move the body and structure perceptions, also structures abstract thought' (Gallese and Lakoff 2005, p. 17), proposing a profound interrelationship between body and mind. In the case of 'grasping', it would appear that that the parts of the brain that are active when physically grasping an object also become active when using words that involve the concept of 'grasping' (Buccino et al. 2005, Gallese and Lakoff 2005). It appears that anatomy determines our fundamental perception of reality, playing a defining role in the development of our psyche and our sense of self (Deacon 1997, Knox 2011) and providing the psychoidal templates that we can describe as archetypal. Perhaps it is the existence of the thumb that has given us the archetypal symbol of the magician, manipulating and changing our perceived reality across the ages.

We cannot then easily separate the development of psyche from the physical experiences in which it is rooted. There is always an intimate relationship between the perceiving body and the perceiving mind, which we may describe as an 'animal mind'. It is an ability to 'be' in the world and to respond intuitively to it without a preoccupation with rational awareness as the focal point of life. Here we do not need to wonder why sitting by the ocean or under a tree makes us feel better; we simply need to know that it does. In this experience, we can enjoy the symbol for itself or notice that it does not feel right and chose to move away from it. We are thinking like an animal. This response is innate, but in our developed world, we learn to devalue it, focusing instead on the authority of the rational mind. We work hard to understand why rather than simply accepting what is. We learn to justify unnatural situations and then find ways to repress our responses to them. We crowd onto trains or sit in traffic jams, file into airless offices, and drink watery coffee from paper cups while convincing ourselves that none of this experience matters to us, as there are good reasons why we continue with this way of life. We visit a psychotherapist or a coach to help us understand ourselves instead of simply moving away to find somewhere that feels better.

This is not to deny the value of rational thought in any way, as it is through the understanding of the unconscious that we can allow ourselves to make more informed conscious choices about our lives. However, it is worth remembering that the reality of the ego is neither our only reality nor our only aspiration if we hope to move closer to our potential. As human beings, we are not brains in a tank or a form of artificial intelligence. We exist in a complex blend of context, body, and mind, and the more we focus on consciousness alone, the less whole we become.

The Need for Sensation

The importance of immersive somatic experience and symbol has become apparent in recent years with the rising popularity of what is termed Autonomous Sensory Meridian Response (ASMR) Video Culture (Gallagher 2016). ASMR is a term that describes a tingling sensation that some people experience in response to particular audiovisual and interpersonal stimuli, a sensation that is usually accompanied by strong emotions. The phenomenon is not new (Grothe-Hammer 2024) and arises in many intimate experiences such as having a haircut or a massage. However, its appearance in the symbolic form of intentionally curated and widely distributed videos featuring highly amplified physical symbols has been striking. People whisper quietly, brush their hair, eat sensual food, stir bowls full of wooden balls, or slowly rearrange coloured pencils. Filming is done in close up, and the volume of often subtle sounds is emphasised and central to the experience.

> ASMR is often associated with scenes of intimacy and concentrated attention: it might be brought on by watching someone performing a meticulous task, by the cadence of a voice, by whispering and soft sounds or by expressions of care, interest and affirmation.
>
> (Gallagher 2016, p. 1)

These symbols appear to activate a sense of 'technologically mediated intimacy' (Smith and Snider 2019, p. 41) and wellbeing, where individuals seek out an archetypal symbolic proxy that delivers a psychosomatic effect. ASMR seems to offer a calming alternative to the superficial 'attention economy' of the internet and allows viewers the chance to activate an emotional experience by watching a physical one. The videos also form the centrepiece of online communities, suggesting that the symbols can be clustered to represent a shared need and a shared sense of identity. The symbols that evoke ASMR may help individuals create the feeling of connectedness with others and themselves. The popularity of these videos may have been fuelled by a rising lack of physical and relational stimulus in modern society. It was particularly pronounced during the COVID-19 pandemic (Russell 2024), where many people were unable to experience intimacy or the world beyond their homes. Many people now seem to be using ASMR videos in self-treatment for depression, anxiety, stress, and insomnia (Barratt and Davis 2015, Smejka and Wiggs 2022), although research is not yet clear whether they have a measurable medical effect.

Whether an effect is measurable or not, the images of physical experience do appear to matter and may themselves be archetypal images of our relationship with the self. In encountering these symbols, we are encouraged to move beyond the boundaries of the conscious mind and experience the self as a connection through the psychoid to something that lies beyond us. In Jungian psychology, the archetype of the self is an image of potential which can be unlocked in our relationships. As we build relationships with others, we open the door to a deeper understanding of ourselves. The symbols of the physical world may then help us to transcend the isolation and loneliness of the ego and move towards the possibility of wholeness, through the experience of the collective and the psychoid.

Moving Towards the Unconscious

Despite this apparent hunger for symbols of the physical, the focus of coaching and psychotherapy remains for the most part firmly rooted in consciousness with an emphasis on relational interaction, as part of a so-called 'talking cure' (Cooley et al. 2020). While this offers considerable support and advantage, both seem to ignore our need for an archetypal, psychosomatic experience that moves us both psychologically and physically. Even when working at depth within a psychodynamic frame, we are typically moving in an arc from the unconscious to the conscious mind. We may work with the symbols of dreams or fantasies, but we are moving towards a conscious understanding from an unconscious intuition. We are supporting our clients as they make sense of the hidden parts of the psyche in the process of individuation: 'an extension of the sphere of consciousness, an enriching of conscious psychological life' (Jung 1969a, CW8, p. 762). Through individuation, we better understand our underlying motivations and make more deliberate choices in the service of our development.

However, our psychological wellbeing and future development may not be solely defined by the things that we have brought to consciousness and given form to. We may not need to begin to create rational hypotheses in order to be healed (or harmed) by a symbol. We do not need to analyse poetry, music, or even the sensations in our own bodies in order to be moved by them. We simply need to be with them. As Louis Zinkin has suggested, 'the unknowable signified does not need to be known, but it does need to be there' (1998, p. 87). The symbol does not need to be interpreted and analysed or even perhaps brought to conscious awareness in order to have affect upon us; it simply needs to be present and available.

This requires us to adjust our mindset, where the symbolic attitude is not simply a conscious awareness of the world but also an intimate participation in it. In this 'symbolic life', we may begin to return to our 'animal intelligence' moving through conscious choice to a state of 'participation mystique' (Samuels et al. 1986, p. 105). Here we are fully immersed in the world, without a need to observe ourselves. Subject and object have become one, with no differentiation. Jung felt that a critical part of therapy – and, by extension, coaching – was 'becoming animal' (Shamdasani 2003, p. 253), identifying 'animal' with a natural state where we live in harmony with our instincts. We can think of this as living a symbolic life.

> Only the symbolic life can express the need of the soul- the daily need of the soul… Everything is banal, everything is 'nothing but'; and that is the reason why people are neurotic, they are simply sick of the whole thing, sick of that banal life, and therefore they want sensation…. life is too rational, there is no symbolic existence in which I am something else.
>
> (Jung 1977, CW18, para. 627–628)

We can begin this adjustment in the conscious mind by noticing the affect our environment has on us. Perhaps we are not living in a way that feels conducive to our wellbeing. Perhaps there is too much noise or pollution or too little light or fresh air. Perhaps we feel the need to move more or to taste something. We can then choose to allow the unconscious to lead us, following our intuition and impulse without analysing our actions. We can find or create spaces that move us and just enjoy being in them. We can listen to music, dance or sing, eat or drink, and allow these symbols to take us. James Hillman suggests that many of the difficulties we face in life may not be within us at all and that rather than changing our inner world, we can begin with a focus on our outer world. We can recognise that our happiness or unhappiness may be linked to the symbols of our environment and that we do not need an intellectual explanation to benefit from this understanding.

> Alterations in the "external" world may be as therapeutic as alterations in my subjective feelings. The "bad" place I am "in" may refer not only to a depressed mood or an anxious state of mind; it may refer to a sealed-up office tower where I work, a set-apart suburban subdivision where I sleep, or the jammed freeway on which I commute between the two.
>
> (Hillman 1995, p. xx)

To illustrate his challenge to the 'dogma of interiorisation' (Hillman and Ventura 1992, p. 82) that psychology often promotes, Hillman describes a letter he received from a woman who has been in psychotherapy but who was not benefiting from the experience.

> I suffered from a kind of low-grade depression for ten years that I lived in Los Angeles. During eight of those years, I was working with a Jungian

analyst. Three years ago, my company moved to San Diego County. My analyst 'advised me against leaving Los Angeles' because she thought I should continue to deal with it inwardly and not run away from it. I moved to San Diego anyway. And almost immediately, magically, the depression lifted. It returns, however, whenever I visit Los Angeles. I know now that a great deal of the depression I suffered in Los Angeles was due to the effect of the smog and other environmental factors which cannot be worked out inwardly. I also found that once I started freeing myself from the insidious bonds of Jungian thought, which can be just as dogmatic, narrow-minded, and damaging as fundamentalist Christianity, and the internalization of my emotions, I felt more alive, angrier, and yes, more politically motivated, which is where I was when I came in.

(Hillman and Ventura 1992, p. 82)

The woman had been profoundly affected by the symbols of her world, and rather embarking on a lengthy inner journey, she found healing in simply moving house to find a world surrounded by more therapeutic symbols. She may, of course, still have benefitted from reflection on why her environment had such a pronounced impact on her, but this seems secondary to the more immediate and tangible outcome of the move.

Green Therapy

If we want to work developmentally with the symbol in this more immersive and less conscious way, a good place to start is in symbols of the natural world and, in particular, in the significance of plants and green spaces. Human beings have evolved to need plants, which provide us with shelter, food, and concealment, and that memory of our ancestral existence seems to be part of our collective unconscious. Beyond Jungian psychology, this connection is often termed the 'biophilia hypothesis' (Wilson 1984) and suggests that humans have an innate attraction to natural environments. Echoing Jung's observations of the psychoidal impact of greenery, the horticulturalist Charles Lewis suggests:

As we garden, tramp through a field or forest, stroll in city parks, or rest beneath a tree, we may come to an unexpected door that opens inward to the self. What begins as recreation can lead to profound investigation of the questions of human existence. There are deep reasons for our love affair with nature. We are creatures who evolved in an environment already green. Within our cells live memories of the role vegetation played in fostering our survival as a species. Plants reconnect that distant past, calling forth feelings of tranquillity and harmony, restoring mental and physical health in a contemporary, technological world. Whether in pots, gardens, fields, or forests, living plants remind us of that ancient connection.

(Lewis 1996, p. xix)

The forest in particular seems to represent something wild and untamed, beyond the limits of society, and it forms the centrepiece of many myths and fairy tales. In the forest, we find ourselves lost in a deep darkness, hiding from the witch with her terrifying feminine energy, or perhaps discover a small cottage in which we can take sanctuary and refuge. It is an archetypal image of the unconscious (Zimmer 1971), with all its risks and opportunities. In Russian fairy tales, the forests are 'dremúchiye', a word that means dense in modern Russian but comes from a root word related to sleep and dreaming: the realm of the unconscious (Scielzo 1983). The 'deep forest' is the 'dreaming forest' and is a liminal place of possibility, from which we can die and be reborn. Without it, we become creatures of a domesticated mind and become alienated from the impulses of our unconscious 'wildness'. The fertile green spaces beyond remind us of the fertile green spaces within. A colleague of Jung's described a dream where he found himself at the foot of a glacier, facing a dark forest in which there was a single bright star. Jung suggested:

> You must turn back to the simple things, just as your dream says, to the forest. There is the star. You must go in quest of yourself, and you will find yourself again only in the simple and forgotten things. Why not go into the forest for a time, literally? Sometimes a tree tells you more than can be read in books.
>
> (1973b, p. 479)

In response to this archetypal need, recent decades have seen an increasing interest in what is termed 'Ecopsychology', which promotes the idea that our dislocation from the natural world, and the absence of its powerful symbolism in our lives, is a root cause of a great deal of psychological distress (Roszak 1992). An immersion in green spaces as a deliberate therapeutic act has increased in popularity through such movements as 'Forest Bathing' or, as it was first named in Japanese, *shinrin yoku* (Miyazaki 2018). Here we simply spend time intentionally in wooded environments, being mindful of our senses and noticing the world around us, without being distracted by daily life and without attempting to reach for meaning and outcomes. This total sensory experience rests on the development of a symbolic attitude and an intentional focus on the present without conscious judgement (Lim et al. 2020).

Research has consistently shown that activities related to 'forest bathing' (in all its possible forms) have extremely positive effects on human physical and mental health. We see decreased heart rate and blood pressure (Twohig-Bennett and Jones 2018), significant reduction in symptoms of depression and anxiety, and increased feelings of energy and wellbeing (Siah et al. 2023). Importantly, the influence of 'green symbols' may not require access to wild spaces, and smaller symbols in more familiar settings may have similar effects. Patients who have natural views from their windows seem to recover more quickly from surgery than others (Ulrich 1984), and patients in hospital wait-ing rooms feel less stressed when seated next to plants (Beukeboom et al. 2012). Even looking at nature has positive effects on mood, stress, concentra-tion, and self-esteem (Bratman et al. 2012), reminding us of the impact of ASMR videos. Access to urban parks has been shown to have similar effects and has also been linked to a greater sense of community and relatedness (Konijnendijk et al. 2013).

Blue Therapy

Another natural and highly archetypal symbol that we can draw upon is that of water, which like the forest, plays a central role in our collective mythologies, folk tales, and belief systems. Water moves and changes and has as many varia-tions and possibilities as the emotional states it can evoke in us. It sustains life and destroys life, catching light and concealing hidden depths. It can be still and reflective or wild and terrifying. It can fall as rain, flow in rivers and streams, collect in placid pools and lakes, and drain into deep wild oceans. It is hard to imagine a more numinous symbol. As the poet Philip Larkin sug-gested, water would make a perfect centrepiece for a new religion, where the poet could make a sacrament of

A glass of water
Where any-angled light
Would congregate endlessly.

(1971, p. 20)

Rivers seem particularly significant as a suitable symbol for the winding path of life itself. They are constantly changing, flowing fast and slow, retracing their steps, and then finding their course again while moving with a timeless inevitability. They form as the wellsprings of life, emerging from the unknown depths of the earth as the 'fountainhead of the psyche' (Jung 1969b, CW11, para. 935) and returning eventually to the depths of the ocean. Flash floods may overwhelm us and sweep us away, reminding us of the terrifying power of water, and rivers may also run dry. Without the nurturing flow of water, we die, both physically and spiritually. Rivers often then mark the symbolic boundar-ies between life and death and signpost the crossing between the two. In ancient Greek myth, travellers to the underworld had to cross the Styx, a crossing rep-licated by the Gjöll in Norse myth or the Vaitarani in Hindu tradition. Each year, tens of millions of pilgrims bathe in the Ganges to be released from their sins, and its waters provide comfort to the dying, while the dead are cremated on its banks in the hope of redemption (Sen 2019). In Christianity, the river Jordan offers the promise of a spiritual birth or rebirth through baptism, and in traditional African American spiritual/folk songs, a symbolic crossing of the river at death promises an everlasting freedom.

> The symbolism of the waters implies both death and rebirth. Contact with water always brings a regeneration—on the one hand because dissolution is followed by a new birth, on the other because immersion fertilizes and multiplies the potential of life.
>
> (Eliade 1959, p. 130)

Water sits at the centre of many of the creation myths of humanity (Campbell 2000, Schama 1995) perhaps as a shared psychoidal memory of the amniotic fluid of the womb. It seems to remind us of the feeling of wholeness from which we came and to which we will ultimately return. Water may sometimes be a complete embodiment of the divine (as in the case of the goddesses Styx and Ganga) or simply a route through which the divine can be accessed (as an archetypal image). The river Jordan is not a god, but its waters allow Christians to move closer to God. Perhaps not surprisingly for such an archetypal image, the symbolic role of water is not limited to our myths and our religions, and we have found many different ways and reasons to engage with this symbol. For thousands of years, we have bathed in water simply for recreation and have created 'blue spaces' as focal points for our communities, where we come to relax together and strengthen our social bonds. From simple sweat lodges to small bathing pools and vast bathhouses, our love affair with water has been part of the collective history of humanity.

It is surprising then that the psychological benefits of 'blue spaces' seem to have been given considerably less focus than those of green spaces, but the research has still suggested similar therapeutic effects. A backdrop of water appears to offer 'serenity and the opportunity to escape' (Vining and Fishwick 1991, p. 122) and general improvements in psychological wellbeing (Hinds J and Sparks P 2011). Research has also linked 'blue spaces' to decreased rates of psychological distress and depression, along with a renewed sense of purpose and meaning (Nutsford et al. 2016, Hooker et al. 2022). Spa bathing has been shown to decrease stress and fatigue (Toda et al. 2006), and even the gentle massage of stream waters has been shown to have the same effect (Mizuno et al. 2010). Some studies have also suggested that 'blue' environments actually have a greater effect on psychological health and wellbeing than other natural environments (Barton and Pretty 2010, Marselle et al. 2013). Like green spaces, the 'blue space' does not need to be wild, and research suggests that the sight and sound of water can bring benefits even in an urban environment (Ting and Bahauddin 2022).

In his book *Blue Mind*, the marine biologist Wallace Nichols suggests that one reason water is so captivating is that it is simultaneously consistent and dynamic. It is predictable and constant, relaxing the mind and 'normalising' our environment, yet its perpetual motion stimulates us. Water provides 'regularity without monotony' (Nichols 2014, p. 155) and is the perfect recipe for creativity, provoking the intuition and inspiration of the unconscious without overwhelming us. Echoing Larkin's 'any-angled light', he suggests:

We are transfixed by sunlight sparkling on the surface of ponds, lakes, streams, rivers, and oceans. In the motion of water, we see patterns that never exactly repeat themselves yet have a restful similarity to them. Our eyes are drawn to the combination of novelty and repetition.

(Nichols 2014, p. 93)

In reflecting on her own relationship with water, a colleague described the experience of swimming:

> My immersion into my inner world always happens in the water, where I go into a kind of flow, into the territory of liminality, between worlds, in the here and now, deeply rooted in myself and where creativity happens as ideas emerge, reflection takes place, and deep inner balance gives me the energy for the day. Here I access the deeper layer of my being, in a way, the ego shuts up and symbolic knowing emerges. It begins to happen after about 10 minutes in the water and continues for as long as I swim, which is like a threshold into the outer world once again. Maybe it is as if the swimming has become a sacred ritual for myself, a return a kind of homecoming. The same is true with light as if water represents the unconscious and light somehow symbolises consciousness, clarity and transformation. It's a bit like yin and yang, and it recharges not only my body but also my soul.

Being close to water seems to remind us of both the inevitable passing of time (chronos) and the timeless, archetypal nature of our world (kairos). It tells a story of life which is engaging and evocative and yet still familiar and comforting. No matter how turbulent in the moment, the waters tell us that everything will pass, and we will 'go on being'.

Re-Enchantment and a Return to the Self

Simply being exposed to the symbols of nature may then be enough to enrich our lives. In this chapter, I have briefly mentioned the impact of green and blue spaces, but I could equally have focused on mountains or desert or perhaps our relationship with animals or another other physical entity. We may even find inspiration in the built environment, remembering that these too are part of us and that 'city is psyche' (Hillman and Ventura 1992, p. 82). We may encounter moments of delight or surprise in the winding streets of an old city. We may discover our gods in 'places of lust' or 'places of awe' (Ellard 2015), the embrace of community in a theme park, or a deep stillness in an old church. We do not need to bring these images into our conscious awareness in order to benefit from them. They simply need to 'be there', channelling an archetypal energy which provokes and guides inner change. As Jung suggested, 'the numinous in the real therapy and inasmuch as you attain the numinous experiences you are released from the curse of pathology' (1973a, CW2, para. 377), and being in the natural world is an ideal opportunity to do this. Indeed, to bring these images to conscious awareness may, in fact, limit their therapeutic effect, turning them into 'signs', which clumsily point the way to intellectual meaning, while stripping away any 'felt experience'.

In coaching and psychotherapeutic work, we spend much of our time constellating the symbol, in a movement from the impulses of the unconscious to a conscious meaning-making. We notice the symbol and then work consciously with it in a movement that allows us to better understand ourselves and to make more deliberate choices about our lives. However, we may also consider another direction, consciously selecting a symbol and then immersing ourselves in it and allowing ourselves to be changed by it. We may choose not to reflect on the unconscious from the perspective of the conscious mind but to live in it on its own terms. Here we recognise that we do not always need to be burdened by rational thought and can instead allow ourselves to simply 'be'. We can return to the magic of our 'animal mind'. Craig Chalquist, a pioneer of ecopsychology, has described this movement as 'the journey of re-enchantment' (Chalquist 2015), a spiral path from the unconscious to the (self)-conscious mind followed by a return to the unconscious, to face the archetypal self before reemerging in consciousness with a new awareness. Chalquist has proposed ten stages for this journey (Chalquist 2015), which I have abbreviated here to six:

Stage 1: *A Magical World*
 We begin in a 'participation mystique' where the world is full of magic and wonder. It moves us without any need for conscious awareness or a reaching after outcomes. This is a place where 'Animals make magic. Fabulous beasts hide under the bed. Dream and daytime merge' (Chalquist 2015).
Stage 2: *Adaptation and Alienation*
 We get older and the magical is 'schooled' out of us by the modern world. We learn to despise superstition and begin to adapt to a much smaller world, dominated by the authority of the rational mind. Although we never lose our sense of awe and wonder, we learn to compartmentalise and domesticate it, in our books, films, and theatre. The animals stop speaking to us, our dreams become 'just dreams', and fairy tales are only for children.
Stage 3: *Rupture and Descent*
 The unconscious, however, cannot be repressed for ever, and in time its voice becomes louder through dreams, fantasies, and even psychosomatic symptoms. We feel the need to look inside and begin our descent into the unconscious. Here we separate from the conscious mind and allow ourselves to start what Jung termed the 'nekyia' or night journey, a descent into the underworld of the mind (CW15, para. 213).
Stage 4: *Seeking and Reemergence*
 As we find ourselves in a place of confusion and discontent, the conscious mind begins to reassert itself and we begin to question ourselves. We start to

make meaning as symbols begin to constellate, and we can begin to find revelation. We return to consciousness with a sense of relief, and we have begun to lose our 'fear of the dark'. We know we can work with the unconscious and survive, perhaps even emerging with a fistful of shining gold with each successive visit. With each night journey, we discover new insights and new ways to make use of them.

Stage 5: A Magic Door

In time, after many false starts and dead ends, we may discover a symbol that provides a reliable entry to the unconscious, a 'magic door' like Alice's rabbit hole. This symbol could be seen as the transcendent function (Jung 1969a, CW8), a synthesis of the unconscious and conscious mind which creates new perspectives and new ways of being. Through the mediation of this symbol, the magical can become a way of life and our world becomes re-enchanted. We can awaken to the richness of our own intuition and imagination. We can develop a stable 'ego-self axis' (Edinger 1960, p. 9), a conduit that facilitates an open dialogue between the unconscious and the conscious mind, between the rational and the animal. With a stable 'ego-self axis', we can live between worlds being equally present in both.

Stage 6: Holding the Door

The discovery of the door for ourselves then allows us to hold the door for others. Once we have developed a stable ego-self axis and the capacity to move between the unconscious and conscious mind, we can begin to support others as they do the same. We can be coaches, psychotherapists, and mentors, working without a 'fear of the dark'. We can share our journey and invite others to find their own path.

From the perspective of Jungian psychology, we could see this journey as another form of individuation, a labyrinthine path of awareness and development, 'consisting of progress and regress, flux and stagnation in alternating sequence' (Jacobi 1983, p. 34). With each iteration of this spiral dance, we enrich our conscious minds, not losing the magic of the symbolic world but allowing it a space to exist. As Jung suggested:

> Thus, in coming to terms with the unconscious, not only is the standpoint of the ego justified, but the unconscious is granted the same authority. The ego takes the lead, but the unconscious must be allowed to have its say too.
>
> (1969a, CW8, para. 185)

We must remember that this journey of re-enchantment requires then *both* a movement from the conscious to unconscious mind, as we deliberately surrender to sensation and emotion, *and* a return to consciousness as we make meaning from our experience. Sometimes we need to reflect, and sometimes we just need to be.

Reflections and Implications

An integrated psyche then requires an integrated journey, and too much focus on symbol from a purely conscious perspective can only limit its potential to transform. We can, of course, obtain a great deal of value from using symbol to make conscious meaning of our own inner world, and of unconscious dynamics of the systems around us, but to fully experience the self, we must be able to move beyond the limits of the ego and begin to live a symbolic life. We must be able to occasionally immerse ourselves in the world without allowing the ego to anxiously force us prematurely back to consciousness. If we mindfully select a suitable context, we can then 'let go' and allow its symbol to do the work for us. As Jung suggests:

> The symbol becomes my lord and unfailing commander. It will fortify its reign and change itself into a fixed and riddling image, whose meaning turns completely inward, and whose pleasure radiates outward like a blazing fire...Because I sink into my symbol to such an extent, the symbol changes me from my one into my other.
>
> (2009, p. 250)

While sometimes we may need to analyse and explain art, music or poetry, their full effect is really felt only by allowing them to wash over us without close examination and the same is true of the symbols within the spaces we inhabit in our daily lives. Sometimes it is best to simply allow ourselves to experience the world without surrendering to the anxieties of the ego and needing to flee to the safety of thinking. To fully benefit from symbol, we may need to remind ourselves of Zinkin's suggestion that 'the unknowable signified does not need to be known...it only needs to be there' (1998, p. 87). We need to allow the symbol to be present without succumbing to an anxious need to consciously grasp it.

As coaches and psychotherapists, we can perhaps then begin to use the physical world as an integral part of our practice, sometimes working consciously with its symbols and sometimes finding spaces in which our clients can simply 'be'. We don't need to tell our clients that we are going forest bathing or to explain why we are going to walk by the sea. This will create a self-conscious awareness and expectation of what the symbols are 'supposed' to do, turning the symbols into signs and diminishing their numinous energy. Instead, we can just allow the space to guide our conversation without remarking on it. We just need to choose our spaces well and then allow them to change us. We can relearn how to see the world through the eyes of the unconscious as participants rather than bystanders. This is a symbolic life.

Acknowledgements

The excerpt from the poem 'Water' by Philip Larkin is taken from his work *The Whitsun Weddings*, published in 1971. It is included here by permission of Faber and Faber Ltd as the publishers and copyright holders.

Take a walk outside, whether a natural or an urban space:

- Don't think too much about the experience. Just walk slowly and let your gaze wander without settling on anything in particular.
- If you find it hard to stop thinking and making associations, don't worry. Just let the thoughts pass and try to focus on the experience of walking.

After a while, take a seat somewhere and reflect on the experience.

- What sensations did you notice? Where did you feel them in your body? What was the feeling like?
- What emotions came up for you? Try to be as specific as possible.
- What do you remember from the walk? What symbols stay with you? How do they make you feel now?

Don't dwell on the experience any more. Just remember the sensations and get on with your day.

References

Barratt EL and Davis NJ 2015, Autonomous sensory meridian response (ASMR): A flow-like mental state. *PeerJ* 3: e851.

Barton J and Pretty J 2010, What is the best dose of nature and green exercise for improving mental health? A multi-study analysis. *Environmental Science & Technology* 44: 3947–3955.

Beukeboom CJ, Langeveld D and Tanja-Dijkstra D 2012, Stress-reducing effects of real and artificial nature in a hospital waiting room. *The Journal of Alternative and Complementary Medicine* 18(4): 329–333.

Bratman GN, Hamilton JP and Daily GC 2012, The impacts of nature experience on human cognitive function and mental health. *Annals of the New York Academy of Sciences* 1249(1): 118–136.

Buccino G, Riggio L, Melli G, Binkofski F, Gallese V, Rizzolatti G 2005, Listening to action-related sentences modulates the activity of the motor system: A combined TMS and behavioral study. *Brain Res Cogn Brain Res* 24(3): 355–363.

Campbell J 2000, *Primitive mythology: The masks of God*. London: Souvenir Press.

Chalquist C (2015, February 24), Why I seldom teach the hero's journey anymore – and what I teach instead. *HuffPost*. https://www.huffpost.com/entry/why-i-seldom-teach-the-he_b_6739046

Cooley SJ, Jones CR, Kurtz A and Robertson N 2020, 'Into the wild': A meta-synthesis of talking therapy in natural outdoor spaces. *Clinical Psychology Review* 77: 101841.

Deacon TW 1997, *The symbolic species: The co-evolution of language and the brain*. London: WW Norton & Company.

Edinger E 1960, The ego-self paradox. *Journal of Analytical Psychology* 5: 3–18.

Eliade M 1959, *The sacred and the profane: The nature of religion.* San Diego, CA: Harcourt Brace Jovanovich.

Ellard C 2015, *Places of the heart: The psychogeography of everyday life.* New York: Bellevue Library Press.

Gallagher R 2016, 'Eliciting Euphoria Online: The Aesthetics of "ASMR" Video Culture', *Film Criticism* 40(2).

Gallese V and Lakoff G 2005, The brain's concepts: The role of the sensory-motor system in conceptual knowledge. *Cognitive Neuropsychology* 22: 455–470.

Garcia-Pelegrin E, Miller R, Wilkins C and Clayton NS 2023, Manual action expectation and biomechanical ability in three species of New World monkey. *Current Biology* 33(9): 1803–1808.

Grothe-Hammer M 2024, Tingles and society: The emotional experience of ASMR as a social phenomenon. *Sociological Inquiry* 1–20.

Hillman J and Ventura M 1992, *We've had a hundred years of psychotherapy and the world's getting worse.* San Francisco, CA: HarperSanFrancisco.

Hillman J 1995, A psyche the size of the earth. In T Roszak, ME Gomes, and AD Kanner (eds.) *Ecopsychology: Restoring the earth, healing the mind.* Berkeley, CA: Counterpoint.

Hinds J and Sparks P 2011, The affective quality of human-natural environment relationships. *Evolutionary. Psychology* 9: 451–469.

Hooker T, McCool S, Fischer SR, Tysor D and Lackey NQ 2022, Exploring changes in depression and meaning in life through river rafting for veterans with PTSD. *Journal of Outdoor Recreation, Education, and Leadership* 14: 2: Special Issue, Part II: Community Impacts of Outdoor Recreation, Education, and Leadership.

Jacobi J 1983, *The way of individuation.* New York: Meridian.

Jung CG 1964, *Man and his symbols.* New York: Doubleday.

Jung CG 1968, *Psychology and alchemy*, CW12.

Jung CG 1969a, *Structure and dynamics of the psyche*, CW8.

Jung CG 1969b, *Psychology and religion: West and east*, CW11.

Jung CG 1973a, *Experimental researches*, CW2.

Jung CG 1973b, *Letters of C.G. Jung volume 1, 1906-1950.* Abington, Oxon: Routledge.

Jung CG 1977, *The symbolic life*, CW18.

Jung CG 2009, *The red book.* London: WW Norton & Company.

Knox J 2011, *Self-agency in psychotherapy: Attachment, autonomy and intimacy.* London: WW Norton & Company.

Konijnendijk CC, Annerstedt M, Nielsen AB and Maruthaveeran S 2013, *Benefits of urban parks: A systematic review.* A Report for IFPRA. Copenhagen: International Federation of Parks and Recreation Administration.

Larkin P 1971, *The Whitsun weddings.* London: Faber and Faber.

Lewis CA 1996, *Green nature/human nature: The meaning of plants in our lives.* Chicago, IL: University of Illinois Press.

Lim PY, Dillon D and Chew PKH 2020, A guide to nature immersion: psychological and physiological benefits. *International Journal of Environmental Research and Public Health* 17: 5989.

Marselle M R, Irvine KN and Warber SL 2013, Walking for well-being: Are group walks in certain types of natural environments better for well-being than group walks in urban environments? *International Journal of Environmental Research and Public Health* 10: 5603–5628.

Mizuno K, Tanaka M, Tajima K, Okada N, Rokushima K, and Watanabe Y 2010, Effects of mild-stream bathing on recovery from mental fatigue. *Medical Science Monitor* 16(1): 8–14.

Miyazaki Y 2018, *Shinrin yoku: The Japanese art of forest bathing*. Portland, OR: Timber Press.

Nichols WJ 2014, *Blue mind: How water makes you happier, more connected and better at what you do*. London: Abacus.

Nutsford D, Pearson AL, Kingham S and Reitsma F 2016, Residential exposure to visible blue space (but not green space) associated with lower psychological distress in a capital city. *Health & Place* 39: 70–78.

Roszak T 1992, *The voice of the earth: An exploration of ecopsychology*. New York: Simon & Schuster.

Russell F 2024, *Digital media as ambient therapy: The ecological self between resonance and alienation*. Abingdon, Oxon: Routledge.

Samuels A, Shorter B and Plaut F 1986, *A critical dictionary of Jungian analysis*. London: Routledge.

Scielzo C 1983, Other voices: An analysis of Bába-Yagá in folklore and fairy tales. American *Journal of Psychoanalysis* 43: 167–175.

Sen S 2019, *Ganges: The many pasts of an Indian river*. New Haven, CT: Yale University Press.

Shamdasani S 2003, *Jung and the making of modern psychology: The dream of a science*. Cambridge, UK: Cambridge University Press.

Siah CJR, Goh YS, Lee J, Poon SN, Yong JQYO, Tam WSW 2023, The effects of forest bathing on psychological well-being: A systematic review and meta-analysis. *International Journal of Mental Health Nursing* 32(4): 1038–1054.

Smejka T and Wiggs L 2022, The effects of autonomous sensory meridian response (ASMR) videos on arousal and mood in adults with and without depression and insomnia. *Journal of Affective Disorders* 301: 60–67.

Smith N and Snider A-M 2019, ASMR, affect and digitally-mediated intimacy. *Emotion, Space and Society* 30: 41–48.

Schama S 1995. *Landscape and memory*. New York: Alfred A. Knopf.

Ting HY and Bahauddin A 2022, The impact of blue space in the interior on mental health. *Arteks: Jurnal Teknik Arsitektur* 7: 1.

Toda M, Morimoto K, Nagasawa S and Kitamura K 2006, Change in salivary physiological stress markers by spa bathing. *Biomedical Research* 27(11): 11–14.

Twohig-Bennett C and Jones A 2018, The health benefits of the great outdoors: A systematic review and meta-analysis of greenspace exposure and health outcomes *Environmental Research* 166: 628–637.

Ulrich R 1984, View through a window may influence recovery from surgery. *Science* 224: 420–421.

Vining J and Fishwick L 1991, An exploratory study of outdoor recreation site choices. *Journal of Leisure Research* 23(2): 114–132.

Wilson EO 1984, *Biophilia: The human bond with other species*. Cambridge, MA: Harvard University Press.

Zimmer H 1971, *The king and the corpse: Tales of the soul's conquest of evil*. Princeton, NJ: Princeton University Press.

Zinkin L 1998, Paradoxes of the self. In H Zinkin, R Gordon, and J Haynes (eds.) *Dialogue in the analytic setting*. London: Jessica Kingsley Publishers.

Some Final Reflections

Over the last few years, I have run a regular reading group for coaches, consultants, psychotherapists, and psychologists, all of whom have at least some background in depth psychology or a related discipline. Working with the unconscious in some capacity or other is their craft. As I wrote this closing chapter, my final reflections on symbolic working, we had begun to read the Red Book.

The Red Book was written by Jung as a way of making sense of the images and associations that had been evoked within him in the years following his split with Freud. Through his dreams and fantasies, he began to have a deliberate dialogue with his unconscious which he further elaborated with paintings, many of which were ornate mandalas. These images presented him with 'cryptograms concerning the state of the self' in which he was able to discern his 'whole being - actively at work' (Jung 1973, p. 221). His careful analysis of these thoughts and symbols provided the foundations for his model of the psyche. It was here that he first began to develop his theory of the archetypes and the collective unconscious, prompting psychotherapy to evolve beyond being simply a responsive treatment for mental illness to a more progressive means of exploring human potential. In the opening lines of the Red Book, Jung describes his experience during this time and its significance to his later work.

THE YEARS, OF WHICH I HAVE SPOKEN TO YOU,
when I pursued the inner images, were the most important time
of my life. Everything else is to be derived from this.
It began at that time, and the later details hardly matter anymore.
My entire life consisted in elaborating what had burst forth from
the unconscious and flooded me like an enigmatic stream
and threatened to break me. That was the stuff and material for more
than only one life. Everything later was merely the outer
classification, the scientific elaboration, and the integration into life.
But the numinous beginning, which contained everything, was then.
C. G. JUNG, 1957

(Jung 2009)

DOI: 10.4324/9781003463269-12

Although he published excerpts from the Red Book, he was adamant that he did not want it included in his Collected Works as it was not of a 'scholarly character' (Jung 2009, p. viii). It is filled with allusions without citations and seems to have very little in common stylistically with Jung's other works and was only published in 2009, nearly five decades after his death. It represents a raw image of the unconscious, transcribed as it was experienced without a conscious filter or an audience in mind. This was an image of Jung's own psyche, for Jung's own contemplation. As an embodiment of the unconscious, the Red Book is elaborate, labyrinthine, symbolic, opaque, and mysterious. It is an unguarded revelation of Jung's own developmental process, and it cannot be read in the same way as a more consciously constructed text. In their dialogues about the Red Book and its implications, James Hillman and Sonu Shamdasani (whose meticulous curation brought this work to the world) emphasise the significance of Jung's personal experiences as the essential ingredient for meaningful development work:

> In the Red Book you find Jung actually setting aside the guide rails, setting aside his own psychology that he'd developed up to then, seeing to what extent he could let the chaos in without apotropaic magic. It's clear in his subsequent statements that this was what he conceived of as the crux of one's encounter with one's own depths, that this is what he saw as the essence of his therapy, his practice, which was to enable an individual to encounter his or her own depths.
>
> (Hillman & Shamdasani 2013, p. 181)

The reaction to the Red Book in the reading group was striking. Members of the group were shocked and confused, and some were even appalled, questioning why I had recommended it as reading. They suggested:

> 'I wanted context to anchor in the conscious mind, and I felt adrift. I was too lost. I did not know how to apprehend the text or to enter into relationship with it. It was too crazy. I needed rational structure. I eventually went to a YouTube video to explain what the Red Book actually means.'

> 'It physically affected me. I felt a real fear of being overwhelmed. It felt so big. At the same time, I was drawn in. I felt frustrated and curious. It was not a good feeling that I didn't get it. What are we supposed to understand?'

> 'It felt like an unanchored state. I was too lost reading it. I needed some context before I could free myself and begin.'

These responses felt somehow inevitable, and perhaps the most significant thing about them is how honest they were. The unconscious is, after all, filled with the numinous, archetypal energy of collective human experience. It is a vast expanse of 'the other' and the mysteries of not-knowing. The symbols that arise from the unconscious can often remind us of how small and how limited we really are. They have the power to move us beyond the boundaries of ego-consciousness, a move we may not always be ready for. Sometimes they urge us towards places we may rather avoid or feel unprepared for. We may not be able to make sense of them. We may feel as though we are entering a 'non-ordinary state of consciousness' and a world of dreams and phantasies that we cannot easily dismiss. In the first chapter of the Red Book, Jung asks himself, 'What is there, where there is no meaning? Only nonsense, or madness' (2009, p. 235) and describes his early experiences in a poetic but still terrifying account.

> It is all frightfully muddled and interwoven. On this desert path there is not just glowing sand, but also horrible tangled invisible beings who live in the desert. I didn't know this. The way is only apparently clear, the desert is only apparently empty. It seems inhabited by magical beings who murderously attach themselves to me and daimonically change my form. I have evidently taken on a completely monstrous form in which I can no longer recognize myself. It seems to me that I have become a monstrous animal form for which I have exchanged my humanity. This way is surrounded by hellish magic, invisible nooses have been thrown over me and ensnare me.
>
> (2009, p. 240)

The ego defines itself by the difference between 'me' and 'not-me', and the experience of allowing the boundaries between the two to become more permeable may then provoke a great deal of anxiety. We may encounter ourselves in symbolic forms that we cannot recognise or accept. It may even suggest an existential threat of disintegration, that could be described as a 'nameless dread' (Bion 2018) or an experience of 'falling forever' (Winnicott 1974). It is an archetypal terror of fragmentation in the timeless and unbounded void. In the unconscious, we relinquish the familiar and we cease to exist as individuals in any tangible form. The chaotic expanse of the unconscious, unchecked by the mundane methodologies, frameworks, and goals of the conscious mind, is for most people an unsettling experience at the very least and under certain conditions may even 'overpower the conscious mind and take possession of the personality' (Jung CW8, p. 68).

However, while we can repress the unconscious, we can never be free of it, and it will always influence us to some degree: 'The secret participation of the unconscious is everywhere present without our having to search for it, but as it remains unconscious we never really know what is going on or what to expect' (Jung CW8, para. 158). This influence may be regressive, drawing us back into past patterns of behaviour, or it may be progressive, suggesting new ways to be and preventing us from becoming stuck. We can make sense of the unconscious if we are open to its symbols and develop a symbolic attitude, taking a 'definite view of the world which assigns meaning to events...and attaches to this meaning a greater value than bare facts' (Jung CW6, para. 899). The more familiar we are with the energy and imagery of the unconscious, the less likely we are to be overwhelmed by it and the more use we can make of its intuition. We may be better able to make conscious sense of its symbols, to deepen our self-awareness, or we can consciously immerse ourselves in them, allowing them to wash over us and take us where we need to be taken. Whether we are analysing our phantasies and dreams, walking in the forest, visiting an art gallery, or reading poetry, symbols can make us and remake us. It is in the tension between the wild 'nonsense' of the unconscious and the rational structure of the conscious mind that we find the opportunities to grow. For Jung, the constant movement between the 'absurdity' of the unconscious and the 'meaning' of the conscious mind allows us to reach towards our potential:

Meaning is a moment and a transition from absurdity to absurdity, and absurdity only a moment and a transition from meaning to meaning.

(Jung 2009, p. 242)

For coaches, this has significant implications, as our work is, by definition, relational and intersubjective. We are always working in the presence of at least one other who is affected by our presence and whose presence affects us. To any coaching conversation is brought the inner theatre of the coach, the inner theatre of the client, and the curious alchemy of their exchange. The relationship between the unconscious and conscious mind of both then shapes our individual responses and the way in which our relationship develops. The degree of comfort that coaches feel in working with our own unconscious will influence the degree of comfort we have in working with the unconscious of our clients. This will shape how we work as a coach, how the client responds to us, and how our relationship develops. If we are uncomfortable with the turbulence and intensity of the unconscious, then our clients will follow our lead, and our work together will lack the creativity and intuition needed to move towards our potential. If we are too comfortable and perhaps even intoxicated by the numinous power of the unconscious, then our clients may be seduced by our uncritical enthusiasm. We may embark on a form of 'folie à deux', where both coach and client participate in a shared inflation which overwhelms the realities of day-to-day life.

To ensure that the unconscious of either and both can have a constructive influence over the work we do together, a coach must be able to consciously notice the symbols produced by the unconscious and not be overwhelmed by the emotions they evoke. We must be able to work with them, whether they originate from our psyche, from the psyche of our client, or as a product of our developing relationship. We must not repress or deny the symbol or run anxiously for a rational interpretation. We must be able to face the symbol as it is, moving between the unconscious and conscious mind and making deliberate choices about our next steps. As Jung suggested, 'the capacity for inner dialogue is a touchstone for outer objectivity' (CW8, para. 187), and unless we have made this inner journey ourselves, we are unlikely to be able to take a considered and reflective view of the challenges faced by our clients. We cannot support the development of our clients or ourselves unless we can move freely and with a considered awareness between the 'absurdity' of the unconscious and the 'meaning' of the conscious mind. If symbol is the bridge between these two states, then a symbolic attitude is the foundation of an ethical coaching practice.

To prepare ourselves to work with symbol we must first understand what symbol is, knowing it is more than a sign and appreciating the complex array of associations and energy from which it arises. We can then spend time noticing our own unconscious, becoming familiar with the symbols that arise within us and that we discover in the world around us. We can then begin to play with them, exploring the feelings they evoke, before developing a deeper understanding of those feelings and their different nuances. We can explore sadness as disappointment, grief, homesickness, or bereavement. We can consider happiness as contentment, pleasure, glee, or ecstasy. We can give words to these states and wonder about the symbols we associate with them. We may begin to reflect on our dreams, perhaps keeping a dream journal or noticing our fantasies and fears, paying careful attention to the symbols contained with them and the possible clusters in which they appear. We may spend our time in art galleries or reading poetry or listening to music, noticing the images that move us and stay with us. We may take a walk in the wild and mediate on the experience of being in our own bodies. This process may be informal, as part of our daily routine, or we may decide to begin to work with the symbols we encounter in an active imagination, entering an intentional, inner dialogue. We may then immerse ourselves again, allowing ourselves to go as far into the experience of the unconscious as we dare before returning to the safe haven of the conscious mind. With each journey, we become more familiar with symbol, and we begin to develop a stable 'ego-self axis' (Edinger 1960), the psychological 'pipeline' which connects the unconscious and conscious mind, enabling a free movement towards wholeness. We can then begin to work with others while, of course, remembering that we are still working with ourselves. As my colleagues' response to the Red Book shows, the unconscious will continue to provoke us with its images and emotions. It will be exciting and intoxicating, terrifying and overwhelming. However, the more we work with it, the more it will reveal and the more benefit we can derive from it.

Throughout of our journey, we may need support, as this is a challenging and confronting path to walk alone. We will discover joy and fascination but also perhaps things about ourselves that shame us or evoke memories that we have buried for a long time. These memories may not even be ours and may belong to our family systems or cultures. We may discover images and associations that are profoundly archetypal with a numinous, overwhelming energy and which speak to the collective experience of being human. Working with a suitable psychotherapist, coach, or supervisor can provide us with emotional support and help us make sense of the symbols that are constellating within and around us.

In time, we can begin to develop a symbolic practice and begin to live a more symbolic life. We can acknowledge that life isn't made up just of surface-level events but that every encounter and event can carry symbolic significance. That significance may be small and personal or profoundly archetypal and life-changing. Leading a symbolic life ultimately requires us to embrace mystery, listen to the soul, and find meaning beyond the rational. In the symbolic life, we learn to pay attention to the unconscious and to value its contribution on equal terms to that of rational consciousness. It is about not escaping reality but deepening it, living with intention, and recognising that each moment may carry a hidden message waiting to be understood and with the potential to transform us. As Jung suggested:

> If one creates a better relation to the unconscious, it proves to be a helpful power, it then has an activity of its own, it produces helpful dreams and at times it really produces little miracles.
>
> (Jung 1998, p. 604)

These miracles are contained within symbols.

References

Bion WR 2018, *Second thoughts: Selected papers on psychoanalysis*. Abingdon, Oxon: Routledge.

Edinger E 1960, The ego-self paradox. *Journal of Analytical Psychology* 5: 3–18.

Hillman J & Shamdasani S 2013, *Lament of the dead, psychology after Jung's red book*. London: W. W. Norton & Co.

Jung CG 1973, *Memories, dreams, reflections*. London: Fontana.

Jung CG 1998, *Visions: Notes of the Seminar Given in 1930–1934, volume 1*. Princeton, NJ: Princeton University Press.

Jung CG 2009, *The red book*. London: W. W. Norton & Co.

Winnicott DW 1974, Fear of breakdown. In C Winnicott, R Shepherd and M Davis (eds.), *Psychoanalytic explorations* pp. 87–95. Cambridge, MA: Harvard University Press.

Index

52, 56, 65, 105, 167, 173; of the
boundary 101, 103; in coaching 5–6,
33, 35–36, 50, 60–65, 69–70, 75–88,
104–106, 118–121, 140–141, 154–162,
178, 184–187; in complexes 13–14, 20;
in culture 146–150, 152–154; in
dreams 126, 128–129, 131–139,
142–143; form and function 4, 13, 27,
30, 32; in luxury brands 4; of the
natural world 171–179; Red Book
182–184; in relationship 54–60, 65,
67–70; as somatic experience 113,
168–169; in stories 31–32; in symbolic
attitude 40–52; in symbolic life
169–171; transcendent function
34–37, 74–75, 87; *see also* image
symbolic attitude 21, 41–48, 51, 58, 63,
65, 69–70, 75, 91, 97, 101, 113–114,
136, 165, 169, 172, 184, 186
symbolic life 51–52, 170, 178, 187
synchronicity 36, 47–48, 65, 120–121

tango 28–29
Telemachus 36
teleological function of the psyche 110
temenos 102, 105
terror 11, 47, 83; archetypal 184; of the
unknown 17
transcendent function 34–35, 61, 69,
74–75, 77, 132, 177
transference 54–63, 67–70, 83, 131;
countertransference 55, 57–59, 61, 63,
69–70; progressive transference 68, 70;
regressive transference 68
trauma 12, 47, 69, 82, 110, 127–128, 136,
160; ancestral 18; cultural 147,
159–152, 156, 159–161; PTSD 93

tree 95, 98, 133–134, 166–167, 171–172;
magnolia tree 133–134; Yggdrasil 134
tribal unconscious 16, 128–129
Trickster 35–36, 85–87

unconscious 1–6, 9, 17–18, 25–29, 32–38,
40–42, 45–51, 54–65, *57–59*, 67–70,
73–88, 91–104, 109–116, 119,
121–122, 125–137, 148–150, 153–154,
157, 160–161, 165, 168–178, 182–186;
collective 15, 24, 29, 34, 36, 47, 51,
54, 56–57, 65, 114–115, 119, *130*,
131–132, 137–142, 146–147, 171, 182;
cultural 16, 25, 54, 57, 99, 129,
147–148, 152–153; personal 16, 18–21,
54, 129, 137, 147–148; psychoid 9–13,
42, 77, 92, 134; tribal 129
underworld: psychic 94–96, 134, 173, 176
Union Flag 152
unus mundus 92, 99
uroboros 19

vas hermeticum 60
von Franz, M.-L. 59, 80, 102, 129

water 78, 139, 146, 150, 153, 155,
173–175; watercourse 75
Weaver, R 111, 114
Wiener, J 70
Willendorf Venus 15
Winnicott, DW 77, 81, 84–85, 88, 99, 103
witch 16, 116, 137, 140, 172
womb 9–10, 15, 104, 174; as matrix 69, 141

Yggdrasil 134

Zinkin, L 64, 139, 169, 178

For Product Safety Concerns and Information please contact our EU
representative GPSR@taylorandfrancis.com
Taylor & Francis Verlag GmbH, Kaufingerstraße 24, 80331 München, Germany